MASSIVE RESISTANCE

MASSIVE RESISTANCE

SOUTHERN OPPOSITION TO THE SECOND RECONSTRUCTION

EDITED BY

CLIVE WEBB

OXFORD
UNIVERSITY PRESS

2005

OXFORD
UNIVERSITY PRESS

Oxford University Press, Inc., publishes works that further
Oxford University's objective of excellence
in research, scholarship, and education.

Oxford   New York
Auckland   Cape Town   Dar es Salaam   Hong Kong   Karachi
Kuala Lumpur   Madrid   Melbourne   Mexico City   Nairobi
New Delhi   Shanghai   Taipei   Toronto

With offices in
Argentina   Austria   Brazil   Chile   Czech Republic   France   Greece
Guatemala   Hungary   Italy   Japan   Poland   Portugal   Singapore
South Korea   Switzerland   Thailand   Turkey   Ukraine   Vietnam

Copyright © 2005 by Oxford University Press, Inc.

Published by Oxford University Press, Inc.
198 Madison Avenue, New York, New York 10016

www.oup.com

Oxford is a registered trademark of Oxford University Press

Library of Congress Cataloging-in-Publication Data
Massive resistance : southern opposition to the second reconstruction /
edited by Clive Webb.
p. cm.
ISBN-13 978-0-19-517785-5; 978-0-19-517786-2 (pbk.)
ISBN 0-19-517785-1; 0-19-517786-X (pbk.)
1. Southern States—Race relations—Congresses. 2. Whites-Southern States—
Politics and government—20th century—Congresses. 3. Government, Resistance
to—Southern States—History—20th century—Congresses. 4. African Americans—
Civil rights—Southern States—History—20th century—Congresses. 5. Southern
States—Politics and government—1951—Congresses. 6. Southern States—
Social conditions—1945—Congresses. I. Webb, Clive, 1970–
E185.61.M374 2005
305.896'073075'09045—dc22   2004059981

1 3 5 7 9 8 6 4 2

Printed in the United States of America
on acid-free paper

ACKNOWLEDGMENTS

This collection is based upon papers presented at a conference held at the University of Sussex in March 2002. I would like to thank the following for their generous financial support, without which it would have been impossible to bring together scholars from both sides of the Atlantic: Professor Vivien Hart and the Cunliffe Centre for the Study of Constitutionalism and National Identity at the University of Sussex, Professor Tony Badger and the Mellon Professorial Fund at the University of Cambridge, and the British Academy. I am grateful to all those who participated in the conference and made it a memorable occasion. The process of turning the papers from the conference into a published collection has been facilitated by the support, patience, and sharp editorial skills of Susan Ferber at Oxford University Press. My thanks also to Kathleen Kendall, a source of immeasurable intellectual and emotional strength.

CONTENTS

CONTRIBUTORS

KAREN S. ANDERSON is Professor in the History Department at the University of Arizona. Her publications include *Wartime Women: Sex Roles, Family Relations, and the Status of Women During World War II* (1981) and *Changing Woman: A History of Racial Ethnic Women in Modern America* (1996). She is currently working on a book about the Little Rock school crisis, to be published by Princeton University Press.

TONY BADGER is Paul Mellon Professor of American History at the University of Cambridge. He is the author of *Prosperity Road: The New Deal, Tobacco and North Carolina* (1980); *North Carolina and the New Deal* (1981); *The New Deal: The Depression Years, 1933–1940* (1989). He is also the editor, with Brian Ward, of *The Making of Martin Luther King, Jr. and the Civil Rights Movement* (1996), and, with Byron Shafer, of *Contesting Democracy: Substance and Structure in American Political History, 1775–2000* (2001).

DAVID L. CHAPPELL is Associate Professor in the History Department at the University of Arkansas. His publications include *Inside Agitators: White Southerners in the Civil Rights Movement* (1994), a winner of the Gustavus Myers Award, and *A Stone of Hope: Prophetic Religion and the Death of Jim Crow* (2004).

JANE DAILEY is Associate Professor in History at Johns Hopkins University. She is the author of *Before Jim Crow: The Politics of Race in Postemancipation Virginia* (2000), and coeditor, with Glenda E. Gilmore and Bryant Simon, of *Jumpin' Jim Crow: Southern Politics from Civil War to Civil Rights* (2000).

ADAM FAIRCLOUGH is Professor of American Studies at the University of East Anglia. His many published works include *To Redeem the Soul of America: The Southern Christian Leadership Conference and Martin Luther King, Jr.* (1986); *Martin Luther King, Jr.* (1990); *Race and Democracy: The Civil Rights Struggle in Louisiana* (1995), winner of the Lillian Smith Award; *Teaching Equal-*

ity: Black Schools in the Age of Jim Crow (2001); and *Better Day Coming: Blacks and Equality, 1890–2000* (2001).

JOHN A. KIRK is Senior Lecturer in the History Department at Royal Holloway College. He is the author of *Redefining the Color Line: Black Activism in Little Rock, Arkansas, 1940–1970* (2002), which won the J. G. Ragsdale Book Award, and *Martin Luther King* (2004).

MICHAEL J. KLARMAN is James Monroe Professor of Law at the University of Virginia. A prolific scholar, he is the author of the book *From Jim Crow to Civil Rights: The Supreme Court and the Struggle for Racial Equality* (2004) and has also published articles in such journals as the *Journal of American History, Virginia Law Review*, and *Michigan Law Review*.

KEVIN M. KRUSE is Assistant Professor in the History Department at Princeton University. A specialist in the social, political, and legal history of the United States in the twentieth century, he is completing a book entitled *White Flight: Race, Place, and Politics in Atlanta*, which will be published by Princeton University Press in 2005.

GEORGE LEWIS is Lecturer in the Department of History at the University of Leicester. He is the author of *The White South and the Red Menace: Segregationists, Anticommunism, and Massive Resistance, 1945–1965* (2004).

ELIZABETH GILLESPIE McRAE is Assistant Professor of History and Director of Social Science Education at Western Carolina University. She is currently revising her dissertation, "Politics and Power: White Southern Conservative Women in the Age of Jim Crow," for publication. Her research has been published in the journals *Georgia Historical Quarterly* and *Carologue*.

CLIVE WEBB is Reader in American Studies at the University of Sussex. His publications include *Fight Against Fear: Southern Jews and Black Civil Rights* (2001). He is currently working on a collaborative project with William D. Carrigan about the lynching of Mexicans in the United States. Articles based on their research have won the Webb-Smith Essay Award from the University of Texas at Arlington and the Arthur Miller Prize from the British Association for American Studies.

CHRONOLOGY

May 17, 1954   U.S. Supreme Court decision in *Brown v. Board of
                        Education* rules that segregated public schools are
                        unconstitutional.

July 11, 1954   White Citizens' Council organized by Robert Pat-
                        terson in Indianola, Mississippi.

October 24, 1955   Eldon Edwards charters U.S. Klans, Knights of the
                        Ku Klux Klan.

May 31, 1955   U.S. Supreme Court issues implementation ruling,
                        Brown II, ordering school desegregation "with all
                        deliberate speed."

August–September 1955   Emmett Till, a black teenager from Chicago, is
                        murdered in Mississippi for allegedly whistling at a
                        white woman. An all-white jury acquits the accused
                        perpetrators.

December 1, 1955   Arrest of Rosa Parks precipitates bus boycott in
                        Montgomery, Alabama.

February 1956   Autherine Lucy admitted to University of Alabama,
                        but violent reaction leads to her expulsion.

March 12, 1956   Nineteen U.S. senators and eighty-one representa-
                        tives issue the Southern Manifesto in opposition to
                        Supreme Court decision.

August 30–31, 1956   Mobs prevent admission of black students to Mans-
                        field High School in Texas. Governor Allan Shivers
                        dispatches Texas Rangers to uphold segregation.
                        President Eisenhower does not intervene.

August–September 1956   Violent disorders over school desegregation in Clinton, Tennessee, lead to intervention of National Guard.

September 1956   National Guard used to restore order in Sturgis and Clay, Kentucky.

November 13, 1956   U.S. Supreme Court upholds federal district court decision in *Browder v. Gayle* ordering desegregation of Montgomery buses.

January 1957   Southern Christian Leadership Conference (SCLC) founded with Martin Luther King, Jr., as president.

September 1957   Congress passes a Civil Rights Act that provides only limited federal protection of black voting rights.

Eisenhower sends troops to suppress mob violence in Little Rock, Arkansas.

Dorothy Counts hounded from high school in Charlotte, North Carolina.

May 1958   Extremist National States' Rights Party established.

September 12, 1958   U.S. Supreme Court rules in *Cooper v. Aaron* that desegregation in Little Rock must occur without further delay.

1958–1959   Virginia closes nine schools in four counties rather than have them integrated. Plan later ruled illegal.

February 1960   Protests in Greensboro, North Carolina, lead to student sit-ins across the South. A new civil rights organization, the Student Non-Violent Coordinating Committee, emerges from the campaign.

May 6, 1960   Congress passes another weak Civil Rights Act.

November 8, 1960   John F. Kennedy elected president.

November 1960   Whites organize boycott of integrated schools in New Orleans.

December 5, 1960   U.S. Supreme Court rules in *Boynton v. Virginia* that the black patron of a restaurant at an inter-

	state bus terminal has a right to be served without discrimination.
May 4, 1961	The Congress of Racial Equality launches the Freedom Rides to integrate interstate bus routes in the South. Riders suffer a series of violent assaults and arrests. The Interstate Commerce Commission in November bans interstate bus companies from use of segregated facilities.
September 30, 1962	Attempt by James Meredith to register at the University of Mississippi results in riot.
January 14, 1963	During his inaugural address as governor of Alabama, George C. Wallace proclaims: "Segregation now, segregation tomorrow, Segregation forever!"
April-May 1963	SCLC campaign in Birmingham, Alabama, results in dramatic scenes of police violence against protesters.
June 11, 1963	George Wallace stands in doorway of University of Alabama to prevent admission of two black students.
June 12, 1963	Medgar Evers, field secretary of the National Association for the Advancement of Colored People, is assassinated.
September 15, 1963	Bombing of Sixteenth Street Baptist Church in Birmingham causes death of four black girls.
November 22, 1963	John F. Kennedy assassinated in Dallas, Texas. Lyndon B. Johnson assumes the presidency.
May–June 1964	Segregationists violently assault civil rights activists during SCLC campaign in St. Augustine, Florida.
June 20, 1964	Civil Rights Act passed.
June 21, 1964	Three voter registration workers, Michael Schwerner, James Chaney, and Andrew Goodman, reported missing at start of Mississippi Freedom Summer campaign. Bodies later discovered in an earthen dam.

March 1965	SCLC campaign in Selma, Alabama, leads to violence by state troopers. March from Selma to Montgomery ends with largest ever civil rights demonstration in the South.
August 6, 1965	Voting Rights Act signed into law.
September 1965	The Elementary and Secondary Education Act empowers the federal government to enforce compliance with desegregation by threatening to withhold funds to school systems.
June 12, 1967	U.S. Supreme Court in *Loving v. Commonwealth of Virginia* strikes down Virginia's prohibition of interracial marriages.
April 4, 1968	Martin Luther King assassinated during campaign in support of striking sanitation workers in Memphis, Tennessee.
October 29, 1969	U.S. Supreme Court rules in *Alexander v. Holmes County Board of Education* that the "all deliberate speed" time frame has expired and that schools must desegregate "at once."
April 20, 1971	U.S. Supreme Court in *Swann v. Charlotte-Mecklenberg Board of Education* endorses busing as a means to implement school desegregation.
1985	Foundation of the antiintegrationist Council of Conservative Citizens, which traces its roots back to the White Citizens' Councils of the massive resistance era.
2004	A greater percentage of black students attend majority-white schools in the South, but the figure continues to decline. Resegregation of public schools a mounting problem.

MASSIVE RESISTANCE

Introduction

On May 17, 1954, the United States Supreme Court issued its landmark ruling in the case of *Brown v. Board of Education* declaring that segregation in public schools was unconstitutional. Civil rights activists hailed the decision as a decisive watershed in the decades-long struggle against Jim Crow apartheid. Charles Johnson, president of Nashville's black university, Fisk, articulated the excited sense of expectation that the ruling would break down social barriers not just in schools but in all areas of public life: "If segregation is unconstitutional in educational institutions, it is no less so in other aspects of our national life." The *Chicago Defender*, the city's black newspaper, was even more emphatic, proclaiming the decision a "second emancipation proclamation."[1]

The Supreme Court decision drew a diverse response among white southerners. Whites in the Deep South mobilized in almost immediate opposition. The Mississippi State Supreme Court judge Tom P. Brady underlined the strength of white southern intransigence by branding the date of the *Brown* decision "Black Monday." Brady expressed the fears of miscegenation that were fundamental to white opposition against integration. In apocalyptic terms, he prophesied the destruction of the white race that would result from blacks and whites socializing in the same public spaces: "Whenever and wherever the white man has drunk the cup of black hemlock, whenever and wherever his blood has been infused with the blood of the negro, the white man, his intellect and his culture have died."[2] To southerners such as Brady, the *Brown* decision represented a usurpation of constitutional authority by the Supreme Court, a conspiracy by communists to destabilize the social and institutional order of the United States, even the start of a new secession crisis. According to the *Jackson Daily News*, "Human blood may stain Southern soil in many places because of this decision, but the dark red stains of that blood will be on the marble steps of the United States Supreme Court building."[3]

[3]

Yet white southerners were by no means united in their reaction to the Supreme Court decision. Southern politicians were only partially successful in exploiting social anxieties over school desegregation to their electoral advantage. The gubernatorial elections of 1954 offer a clear illustration of the political flux that characterized the southern states. Although white voters in South Carolina and Georgia elected uncompromising segregationist candidates, moderates won the day in Alabama, Florida, North Carolina, and Tennessee. The Upper South reacted with particular circumspection. Although most whites did not accept the moral principle of integration, many reluctantly accepted that the preservation of law and order compelled compliance with the ruling. On occasion there was even emphatic endorsement of the *Brown* decision. As the *Knoxville Journal* asserted, "No citizen, fitted by character and intelligence to sit as a Justice of the Supreme Court, and sworn to uphold the Constitution of the United States, could have decided this question other than the way it was decided."[4] Implementation of the court ruling proceeded without incident during 1955 and 1956 in parts of Arkansas, Kentucky, and Texas.

The Supreme Court took a further twelve months after its decision in the *Brown* case to issue an implementation decree. In May 1955, the court entrusted federal district and appeals courts with the responsibility for ensuring compliance with the initial ruling. The court did not establish a deadline for the termination of segregated schooling. Chief Justice Earl Warren, in one of the most controversial phrases in American legal history, wrote only that integration should be implemented "with all deliberate speed." The National Association for the Advancement of Colored People (NAACP) responded to what became known as *Brown II* by launching a series of legal actions intended to enforce school integration. Confronted by this threat, segregationists mobilized en masse.

Southern resistance assumed its most potent organizational shape in the White Citizens' Councils. Founded by Robert Patterson at Indianola, Mississippi, in July 1954, the Councils attained a membership estimated at 250,000. Most of these members were recruited from the middle classes, a deliberate strategy intended to promote an image of political respectability. The Citizens' Councils attempted to promote the legitimacy of their opposition to racial integration by disavowing violent resistance of the law and demagogic appeals to white prejudice. Instead, they tried to appeal to issues of high political principle by framing their opposition to the Supreme Court decision within the strict doctrine of states' rights. Nonetheless, the Councils' use of economic intimidation in particular contradicted their claims of political moderation. African Americans who attempted to register as voters or enroll their children at all-white schools suffered financial reprisals. Some were fired from their jobs; others had their names removed from the welfare rolls. Loans were called in and further credit refused. In these and other ways, white segregationists exploited the economic dependency of poor blacks as a means of repressing incipient civil rights protest.

Politicians reacted to the rightward shift in southern politics by pandering to the basest prejudices of the electorate. The governor of Arkansas, Orval Faubus, cynically abandoned his racially progressive position in pursuit of a third term. His defiant stance over school desegregation in Little Rock won over the segregationist doubters who had described him as "Awful Faubus" and secured his reelection. In 1958, meanwhile, the Alabama politician George Wallace lost the Democratic gubernatorial nomination to a hard-line segregationist. "Well boys," Wallace informed his supporters, "no other son-of-a-bitch will ever out-nigger me again." Four years later Wallace ran a blatantly race-baiting campaign and won the governorship in an unprecedented landslide.[5]

Confronted by the federal assault on state autonomy, southern politicians closed ranks. In March 1956 more than one hundred members of the House and Senate signed a "Declaration of Constitutional Principles" asserting their intention to use every legal means to resist school desegregation. "This unwarranted exercise of power by the court, contrary to the Constitution, is creating chaos and confusion in the states principally affected. It is destroying the amicable relations between the white and Negro races that have been created through ninety years of patient effort by the good people of both races."[6] The "Southern Manifesto," as it popularly came to be known, forced the hand of racially moderate politicians who feared electoral reprisals if they refused to add their signatures. The only southern senators who did not sign were Lyndon Johnson of Texas and Estes Kefauver and Albert Gore of Tennessee, all of whom had national ambitions that would suffer if they were associated with southern racism.[7]

The Southern Manifesto acted as a clarion call to the forces of white resistance. Defiance of the Supreme Court decision became the litmus test of white southerners' racial and regional loyalties. In the words of the journalist Hodding Carter, "the white South is as united as 30,000,000 people can be in its insistence upon segregation."[8] Despite such contemporary attempts, it is difficult to quantify the size and scale of massive resistance in the southern states. Although organizations such as the White Citizens' Councils recruited only a small share of the overall white southern population, the political inertia of many people should not be interpreted as a sign of their equivocation over segregation. A poll conducted by the American Institute of Public Opinion in 1956 showed that only 16 percent of southern whites approved of the *Brown* decision, compared with 80 percent who disapproved. In the core states of the Deep South—Alabama, Georgia, Louisiana, and Mississippi, and South Carolina—the percentage of those respondents opposed to the ruling was even higher, at around 90 percent.[9] In moments of crisis, when a community was confronted with court-ordered integration, ordinary citizens who had seldom or never participated in civic affairs were prepared to take to the streets in protest. The mobs that threatened black students attempting to integrate white institutions were not composed simply of a rabble element of the white, rural laboring class, or "rednecks," but included people drawn from a broad cross-section of the community.

One of the most aggressive forms of defense by white southerners was their use or misuse of the law to circumvent civil rights reform. Within a few years of the Supreme Court decision, southern state legislatures had enacted nearly five hundred laws intended to obstruct the already sluggish implementation of school desegregation. In the words of the *Richmond News Leader*, "if one remedial law is ruled invalid, then let us try another; and if the second is ruled invalid, then let us enact a third."[10] This strategy included "pupil placement" laws, which allowed local districts to assign students to schools according to complicated criteria that avoided mention of race but were clearly intended to maintain segregation. Southern lawmakers also threatened to withdraw state funds for educational institutions that complied with the Supreme Court, and approved payment of tuition grants to white parents who removed their children from integrated schools.

Southern authorities also took ruthless measures to repress the NAACP, which stood almost alone in its struggle to secure school desegregation. State prosecutors in some instances forced the organization to surrender its membership lists, exposing those people whose names appeared in the public domain to threats, harassment, and violence. When the NAACP refused to relinquish the names of its members, as was the case in Alabama, the courts imposed an outright ban on the organization. As soon as local branches of the NAACP filed desegregation suits against school boards, segregationists retaliated by threatening the signatories with physical harm or firing them from their jobs. By 1958 the NAACP had lost 246 branches in the South, and its litigation strategy was in disarray. The white power structure had succeeded in utilizing its superior resources to curtail school desegregation across the South.[11]

Southern politicians insisted that they acted within a strictly legal and constitutional framework in resisting school desegregation. Their defiance of federal authority nonetheless contributed to a political climate that encouraged acts of mob intimidation and racial terrorism. The refusal of elected officials to respect the law of the land, their threats of interposition, and their disavowal of responsibility for the violence they claimed would occur in reaction to federal efforts to enforce desegregation emboldened racial extremists to believe they could act with impunity in brutally repressing black civil rights. Between January 1, 1955, and January 1, 1959, the southern states experienced 225 incidents of anti–civil rights violence. That total included acts of intimidation, assault, and murder of black and white individuals, as well as the burning or bombing of schools, churches, synagogues, and private homes.[12] Educational institutions that attempted to integrate saw their campuses turned into battlegrounds. A mob of one thousand students rioted in protest at the admission of a black student, Autherine Lucy, to the University of Alabama in February 1956. Similar demonstrations met the enrollment of James Meredith at the University of Mississippi in September 1962. In the intervening years, racial violence erupted at locations from college campuses to elementary schools, from Charlotte to Nashville to New Orleans. The National Guard were dispatched to other less well documented trouble spots, including Clinton, Tennessee, and Clay and Sturgis, Kentucky.

Responsibility for these disturbances rests with the racist demagogues who stirred whites into open revolt. It should nonetheless be stressed that the failure of the federal government to enforce the Supreme Court decision gave implicit sanction to the forces of massive resistance. Dwight Eisenhower used neither his prestige as a military hero nor his presidential power to push for compliance with the ruling. This lack of moral leadership encouraged southern politicians to take measures in willful disobedience of federal law. In August 1956, the governor of Texas, Alan Shivers, used state troopers to prevent the admission of African American students to a public school in Mansfield. When black activists appealed to Eisenhower, he insisted that he did not have the jurisdiction to intervene. The Mansfield incident emboldened other politicians to believe they could resist court-ordered integration without risk of federal reprisal. On September 4, 1957, Governor Orval Faubus of Arkansas ordered National Guardsmen to obstruct the entrance of nine black students to Central High School in Little Rock. Following a meeting with the president at which he agreed not to cause further problems, Faubus withdrew the militia from the school. Disclaiming responsibility for any breakdown in law and order, he then left Little Rock for a southern governors' conference. On September 23, a mob of more than one thousand people confronted the black students. A frustrated and embarrassed Eisenhower was compelled to federalize the National Guard and dispatch U.S. paratroopers to enforce the law. Much of the responsibility for the Little Rock crisis nonetheless rested with federal authorities for their failure to take interventionist action until confronted by a flagrant challenge to their authority. The administration of John F. Kennedy was initially no more assertive in pushing for implementation of the Supreme Court decision. Kennedy held the complacent conviction that white southerners could through moral suasion be made to see reason. It took incidents such as the riotous reaction to the admission of James Meredith to the University of Mississippi in September 1962 to persuade Kennedy of the error of such a tactic.

By the early 1960s the strength of white southern opposition to school integration still appeared deep and pervasive. Ten years after the Supreme Court
handed down the *Brown* decision, less than 2 percent of black schoolchildren
in the southern states attended formerly all-white institutions. In the Deep
South, the figures were so small as to scarcely register on the political radar:
0.007 percent in Alabama, 0.004 percent in South Carolina, and not a single
child in Mississippi.[13] Racist demagogues such as Ross Barnett in Mississippi
and George Wallace in Alabama occupied governors' mansions across the
region. The White Citizens' Councils remained a potent political force. Many
other more extreme white supremacist organizations such as the Ku Klux Klan
and National States' Rights Party continued to brook no compromise over the
race issue.

Massive resistance, therefore, represented a potent challenge to the advancement of racial equality. Its influence pervaded the social, intellectual, and
political discourse of the southern states. Despite this, scholars have shown a
reluctance to treat segregationists seriously. Such is the persistent outpouring
of scholarship on the civil rights movement that it can threaten to submerge
readers. By contrast, research on massive resistance has amounted to little more
than a slow drip.

It is more than thirty years since Numan V. Bartley published his seminal
work *The Rise of Massive Resistance: Race and Politics in the South During the
1950s*. Since then, only a relatively small number of scholarly and journalistic works have been published on white southern opposition to desegregation.
This literature consists essentially of three elements. The most common are the
biographies of leading segregationist politicians, including Harry Byrd, Orval
Faubus, Strom Thurmond, and George Wallace.[14] A second element encom-
passes organizational histories of racial supremacist groups such as the White
Citizens' Council and the Ku Klux Klan.[15] The third consists of case studies of
southern communities that staged the most dramatic confrontations over the
desegregation of public schools and universities.[16]

Southern white opposition to the civil rights movement has nonetheless suffered relative neglect by scholars. The literature on the African American struggle for racial equality focuses primarily on the strategy and ideology of civil
rights protesters. As important as this is, it is only one side of the story. As the
historian Charles Eagles observes, the scholarship on the civil rights movement
"suffers from an asymmetry."[17] The comparative lack of attention bestowed on
segregationists has stripped the story of civil rights protest of its proper historical context. Only by understanding the nature of the opposition can scholars
accurately assess the accomplishments of the civil rights movement.

There are many potential issues where points of comparison and contrast can be made. Numerous studies emphasize the fractious nature of the

civil rights coalition. Martin Luther King attempted to act as the "vital center" between the moderate and radical factions of the movement. By contrast, white opposition to the movement is still commonly portrayed in monolithic terms. Yet ideological and strategic dissent also beset the ranks of segregationists. The issue that needs to be determined is whether or not these tensions were even more serious than those that threatened to unravel the civil rights coalition, and how important this was to segregationist defeat.

The study of white segregationists is important not simply as a means to enhance our understanding and appreciation of black civil rights activism but should be of intrinsic interest to any serious student of the American South. Historians have exposed the proslavery ideologies of nineteenth-century southern whites to rigorous critical examination.[18] The essays in this collection offer similar scrutiny of segregationist thought in the twentieth century. In some instances, the authors interpret the same issues and events but from different critical perspectives. This is true of the essays on the origins of massive resistance by Michael Klarman and Tony Badger, the assessment of school desegregation in Little Rock by John Kirk and Karen Anderson, and the analysis of the role of religion in the defense of segregation by David Chappell and Jane Dailey. Whatever their differences of opinion, the contributors to this collection all help to capture more clearly the political dynamics of the massive resistance movement.

Part I of this collection assesses how the political center in southern politics was eroded in the years that followed the Supreme Court decision. The authors examine the political strategies used by southern political leaders to oppose desegregation of the public school system and evaluate their success or failure.

Michael Klarman assesses how the forces of massive resistance overwhelmed more liberal opinion on racial integration. He asserts that those white southerners who were opposed to the *Brown* decision were more politically committed than were those who accepted or supported it. Moreover, die-hard segregationists used the apparatus of local and state government to crush political dissent among southern whites. Klarman emphasizes the importance of legislative malapportionment, which provided disproportionate political power to rural districts where white racism was most virulent. In the end, he paints a dramatic portrait of the southern states in the grip of reactionary racial politics.

Where Michael Klarman sees the Supreme Court decision as having galvanized white supremacist politics in the South, Tony Badger asserts that conservative resistance to racial change was already entrenched before 1954. He also claims that moderate southern politicians were too fearful of an electoral backlash to formulate a strategy to promote gradual racial reform once the Supreme Court had issued its ruling. The implication of this argument is that massive resistance only became inevitable because of the timidity and fatalism of liberal leaders.

To complement the broad regional analyses of Klarman and Badger, Adam Fairclough provides a specific state study of segregationist politics in Louisiana. Fairclough shows how the racially moderate state leadership was confronted with an intense political challenge from the forces of massive resistance. Although the gubernatorial election of Earl Long in 1956 appeared to represent the triumph of racial moderates, within months hard-line segregationists reclaimed the political initiative, launching a multipronged assault on black civil rights. The forces of massive resistance would nonetheless ultimately fail, particularly in their attempt to purge black voters from the electoral rolls, which resulted in a federal backlash. In addition, Fairclough depicts the massive resistance movement as less a grassroots revolt against an unrepresentative government than a conspiracy by a small but fanatical band of politicians.

Historians of the civil rights movement have focused on the more obvious flash points of white southern resistance, none more so than the Little Rock school crisis of 1957. John Kirk asserts that scholars who focus on the scenes of violent unrest precipitated by the political antics of Governor Orval Faubus misrepresent the real character of the crisis. Kirk focuses less on the public scenes of massive resistance than on the policy of minimum compliance pursued by Arkansas's superintendent of schools, Virgil T. Blossom. Although Blossom claimed to steer a politically moderate course between what he called the extremists on both sides of the integration issue, his strategy was simply a more insidious means of undermining implementation of the Supreme Court decision.

Whites in Atlanta also pursued an alternate strategy to open confrontation in resisting school desegregation. Kevin Kruse reveals how white parents used the rationale of "freedom of association" to protect their children from attending school with African Americans. When it became apparent that the public school system would be desegregated, whites applied the same line of reasoning in reenrolling their children at private religious academies. These institutions succeeded in maintaining segregation long after the forces of massive resistance had supposedly suffered defeat. The two case studies by Kirk and Kruse show that while segregationists could not win a showdown with federal authorities over school desegregation, they could still successfully circumvent the Supreme Court decision.

Kruse argues that the emphasis white Atlantans placed on the right to make choices for their children free of governmental interference was not merely a conceit intended to conceal their crude racial prejudice. Part II of this collection demonstrates in further detail that southern opposition to the Supreme Court decision was a complex phenomenon. Through a focus on the political thought of segregationists, the authors show how not only race but also religion, class, gender, and global politics impacted on massive resistance politics.

In recent years historians have enhanced our understanding of the civil rights revolution by placing it within the larger political context of the Cold War. The persistence of racial discrimination at home compromised the capacity of the federal government to fight communism abroad. Soviet propaganda emphasized the hypocrisy of the United States for proclaiming to be the leader of the free world while tolerating the repression of its own citizens on the basis of race. Apprehension over the potential impact to its international reputation forced the United States government to take a more committed stance in support of black civil rights. George Lewis pursues an alternate line of analysis by assessing how segregationists also attempted to manipulate Cold War tensions to their own political advantage. The parochial self-interest of segregationists seemed to their political opponents "un-American," since it destabilized the United States at a time when the country was already faced with an unprecedented foreign threat. Segregationists, therefore, attempted to reclaim their political legitimacy by arguing that civil rights activism was a communist conspiracy to destroy the social fabric of the nation. This exploitation of Cold War rhetoric transformed the struggle to preserve Jim Crow into a patriotic crusade. The irony lost on segregationists was that their supposed protection of American traditions and ideals made it permissible for them to disobey their own democratically elected government.

The chapters by David Chappell and Jane Dailey provide a provocative dialogue on the religious defense of racial segregation. Chappell argues that the southern states did not withstand the tide of political reform in part because white religious leaders failed to commit complete ideological and institutional support for segregation. The equivocation of white southern clergymen denied segregationists the cultural legitimacy they needed to sustain their cause. This was in pronounced contrast to the pivotal role of the black church in promoting civil rights reform. The church not only served as an organizational base and important source of income but also, through its leaders, instilled activists with a sense of divine purpose. Chappell summarizes his challenging thesis by saying that white churches, in contrast, "did not care deeply enough about segregation to make its defense the most important thing in their lives." Dailey takes issue with this analysis. She asserts that segregationists were motivated by their fear of miscegenation to seek divine sanction for the separation of the races. They found in their reading of the Bible theological justification for their opposition to the atheistic Supreme Court decision. Despite their interpretative differences, Chappell and Dailey share some common ground. Both historians accept that there were serious tensions over the issue of segregation between liberal clergymen and their more conservative congregations. Although many religious leaders may not have sustained the southern cause, at a grassroots level the Bible seems to have been a potent ideological weapon in the segregationist arsenal.

Dailey observes that many of the ordinary white southerners who quoted Holy Scripture in support of segregation were women. While case studies of local and state civil rights activism have revealed the central role of African American women, historians have largely neglected the contribution of female segregationists to the protection of Jim Crow. The last two chapters in this collection address this lacuna in civil rights historiography.

Elizabeth McRae expands on this point in her biographical profile of the Mississippi segregationist Florence Sillers Ogden. Ogden drew on traditional constructions of maternal responsibilities in constructing a public role as defender of white supremacy. She argued that women had a duty to campaign against racial integration in order to protect the welfare of current and future generations of white southerners. This increased public activism on the part of white southern women was by implication a criticism of the incompetence of the male power structure. Although Ogden does not appear to have been aware of it, her arguments were riddled with inconsistencies. She proclaimed the need for women to assume a more substantial role in political affairs while disparaging gender equality in the workplace. While she saw the preservation of segregation as essential to protect the privileges of white women, the male leadership of the massive resistance movement chauvinistically marginalized their female members. The story of Florence Sillers Ogden is nonetheless significant in showing that white women served more than a rhetorical purpose for the segregationist cause as passive victims in need of male protection.

In a similar vein, Karen Anderson reassesses the Little Rock school crisis through the lens of gender. She asserts that white working-class men interpreted desegregation as a challenge to their manhood. As whites they were alarmed at the elimination of their social privileges. As workers they were threatened by the removal of racial barriers that protected them against job competition. And as fathers they feared that the admission of African Americans to integrated public schools would lead to a loss of patriarchal control over the sexual choices of their children. Their opposition to integration was therefore not only a means to retain white racial dominance but also to restore masculine pride. Ironically, the intervention of white women in the school crisis bolstered the ability of men to reclaim their traditional role as protectors of their wives and daughters. The Mothers' League of Central High portrayed women as the passive victims of federal government aggression, necessitating the intervention of male segregationists. As Anderson shows, the Mothers' League paradoxically succeeded in pandering to traditional gender stereotypes while empowering white women to take a more active role in civic affairs.

. . .

Although this collection provides important new perspectives on massive resistance, there are numerous areas of research still in need of investigation. First, while scholars continue to study the Little Rock crisis in intimate detail, the stories of other communities that suffered serious disorder over school desegregation have still to be told. The two chapters on Little Rock in this collection are testimony to its enduring scholarly interest. Nonetheless, we need to learn the extent to which the analysis of that crisis can be applied to other cities affected by violent racial unrest. There are, for instance, interesting points of comparison and contrast between Little Rock and Nashville. Desegregation of public schools occurred simultaneously in the two cities. Both Little Rock and Nashville had reputations for racial progressivism. Despite this, the school boards in both cities pursued a policy of minimum compliance with court orders to integrate their public schools. The Nashville school board implemented a plan similar to that described by John Kirk in his essay on Little Rock to restrict the number of black students admitted to white institutions. Both cities were also the scene of mob violence when African Americans attempted to enter the schools. Yet here the comparison ends. While the turmoil in Little Rock necessitated the intervention of the National Guard, the city administration in Nashville moved swiftly to dispel the rabble element within their midst. The issue that needs to be assessed is why extremism prevailed in one community and moderation in the other. It is also necessary to ask whether the negative impact of the Little Rock crisis served as an instructive lesson to the white leadership of other cities such as Nashville.

A case study could also be made of the Kentucky towns of Sturgis and Clay. In September 1956, nine black students attempted to integrate the high school in the small mining community of Sturgis. Their entry was blocked by a mob brandishing shovels and baseball bats. Trouble also erupted in the nearby town of Clay, where the local school board had publicly opposed desegregation. When Governor Albert B. Chandler sent in the National Guard to restore order in both communities, white parents withdrew their children from the schools. Many teaching staff also resigned or failed to report to class. Efforts to enforce integration were further undermined when the attorney general of Kentucky, Jo M. Ferguson, issued an opinion that the admission of the black students was illegal. The frustrated attempt to integrate public schools in western Kentucky is omitted from many studies of massive resistance. Nonetheless, the experiences of Sturgis and Clay raise a range of issues. The towns stood in a border state and had predominantly white populations. How, therefore, do we account for the violent hostility toward desegregation? Was class as much a factor as race for the working people of these mining communities? The intransigence of the school boards and the resignations of some teachers also underlines the need to study more closely how the desegregation crisis impacted on men, women, and children in the classroom. Almost nothing, for instance, has been written on school integration from the perspective of the teachers who had to contend with their own prejudices while overseeing the admission of black students.

Second, other scholars need to add their voices to the debate between David Chappell and Jane Dailey about the role of religion in the defense of segrega-tion. Chappell supports his claim that white church leaders were a hindrance rather than a help to the massive resistance cause by citing the resolutions issued by southern religious organizations in support of the Supreme Court. The fact that these resolutions were made at all is significant, but what still needs to be determined is whether they led to the actual implementation of racial reform within southern churches. If one accepts that white southern cler-gymen equivocated over segregation, the issue that must also be addressed is why and when the church ceased to serve the defense of the status quo. When southern institutions were under threat from the federal government in the 1850s, church leaders provided powerful ideological defenses of slavery and secession. Yet when the South faced similar challenges from Washington in the 1950s, clergymen offered little resistance. This shift over the course of a century in the racial attitudes of southern white churches needs to be explained.

Third, we need to learn more from a secular perspective about the battle between segregationists and civil rights activists for the hearts and minds of the American people. One of the most successful strategies pursued by civil rights protesters was their manipulation of the media. The Southern Christian Leadership Conference was particularly skillful in using the press to its political advantage. The presence of cameras at its demonstrations acted as a control on local authorities who feared that the use of excessive force would generate negative publicity. While law enforcement officials were willing to take physical action against demonstrators, they did not act with a reckless disregard for life. Through their careful control of the situation, civil rights activists were there-fore able to dramatize the virulence of white racial violence without excessive risk to themselves. While historians have long recognized the importance of the print media and television to the civil rights cause, they are also now start-ing to appreciate the importance of radio. Brian Ward has brilliantly demon-strated how black radio stations played a pivotal role in the dissemination of propaganda and organization of civil rights demonstrations.[19] By contrast, far less known is about how southern segregationists used channels of commu-nication to influence public opinion. No scholar, for instance, has attempted a systematic study of the Citizens' Council Forum Films, broadcast between

1955 and 1966. These fifteen-minute propaganda films preached not only to the converted but also were screened by television stations across the country in an attempt to enlist the support of northern conservatives. The failure of southern segregationists to sell their message to a national audience places the successful media strategy of the civil rights movement in even sharper perspective.[20]

Fourth, much of the literature on massive resistance focuses on the southern political elites who pursued a strategy of "respectable resistance" against desegregation. Far less attention has been given to the more militant white supremacists who made less pretense of operating within the democratic political process. If we know comparatively little about elite segregationist groups like the White Citizens' Council, then we know almost nothing at all about racial extremists such as Americans for the Preservation of the White Race, the National States' Rights Party, and the National Association for the Advancement of White People. The members of these organizations are usually dismissed as uneducated, marginal members of society who suffered from some form of clinical psychosis. Yet many radical racist leaders were actually from more stable and privileged family backgrounds than scholars have often assumed. More research is need on the motivations of these extremists and their methods of mobilizing popular support. Moreover, further study of the fraught relationship between moderate and radical segregationists will help to challenge common notions of a monolithic massive resistance movement.

History, it is often said, is written by the victors. The story of the civil rights movement has too often been told from the sole perspective of the activists who attempted to destroy the institution of Jim Crow apartheid. It is all too easy to dismiss segregationists as a relic of an earlier, less tolerant era in American race relations. At a time when social scientists report that the resegregation of public schools is occurring at the fastest rate since the *Brown* decision, we should perhaps consider more carefully the enduring significance of massive resistance.[21]

Notes

1. James T. Patterson, *Brown v. Board of Education: A Civil Rights Milestone and Its Troubled Legacy* (New York: Oxford University Press, 2001), 71.

2. Judge Tom P. Brady, *Black Monday* (Winona, Miss.: Association of Citizens' Councils, 1955).

3. *Jackson Daily News*, May 18, 1954.

4. Hugh Davis Graham, *Crisis in Print: Desegregation and the Press in Tennessee* (Nashville: Vanderbilt University Press, 1967), 32.

5. Dan T. Carter, *The Politics of Rage: George Wallace, The Origins of the New Conservatism, and The Transformation of American Politics* (New York: Simon and Schuster, 1995), 96.

6. *New York Times*, Mar. 12, 1956.

7. Tony Badger, "Southerners Who Refused to Sign the Southern Manifesto," *Historical Journal* 42 (1999): 517–34.

8. David R. Goldfield, *Promised Land: The South Since 1945* (Arlington Heights, Ill.: Harlan Davidson, 1987), 52.

9. Numan V. Bartley, *The Rise of Massive Resistance: Race and Politics in the South During the 1950s* (Baton Rouge: Louisiana State University Press, 1969), 13–14.

10. John Bartlow Martin, *The Deep South Says "Never"* (New York: Ballantine Books, 1957), 11–12.

11. Adam Fairclough, *Better Day Coming: Blacks and Equality* (New York: Viking Penguin, 2001), 221–24.

12. Michal R. Belknap, *Federal Law and Southern Order: Racial Violence and Constitutional Conflict* (Athens: University of Georgia Press, 1987), 28–29.

13. Martin Gilbert, *The Dent Atlas of American History* (London: Dent, 1993), 105.

14. Ronald L. Heinemann, *Harry Byrd of Virginia* (Charlottesville: University Press of Virginia, 1996); Roy Reed, *Faubus: The Life and Times of an American Prodigal* (Fayetteville: University of Arkansas Press, 1997); Nadine Cohodas, *Strom Thurmond and the Politics of Southern Change* (New York: Simon and Schuster, 1993); Stephan Lesher, *George Wallace: American Populist* (Reading, Mass.: Addison-Wesley, 1993); Carter, *Politics of Rage*.

15. Neil R. McMillen, *The Citizens' Council: Organized Resistance to the Second Reconstruction, 1954–64* (Urbana: University of Illinois Press, 1971); David Chalmers, *Backfire: How the Ku Klux Klan Helped the Civil Rights Movement* (Lanham, Md.: Rowman and Littlefield, 2003).

16. Matthew D. Lassiter and Andrew B. Lewis, eds., *The Moderates' Dilemma: Massive Resistance to School Desegregation in Virginia* (Charlottesville: University Press of Virginia, 1998); Jeff Roche, *Restructured Resistance: The Sibley Commission and the Politics of Desegregation in Georgia* (Athens: University of Georgia Press, 1998); Elizabeth Jacoway and C. Fred Williams, eds., *Understanding the Little Rock Crisis: An Exercise in Remembrance and Reconciliation* (Fayetteville: University of Arkansas Press, 1999); William Doyle, *An American Insurrection: The Battle of Oxford, Mississippi, 1962* (New York: Doubleday, 2001).

17. Charles W. Eagles, "Toward New Histories of the Civil Rights Era," *Journal of Southern History* 66 (2000): 842.

18. Studies of proslavery ideology include Drew Gilpin Faust, ed., *The Ideology of Slavery: Proslavery Thought in the Antebellum South, 1830–1860* (Baton Rouge: Louisiana State University Press, 1981); Larry E. Tise, *Proslavery: A History of the Defense of Slavery in America, 1701–1840* (Athens: University of Georgia Press, 1987); John David Smith, *An Old Creed for the New South: Proslavery Ideology and Historiography, 1865–1918* (Athens: University of Georgia Press, 1991); David F. Ericson, *The Debate over Slavery: Antislavery and Proslavery Liberalism in Antebellum America* (New York: New York University Press, 2000); John Patrick Daly, *When Slavery Was Called Freedom: Evangelicalism, Proslavery, and the Causes of the Civil War* (Lexington: University Press of Kentucky, 2002); Paul Finkelman, *Defending Slavery: Proslavery Thought in the Old South, A Brief History with Documents* (Boston: St. Martin's, 2003).

19. Brian Ward, *Radio and the Struggle for Civil Rights in the South* (Gainesville: University Press of Florida, 2004).

20. The Citizens' Council Forum Films Collection, consisting of 132 reels of film, is housed at the Mississippi Department of Archives and History, Jackson, Mississippi.

21. For a detailed statistical analysis of the current racial balance in public schools, see Gary Orfield and John T. Yun, "Resegregation in American Schools," Civil Rights Project, Harvard University, available online at: www.civilrightsproject.harvard.edu/research/deseg/Resegregation_American_Schools99.pdf. Consulted October 14, 2004. No print source known.

PART ONE

The Origins and Impact
of Southern Resistance

ONE

Why Massive Resistance?

Michael J. Klarman

On May 17, 1954, the United States Supreme Court invalidated public school segregation in *Brown v. Board of Education*. Most politicians outside of the Deep South reacted to *Brown* with restraint. Governor Francis Cherry of Arkansas promised that his state would "obey the law. It always has." The governor of Virginia, Thomas B. Stanley, guaranteed a "calm" and "dispassionate" response to *Brown*, and the state's superintendent of public education predicted "no defiance." That spring and summer, *Brown* attracted little attention in Democratic primaries in Arkansas, Alabama, Florida, and Texas. Throughout most of the South, newspaper editors urged calm and avoided talk of defiance. The *Nashville Tennessean* declared that southerners "have learned to live with change. They can learn to live with this one." Ralph McGill of the *Atlanta Constitution* was reported to have said: "Segregation is on the way out . . . and he who tries to tell the people otherwise does them great disservice." The day after *Brown*, the school board of Greensboro, North Carolina, voted six to one to instruct the superintendent to study means of compliance, and within a week the Little Rock school board had followed suit.[1]

Political reaction in the Deep South was often more defiant. Governor Herman Talmadge declared, "Georgia is going to resist mixing the races in the schools if it is the sole state of the nation to do so." Senator James Eastland of Mississippi announced that "the South will not abide by or obey this legislative decision by a political court," and Mississippi officials warned that they would abolish public education before integrating. The Louisiana legislature, in session when *Brown* was decided, overwhelmingly resolved to censure the Court's "usurpation of power" and adopted a new school segregation law. That fall, voters in Georgia and Mississippi passed constitutional amendments that authorized legislatures to close schools rather than desegregate them. By September, Talmadge was declaring that "no amount of force whatever can compel desegregation of white and Negro schools," while Governor-elect Marvin Griffin was announcing that "come hell or high water, races will not be mixed in Georgia schools."[2]

Over the next eighteen months, most of the region fell in line behind the defiant Deep South. Citizens' Councils, new organizations committed to preserving white supremacy by all means short of violence, began forming in Mississippi in the summer of 1954, quickly spread to Alabama, and then expanded across the South, achieving a maximum membership of perhaps 250,000. Whites flocked to the councils as southern blacks began filing desegregation petitions with school boards; many whites reasoned, "we must make certain that Negroes are not allowed to force their demands on us." The Supreme Court's enforcement decision in *Brown II* fueled further resistance, as many southern whites detected weakness or "backtrack[ing]" in the justices' efforts to be conciliatory. A Florida segregationist thought the court had "realized it made a mistake in May and is getting out of it the best way it can." When lower courts began ordering desegregation, violence erupted, which further radicalized white opinion. The admission of Autherine Lucy to the University of Alabama in February 1956 produced a race riot, and Alabama whites, already riled over the Montgomery bus boycott, now joined Citizens' Councils in droves. That month a segregationist rally in Montgomery drew ten thousand people. Early in 1956, several state legislatures in the South adopted interposition resolutions that purported to nullify *Brown*. They also passed dozens of laws designed to avoid desegregation—measures that authorized school closures, repealed compulsory attendance requirements, cut off public funding for integrated schools, provided public money for private schools, and attacked the NAACP. In March 1956, most southern congressmen signed the Southern Manifesto, which assailed the court's "clear abuse of judicial power" and pledged all "lawful means" of resistance.[3]

Political contests in southern states quickly assumed a common pattern: candidates tried to show that they were the most "blatantly and uncompromisingly prepared to cling to segregation at all costs." "Moderation" became "a term of derision," as the political center collapsed, leaving only "those who want to maintain the Southern way of life or those who want to mix the races." Moderate critics of massive resistance were labeled "double crossers," "sugar-coated integrationists," "cowards," and "traitors." Most officeholders either joined the segregationist bandwagon or were retired from service. A Virginia politician observed that it "would be suicide to run on any other platform [than segregation]."[4]

Why did *Brown* so radicalize southern politics, leading candidates for public office to compete for the most extreme segregationist positions? Politics does not usually work this way. Rather, politicians generally strive for the middle, seeking to assemble majority coalitions by appealing to median voters, who, by definition, are moderates rather than extremists. There *were* white racial moderates in the South—people who favored compliance with court orders, opposed school closures, and would have tolerated gradual desegregation. The justices in *Brown II* had consciously appealed to such moderates and sought to empower them. Why did that strategy fail so abysmally? Why were so few moderate voices heard in the South after *Brown*?

One explanation focuses on southern politicians. Either because they miscalculated their constituents' preferences or because they demagogically capitalized on their constituents' fears, politicians became extremists and created an environment that chilled the expression of moderate sentiment. In this view, massive resistance was not inevitable, at least outside of the Deep South. Politicians could have espoused more moderate positions without losing office, as evidenced by electoral results in Tennessee and Texas. Had they chosen this route, politicians might have mobilized more vocal support from the large bloc of moderates, who instead fell silent.[5]

It is true that some politicians had incentives for extremism, regardless of their constituents' preferences. In Virginia, the Byrd machine had reason to drum up massive resistance to school desegregation, which could distract voters from debates over public services that were gradually weakening its political position. But in most of the South, it was not politicians who were primarily responsible for massive resistance. The political dynamics of the segregation issue, combined with certain features of southern politics, propelled public debate toward extremism, independently of the machinations of politicians. Most officials, including those who were ordinarily inclined toward racial moderation, became more extremist to survive, and those few who resisted were generally destroyed.[6]

Several factors helped foster massive resistance. Die-hard segregationists had stronger preferences than did most moderates. They also had the capacity and the inclination to use repressive tactics to create the appearance that southern whites were united behind massive resistance. Die-hard states similarly exerted pressure on more moderately inclined neighbors to support massive resistance. Further, legislative malapportionment exaggerated the political power of extremists. Perhaps most important, the desire of nearly all southern whites to preserve segregation if possible virtually ensured an attempt at massive resistance. Differences among whites concerned the costs that they were willing to bear to preserve segregation, not their preference for it. Finally, the use of federal troops, which proved necessary to suppress massive resistance, ironically bolstered it in the short term.

Although many white southerners were prepared to comply with *Brown*, and a few actually agreed with it, hard-core segregationists tended to be more intensely committed. Some white moderates came from regions with small black populations, so that school desegregation would not greatly affect them. Ardent segregationists tended to come from rural areas with large black populations or from working-class urban neighborhoods without rigid residential segregation. Those who were most committed on the segregation issue tended to be most adamantly opposed to *Brown*. By virtue of their strong preferences, they were also likely to control southern racial policy. Black-belt segregationists generally dominated legislative commissions that were appointed to recommend responses to *Brown*. The legislator who chaired Virginia's commission, Garland Gray, came from the Southside region of Virginia, and he had already recorded his "unalterable opposition" to the court's "monstrous" decision. All five members of the Arkansas legislative committee that recommended policy on school segregation represented the Delta region, home to the state's largest black populations.[7]

Die-hard segregationists were not only more intensely committed than their adversaries were but also had the inclination and the capacity to silence dissent. Massive resisters wanted to suppress opposition because they believed that only by presenting a united front could they induce the court and the nation to retreat from *Brown*. This issue arose mainly in the context of whether to allow local-option desegregation. If given a choice, portions of many southern states—northwestern Arkansas, West Texas, northern and western Virginia, East Tennessee, and the city of Atlanta—were prepared to comply with *Brown*. But massive resisters in state government were determined to eliminate that choice for fear that any deviation from universal segregation would make integration appear inevitable, embolden the NAACP, and undermine the campaign to convince northern integrationists that the South would never tolerate *Brown*. Thus, the Virginia legislature revoked Arlington County's right to elect school board members as punishment for the board's 1956 vote to desegregate, and it rejected the Gray Commission's initial proposal for local-option desegregation. In 1957 the Texas legislature required local communities to conduct referenda before desegregating or else lose their state education funds. More than 120 school districts in Texas had desegregated before this law was passed, but almost none did so for several years thereafter. Massive resisters in Georgia worried that Atlanta, with its "wrecking crew of extremists, ultra-liberals and renegade politicians," could prove to be the "Achilles' heel in the fight to keep segregation." When Mayor William B. Hartsfield asked the state legislature to adopt local option, Governor Griffin declared that the mayor "cannot throw in the towel for me or any other Georgian," and Senator Richard B. Russell warned against "surrender" talk. The Southern Manifesto was a highly successful effort by senators such as Russell and Harry Byrd to coerce moderates—Lister Hill, John Sparkman, William Fulbright, Brooks Hays—into maintaining a united front.[8]

Their incentive to suppress dissent is clear, but why were massive resisters so effective at doing so? The answer, in short, is that the South was not an open society characterized by robust debate on racial issues. In 1960 a law school dean in Mississippi pointed out: "Friends won't argue among themselves" about segregation, and "you can't think out loud hardly." James Silver, a history professor at the University of Mississippi, charged that Mississippi had "erected a totalitarian society which has eliminated the ordinary processes through which change can come about." A South Carolina minister, noting that people were afraid even to protest the beating of a local band teacher who had allegedly made integrationist statements, observed that "fear covers South Carolina like the frost." In such an environment, white moderates were "immobilized by confusion and fear," and they mostly went into hiding.[9]

In the mid-1950s, massive resisters were a majority in much of the South, and thus they could use the levers of government to suppress dissent. Public school teachers and university professors lost their jobs or were harassed by legislative investigating committees for daring to support integration or even for urging obedience of the law and criticizing mob violence. Unwilling to tolerate such assaults on academic freedom, many of them resigned and moved elsewhere, which only exacerbated the problem of the closed society. Integrationist university students faced similar harassment and expulsion. Some southern states targeted speech as well as speakers, removing offensive books from circulation. When the Georgia board of education banned textbook statements that charged whites with discrimination against blacks, the chairman explained: "There is no place in Georgia schools at any time for anything that disagrees with our way of life." An Alabama legislator sparked a national controversy by demanding that public libraries ban a popular children's book about the marriage of two rabbits, one white and one black. Even the staunchly segregationist *Montgomery Advertiser* thought this was "idiocy," but the legislator defended himself on the ground that "the South has room for only one viewpoint."[10]

Private suppression of dissent supplemented public suppression. Citizens' Councils applied economic pressure to blacks who pursued integration and to whites who were deemed insufficiently committed to segregation. The U.S. Civil Rights Commission had difficulty enlisting Mississippi whites to serve on the state's advisory committee after a Citizens' Council editor warned that "any scalawag southerner who fronts for our mortal enemies will face the well-deserved contempt and ostracism that any proud people would feel for a traitor." White students who initially befriended the Little Rock Nine were condemned

THE ORIGINS AND IMPACT OF SOUTHERN RESISTANCE

as "Nigger lovers," as were Ole Miss faculty and administrators who were civil to James Meredith. When a few white families refused to boycott desegregated schools in New Orleans in 1960, they received death threats, homes were vandalized, and the parents were fired from their jobs. One family gave up and moved north. Violence was the last resort for compelling white conformity. A mob beat up a white minister in Clinton, Tennessee, for escorting black students to the desegregated school. When a white woman contributed an essay to the moderate publication *South Carolinians Speak* in which she urged gradual desegregation, her home was bombed.[11]

Such pressure suppressed the traditional organs of moderate racial opinion. Newspapers that advocated desegregation or simple obedience of the law were boycotted and sometimes shut down. The editor of the only South Carolina newspaper that urged compliance with *Brown* was driven out of the state, as was the editor of one of the few Mississippi newspapers that criticized Governor Ross Barnett's antics at the University of Mississippi. Southern ministers who advocated integration, or simply protested against extremist resistance, were usually evicted by their congregations. In 1963, twenty-eight Methodist ministers in Mississippi signed a statement supporting school desegregation, and all but seven of them were gone within a year. Many other ministers simply suppressed their private convictions that segregation was immoral. Under pressure from public officials, some southern universities stopped inviting integrationist speakers. Citizens' Councils harassed social clubs that expressed interest in hearing opposing viewpoints. Some television stations refused to air national programs that discussed integration, explaining that they were not "running a propaganda machine for the NAACP."[12]

If southern society was closed for whites, it was hermetically sealed for blacks. Because blacks were the most integrationist of southerners, suppressing their viewpoint was critical to maintaining the veneer of solid support for segregation. Blacks were subject to the same forms of segregationist pressure as whites but often more intense versions. Citizens' Councils announced: "We intend to make it difficult, if not impossible, for any Negro who advocates desegregation to find and hold a job, get credit, or renew a mortgage." Police harassed integrationist blacks, disbanding their meetings, arresting them on fraudulent charges, and sometimes beating them. During the Montgomery bus boycott, public officials who were pursuing a "get tough" policy arrested scores of blacks on phony traffic charges and tried to disbar the black lawyer who filed the bus desegregation suit and to alter his draft classification. A black man in Bessemer, Alabama, was sentenced to six months in jail for breach of the peace and inciting to riot for reproducing a picture from a northern newspaper of a black man praying to God that equal rights would be extended to all. The most aggressive black integrationists were targets of extraordinary white violence.

Daisy Bates, leader of Little Rock's desegregation forces, had her home fire-bombed seven times within two years.[13]

Southern society was closed, but Mississippi verged on totalitarianism. The state sovereignty commission spied on civil rights workers and channeled public funds to Citizens' Councils. The legislature made it a crime to incite a breach of the peace by urging "nonconformance with the established traditions, customs, and usages of the State of Mississippi," and Governor James Coleman threatened to prosecute speakers who entered Mississippi to agitate the race issue. A white newspaper editor, who was sued for libel for criticizing law enforcement officers who mistreated blacks, observed that "in much of Mississippi, we live in an atmosphere of fear." When the longtime University of Mississippi history professor James Silver criticized the state as a "closed society" in 1963, public officials, failing to perceive the irony, announced that "it is time to get rid" of Silver and "to stifle his degrading activities." Mississippi officials concocted phony charges against blacks who pursued integration. Clyde Kennard, who tried to desegregate Mississippi Southern University, was later sentenced to seven years at hard labor for allegedly trying to buy twenty-five dollars' worth of stolen chicken feed. When the NAACP field secretary Medgar Evers called Kennard's sentence "a mockery of judicial justice," he received thirty days in jail for contempt. Nobody ruled Senator Eastland in contempt, though, when he told white Mississippians: "You are not required to obey any court which passes out such a ruling [*Brown*]. In fact, you are obligated to defy it." In many parts of Mississippi, blacks still faced "systematic racial terrorism." A visitor to Jefferson County reported: "It is all but unbelievable to see the fear that is shown by the Negro people." In many counties, not a single black person dared register to vote. In the early 1960s, civil rights workers in Mississippi were routinely beaten, bombed, shot at, and occasionally killed.[14]

Racial moderates had neither the inclination nor the capacity to use such methods. They did not control state or local governments, and thus they could not fire segregationist teachers, expel segregationist students, or use law enforcement apparatus to harass Citizens' Council members. Nor did moderates make harassing phone calls to segregationists, burn crosses on their lawns, or blow up their homes. When Robert Williams, the president of the NAACP branch in Union County, North Carolina, advocated that blacks meet "violence with violence" in the wake of Mack Parker's lynching in Mississippi in 1959, the national office immediately suspended him. Thus, hard-core segregationists were not only more intensely committed to their position than were moderate whites but also were more willing to use coercive measures to achieve victory. The suppression of moderate opinion had a cascading effect: as some people were intimidated into silence, the pressure on others to conform intensified.[15]

Just as die-hard segregationists in one state could pressure moderates by denying the inevitability of desegregation, so could extremist states pressure their moderate neighbors. Politicians had difficulty explaining to constituents why they had to desegregate when neighboring states were not doing so. This dynamic partially explains Governor Orval Faubus's dilemma over school desegregation in Little Rock in 1957. Alabama and Texas had flouted desegregation orders the previous year, and the segregationist governor of Georgia, Marvin Griffin, visited Little Rock two weeks before schools were scheduled to open, expressing shock that any governor with troops at his disposal would allow integration. Citizens approached Faubus on the street, demanding to know "if Georgia doesn't have integration, why does Arkansas?" On other occasions, Citizens' Council members asked why Faubus remained silent while governors in South Carolina and Georgia were denouncing court decisions that banned segregation in public parks, playgrounds, and golf courses. Alabama Citizens' Councils pressured their congressmen "to join us in this fight, so we won't have to go to Mississippi, Georgia or South Carolina" to find real segregationists.[16]

Comprehending this dynamic and the importance of maintaining regional unity, die-hard states in the Deep South pressured their more moderate neighbors to conform to massive resistance. The *State* of Columbia, South Carolina criticized states that were abandoning segregation without a fight, because "surrender of some states makes it harder for the others to hold the line." Soon after he had fomented violent resistance to desegregation in Clinton, Tennessee, John Kasper, the South's leading peripatetic troublemaker, told Birmingham segregationists: "We want trouble and we want it everywhere we can get it." When sixteen Clintonians were arrested in connection with Kasper's disturbances, several attorneys general from southern states agreed to defend them—an expression of regional solidarity. Senator Eastland also traveled through the South, speaking to mass segregationist rallies, warning against efforts "to pick them off one by one under the damnable doctrine of gradualism," and criticizing "border states [that] have weak-kneed politicians in the capitol ... [and] weak governors." Both the interposition movement and the Southern Manifesto were partially aimed at pressuring moderate states to support massive resistance. The perceived importance of maintaining regional unity led Virginians to criticize North Carolina's token integrationism as "abject surrender" and Alabamians to regard Virginia's later abandonment of massive resistance as a "crippling blow."[17]

Extremists also benefited from legislative malapportionment, which in every state favored rural districts that contained the most committed white supremacists. In Alabama and Georgia, black-belt counties enjoyed nearly twice the representation that their populations warranted, meaning that whites in those counties, where blacks were generally disfranchised, exercised even more disproportionate political power. Moreover, such counties tended to reelect the same representatives for decades, which enhanced their legislative seniority and thus further augmented the political power of die-hard segregationists. Moderate racial opinion in cities was often nullified by malapportionment. For example, Atlanta had little clout in the rural-dominated Georgia legislature. Georgia's unique county-unit system, which extended malapportionment to elections for state executive office, explains the extremism of governors such as Talmadge and Griffin. In other states, which elected executive officers on the principle of one person, one vote, governors often tried to force legislative reapportionment, but their efforts came to naught. When governors James Folsom and Leroy Collins called special legislative sessions in Alabama and Florida in the mid-1950s to consider reapportionment, legislators instead enacted massive-resistance measures. Had *Brown* been decided after *Reynolds v. Sims* (1964) invalidated malapportionment in state legislatures, rather than before, massive resistance might have played out rather differently.[18]

Yet the most important explanation for the temporary triumph of massive resistance may be this: many southern whites—perhaps a majority outside of the Deep South—preferred token integration to school closures, but very few favored token integration over segregation. Thus, opinion polls on *Brown* revealed minimal support among southern whites, but referenda on school closures showed substantial white opposition. Consequently, until it became clear that preserving segregation entailed school closures, moderate whites had every reason to allow massive resistance to run its course, as they, too, preferred to avoid desegregation. The difference between white "moderates" and "extremists" was in the costs they were prepared to bear to maintain segregation, not in their preference for it.[19]

From this perspective, the crucial development of the mid-1950s was the growing conviction among white southerners that *Brown* could be successfully defied and segregation preserved. Massive resisters may have been emboldened by the fierce and successful opposition to desegregation put up by whites in Milford, Delaware, in the fall of 1954. If border-state whites could frustrate desegregation, how could it possibly be imposed on the real South? *Brown II* furthered this conviction, as many southern whites sensed the beginnings of a judicial retreat. President Dwight Eisenhower's obvious lack of enthusiasm for *Brown*, his statements rejecting the use of federal troops to enforce desegregation orders, and his refusal to intervene against violent resistance to desegregation in Texas, Alabama, and Tennessee in 1956 encouraged southern whites to question the inevitability of integration. Historical memories of the first Reconstruction, when southern whites had worn down the (never intense) commitment of northern whites to protecting the political and civil rights of southern blacks, inspired hope that determined resistance could nullify *Brown*. One segregationist editor, urging white southerners to "shape their destiny and control their way of life, just as they did in the far more dangerous period of Reconstruction," triumphantly concluded: "Our forefathers saved white men's civilization. We can do it again." Analogies to Prohibition also offered solace to southern whites: many Americans, in the North as well as the South, had drawn the lesson from that historical episode that national efforts to coerce social reform against strong resistance were doomed to failure.[20]

One cannot know how many white southerners genuinely believed that *Brown* could be nullified and segregation preserved. But many southern politicians spoke this way, and constituents may well have believed what they wanted to. Governor Lindsay Almond of Virginia had "faith that the decision ultimately will be reversed," and Senator Byrd thought that "if people are firm enough and determined enough," the justices might change their minds. A Louisiana legislator observed: "When those birds in the Supreme Court realize we mean business, we'll find we won't have to change our entire school system." A South Carolina judge expressed confidence that "this decision will be eventually reversed, though it may take years." Countless other southern politicians insisted that desegregation would not come "in a thousand years" or in their "lifetime." The principal purposes of the Southern Manifesto included convincing white southerners that desegregation was not inevitable and convincing northerners that the South would not capitulate. Efforts at undermining the perceived inevitability of desegregation also had a cascading effect: the fewer people who accepted desegregation as inevitable, the less so it became.[21]

Such political rhetoric convinced at least some people. A circular from a white supremacist organization declared: "The fact that the Supreme Court has ruled as it has, in favor of the black man, is no sign that the whole thing is settled. Many times in the past the Supreme Court has reversed itself, and many other times it has merely overlooked enforcing its rulings." A reporter from Norfolk, Virginia, noted that after the "general air of calm resignation" following *Brown I*, the notion had developed "that the fatal day would be delayed for many years," and "in some quarters there was actual belief that integration would never come." The political journalist Samuel Lubell, who was interviewing white southerners during this period, reported: "By the spring of 1957 the segregationists, emboldened by the lack of opposition to their efforts, had come to believe that nullification of the Supreme Court's decision was in sight." According to Gallup polls, the number of white southerners who believed that school desegregation was inevitable fell from 55 percent early in 1956 to 43 percent in August 1957.[22]

Once Eisenhower used federal troops at Little Rock, however, only school closures could prevent desegregation. As several schools closed in Virginia and in Little Rock in 1958, white southerners had to confront a previously avoided question: What costs were they prepared to bear in order to preserve segregation? Many had supported massive resistance as a bluff or as an initial response but were unwilling to pursue it to its logical conclusion—the abolition of public schools. Parents' groups that were dedicated to saving public education sprang up across the South, and some local chambers of commerce mobilized against school closures.[23]

The speed with which massive resistance crumbled outside of the Deep South after schools were closed suggests one of two possibilities: either many whites had endorsed school closures only as a bluff to induce a retreat by the Supreme Court and by integrationist northerners, or they had genuinely supported closures but without carefully calculating the costs. Once the bluff was called, and the costs of school closures were made concrete, the attitudes of white southerners toward school desegregation changed rapidly.

A post–Little Rock poll revealed that two out of three whites in Virginia would rather close schools than integrate them. Reflecting that opinion, in 1958 Governor Almond closed schools in Charlottesville, Norfolk, and Warren Counties, while continuing to give fiery speeches that endorsed massive resistance. But private-school arrangements quickly proved unsatisfactory, especially in Norfolk, where a federal judge enjoined public employees from teaching in private schools and thousands of children went uneducated. Public opinion in Virginia changed rapidly as a result. By November, newspapers that had formerly supported massive resistance were calling for "speedy abandonment" of that "futile" strategy and the adoption of "a new approach." Public officials soon reflected that opinion shift. Although politicians in the heavily black Southside region continued to endorse "massive resistance all the way," Governor Almond changed his tune virtually overnight. After federal and state courts invalidated school closures in January 1959, Almond repudiated massive resistance in favor of local option and token integration. He criticized proposals to abandon public education as "going back to the dark ages" and warned that Virginia "cannot secede from the Union [or] overthrow the federal government." An opinion poll showed that two out of three Virginians supported the governor's new policy.[24]

Attitudes toward school desegregation also changed quickly in Little Rock. Governor Faubus had promised an easy transition from public to private education, and in September 1958 Little Rock voters supported school closures in a referendum by a margin of greater than five to two. But the white private school quickly proved unsatisfactory, especially after a federal court blocked its use of public money and public school buildings. In December, school board elections showed that voters were evenly divided between candidates of the Citizens' Council and those of more moderate businessmen. In February 1959, the two thousand members of the Little Rock Chamber of Commerce voted by a margin of better than three to one to reopen high schools with token integration. The businessmen could easily count the costs of school closures: ten businesses had relocated to Little Rock in the two years before September 1957, but not a single one since. In May 1959 voters narrowly recalled segregationist school board members in retaliation for their purges of moderate teachers and replaced them with token integrationists. By the time Little Rock public high schools reopened with a few blacks that fall, the private-school corporation had gone bankrupt. In 1960 Samuel Lubell discovered that the same Little Rock whites who two years earlier had preferred to see Central High burned down rather than "infested with niggers" now favored token integration over school closures.[25]

Because their moment of truth arrived later, Georgians were able to learn vicariously from the tribulations of others. Little Rock officials and businessmen visited Atlanta to warn of the economic and social costs entailed by diehard segregationism. In his 1958 gubernatorial campaign and then repeatedly over the next two years, Governor Ernest Vandiver had rejected local option and token integration in favor of school closures. Yet public opinion began to shift as school closures loomed, once Judge Frank Hooper ordered Atlanta to desegregate in 1960, which he later postponed until 1961. Parents' organizations, business leaders, and most newspapers preferred token integration to school closures. Reflecting this opinion shift, Vandiver encouraged the legislature to appoint the Sibley Commission, which searched for an honorable means of retreat. By early 1961, as the desegregation crisis hit the University of Georgia, Vandiver was declaring, "we cannot abandon public education" and urging the repeal of statutes that required integrated schools to close and their replacement with provisions for local option and public tuition grants for students to attend private schools. Henceforth, Vandiver insisted that federal court orders must be obeyed, and he bragged that his administration had kept the schools open.[26]

These dramatic turnabouts in Virginia, Arkansas, and Georgia help explain the political dynamics of massive resistance. Until attempted, nobody knew whether it could succeed. After Little Rock, however, only school closures could preserve segregation. Once that strategy was tried, public opinion turned rapidly against it because of the harm to education and to business development. Moderates, who had previously possessed little incentive to oppose massive resistance, now asserted themselves, and the debate rapidly swung in their favor. Token integration, though "still . . . objectionable," was "not intolerable," and it was preferable to school closures. Moreover, this dynamic favoring moderation was as self-reinforcing as the earlier one that supported extremism. As the first moderates asserted themselves and demanded open schools, others found it easier to follow.[27]

Yet the realism that was impelled by Little Rock, New Orleans, and the University of Mississippi had little immediate effect on governors John Patterson, George Wallace, and Ross Barnett. In the late 1950s, die-hard resisters may genuinely have believed that desegregation could be avoided and the Supreme Court induced to back down. Explaining their behavior in 1962–63 is more difficult, as they surely understood by then that they could not preserve "segregation forever" and that to "fight harder next time" was no formula for success. The reason that politicians continued to make such pledges is probably that voters in Alabama and Mississippi continued to reward them for doing so. For example, Wallace plainly anticipated political gain from fomenting a desegregation fight with the federal government, even though his stand in the schoolhouse door in Tuscaloosa was a carefully orchestrated charade. The real question is why voters rewarded such irresponsible pledges once desegregation had become inevitable. Perhaps they were so embittered at the prospect of externally coerced racial change that they preferred, in the best southern tradition, to fight futile battles rather than to capitulate. Many whites in Mississippi and Alabama, though conceding that "you can't fight the Federal government and win," still insisted that "we'll never accept it voluntarily" and "they'll have to force it on us." As the novelist William Faulkner pointed out, Mississippi whites "will accept another civil war, knowing they're going to lose."[28]

Finally and ironically, massive resistance could end only after Eisenhower had proved his willingness to use federal troops to enforce desegregation orders, yet the deployment of these forces bolstered massive resistance in the short term. As a general rule, external threats tend to unify a polity. When NATO forces bombed Serbia in 1999, even critics of President Slobodan Milosevic temporarily rallied behind him in opposition to outside attacks. Historically, white southerners were especially sensitive to outside interference with their "way of life." Thus, when Eisenhower sent federal troops into Little Rock, moderate white southerners united with extremists in assailing the president. Ironically, though Little Rock should have discouraged extremism by demonstrating the futility of massive resistance, its immediate effect was to further radicalize southern opinion and to empower politicians who promised defiance of "federal tyranny."[29]

On statewide television, Faubus referred to Little Rock as an "occupied" city, implicitly appealing to the bitter historical memories that Arkansas whites had of the Civil War and of Reconstruction, when federal troops had invaded the South. Southern political opinion overwhelmingly supported Faubus and condemned Eisenhower. A North Carolina congressman asserted: "The issue of integrated schools is dwarfed by the precipitous and dictatorial stab at the rights of an individual state." Several southern politicians compared the use of federal troops at Little Rock to the Soviet Union's invasion of Hungary in 1956. Governor George Timmerman of South Carolina criticized the president for "trying to set himself up as a dictator," and he resigned his commission in the naval reserves. Senator Russell condemned the use of "storm troopers." Circuit Judge George Wallace compared Eisenhower to Hitler and accused the president of substituting "military dictatorship for the Constitution of the United States."[30]

. . .

It is ironic that after *Brown,* southern whites abandoned tried-and-true evasive techniques that for decades had successfully nullified the constitutional rights of blacks, in favor of outright defiance. Southern whites had eschewed open confrontation with the Supreme Court over black jury service and black suffrage, while completely sabotaging those rights through the discriminatory exercise of administrative discretion. But rather than using similarly fraudulent mechanisms to circumvent school desegregation, the white South declared war on the Court, nullified *Brown,* and used state troops and vigilante mobs to block the enforcement of desegregation orders. Such open defiance forced President Eisenhower's hand, alienated national opinion, radicalized southern politics, fostered violence, and irritated Supreme Court justices. One cannot know how long token school desegregation might have persisted had white southerners played their hand differently, but in retrospect massive resistance almost certainly proved a mistake from their perspective. The nature of southern politics may have impelled that mistake. Southern politicians reaped rewards for adopting extremist positions. Governor Faubus won four more terms in office because he called out the militia to block the desegregation of Little Rock schools, and state legislators across the South saw political profit in passing interposition resolutions. The electoral incentives of southern politicians led them to respond to *Brown* in ways that ultimately facilitated its enforcement. The harder southern whites fought to maintain Jim Crow, the more they seemed to accelerate its demise.

Notes

1. *Southern School News (SSN),* Sept. 1954, 2, 5, 10, 13, 14; R. Ray McCain, "Reactions to the United States Supreme Court Segregation Decision of 1954," *Georgia Historical Quarterly* 52 (Dec. 1968): 371–72, 376, 378; C. Vann Woodward, "The 'New Reconstruc-

tion' in the South: Desegregation in Historical Perspective," *Commentary* 21 (Jun. 1956): 503; Benjamin Muse, *Ten Years of Prelude: The Story of Integration Since the Supreme Court's 1954 Decision* (New York: Viking Press, 1964), 17, 20–21, 124; William H. Chafe, *Civilities and Civil Rights: Greensboro, North Carolina, and the Black Struggle for Freedom* (New York: Oxford University Press, 1980), 16; J. W. Peltason, *Fifty-Eight Lonely Men: Southern Federal Judges and School Desegregation* (New York: Harcourt, Brace and World, 1961), 31–32.

    2. *Chicago Defender*, Sept. 25, 1954, 3; *SSN*, Sept. 1954, 5, 8, 12, 13; Oct. 1954, 6; Dec. 1954, 6; Jan. 1955, 10; *New York Times*, May 18, 1954, 1, 20; Muse, *Ten Years of Prelude*, 20–22, 24; James T. Patterson, *Brown v. Board of Education: A Civil Rights Milestone and Its Troubled Legacy* (New York: Oxford University Press, 2001), 78; McCain, "Segregation Decision," 381–83.

    3. *SSN*, Feb. 1956, 6; Jun. 1955, 3, 9; Mar. 1956, 1, 6–7, 9, 10, 14; Apr. 1956, 1, 5, 9, 14; David Halberstam, "The White Citizens Councils," *Commentary* 22 (Oct. 1956): 293–302; Neil R. McMillen, *The Citizens' Council: Organized Resistance to the Second Reconstruction* (Urbana: University of Illinois Press, 1971), 19–31, 42–50, 59–68, 74–77, 268–69; Muse, *Ten Years of Prelude*, 62–72; Patrick E. McCauley, "'Be It Enacted': The Legislative Record," in *With All Deliberate Speed: Segregation-Desegregation in Southern Schools*, ed. Don Shoemaker (New York: Harper, 1957), 130–46.

    4. Muse, *Ten Years of Prelude*, 161, 168; *SSN*, Feb. 1959, 11; Nov. 1954, 15; Jul. 1956, 3; Jul. 1957, 3; Weldon James, "The South's Own Civil War: Battle for the Schools," in Shoemaker, *All Deliberate Speed*, 23; Numan V. Bartley, *The Rise of Massive Resistance: Race and Politics in the South During the 1950s* (Baton Rouge: Louisiana State University Press, 1969), 68, 192, 247.

    5. Tony Badger, "Southerners Who Refused to Sign the Southern Manifesto," *Historical Journal* 42 (Jun. 1999): 528, 532–33; Tony Badger, "'The Forerunner of Our Opposition': Arkansas and the Southern Manifesto of 1956," *Arkansas Historical Quarterly* 56 (autumn 1997): 356–58.

    6. J. Harvie Wilkinson, *Harry Byrd and the Changing Face of Virginia Politics 1946–1966* (Charlottesville: University Press of Virginia, 1968), 112–14, 151–54; Benjamin Muse, *Virginia's Massive Resistance* (Bloomington: Indiana University Press, 1961), 46–47, 168, 176.

    7. *SSN*, Oct. 1954, 14; Nov. 1954, 15; Sept. 1954, 13; Mar. 1956, 4; Lewis M. Killian and John L. Haer, "Variables Related to Attitudes Regarding School Desegregation Among White Southerners," *Sociometry* 21 (Jun. 1958): 161, table 1; Bartley, *Massive Resistance*, 13–14, 253–54, 337; James W. Ely, Jr., *The Crisis of Conservative Virginia: The Byrd Organization and the Politics of Massive Resistance* (Knoxville: University of Tennessee Press, 1976), 30, 34–37; McMillen, *Citizens' Council*, 6–7, 45–46, 93–94, 103–5, 292–93; Thomas F. Pettigrew and Ernest Q. Campbell, "Faubus and Segregation: An Analysis of Arkansas Voting," *Public Opinion Quarterly* 24 (autumn 1960): 442–45.

    8. *SSN*, Jun. 1958, 3; Jun. 1956, 16; Dec. 1958, 15; Feb. 1956, 14; Mar. 1956, 14; Sept. 1956, 8; Aug. 1957, 8; Muse, *Ten Years of Prelude*, 147–48, 214; Matthew David Lassiter, "The Rise of the Suburban South: The 'Silent Majority' and the Politics of Education, 1945–75" (Ph D. diss., University of Virginia, 1999), 241, 253; Peltason, *Fifty-Eight Lonely Men*, 43–45, 130; Badger, "Southerners Who Refused to Sign," 517–18; Wilkinson, *Harry Byrd*, 132–33, 151–52.

9. *SSN*, Mar. 1960, 7; Dec. 1963, 10; Stan Opotowsky, "Dixie Dynamite: The Inside Story of the White Citizens Councils" (reprinted from *New York Post*, Jan. 6–20, 1957), 12, in Papers of the National Association for the Advancement of Colored People (hereafter NAACP Papers), ed. August Meier, microfilm, 28 parts (Frederick, Md.:University Publications of America, 1982), part 20, reel 13, frame 679; Stewart Burns, ed., *Daybreak of Freedom: The Montgomery Bus Boycott* (Chapel Hill: University of North Carolina Press, 1997), 168, 208, 303; James W. Silver, *Mississippi: The Closed Society* (New York: Harcourt, Brace and World, 1964), 151–55; Muse, *Ten Years of Prelude*, 48–49, 161, 168.

10. *SSN*, Jun. 1955, 18; Jun. 1959, 12; Dec. 1955, 6; Mar. 1956, 7, 9; Oct. 1956, 10; Muse, *Ten Years of Prelude*, 160–61, 168–72; McMillen, *Citizens' Council*, 240–42; Bartley, *Massive Resistance*, 227–33; Silver, *Closed Society*, 81–82, 111–12.

11. *SSN*, Mar. 1960, 7; Jan. 1958, 8; Dec. 1963, 10; McMillen, *Citizens' Council*, 246–47, 290, 313–15, 319, 326–28, 334, 336–37; Opotowsky, "Dixie Dynamite," 11 (frame 678); Margaret Price, "Joint Interagency Fact Finding Project on Violence and Intimidation" (draft), 14–36, 54, 65–66, in NAACP Papers, part 20, reel 11, frames 351–73, 398, 401–2; Muse, *Ten Years of Prelude*, 50, 161–62; Pete Daniel, *Lost Revolutions: The South in the 1950s* (Chapel Hill: University of North Carolina Press, 2000), 239–42.

12. *Birmingham Post-Herald*, Dec. 22, 1960, in NAACP Papers, part 21, reel 22, frame 399; *SSN*, Oct. 1955, 3; Dec. 1955, 7, 11; Mar. 1956, 3; Aug. 1957, 13; H. L. Mitchell, preliminary report on the rise of the White Citizens' Council movement, Jan. 30, 1956, 2–3, NAACP Papers, part 20, reel 13, frames 325–26; "Bilbo's Ghost Haunts a Mississippi Educator," unidentified press clipping, Mar. 14, 1958, NAACP Papers, part 20, reel 2, frame 118; John Dittmer, *Local People: The Struggle for Civil Rights in Mississippi* (Urbana: University of Illinois Press, 1994), 61–69, 463–64 n. 62; Silver, *Closed Society*, 37–39, 57–58.

13. NAACP press release, Jul. 25, 1956, 1–2, NAACP Papers, part 20, reel 4, frames 639–40; Asbury Howard, Jr., statement, undated, NAACP Papers, frames 468–69; Gloster Current to NAACP officials, memo, Jan. 31, 1956, NAACP Papers, part 20, reel 5, frames 120–21; Orzell Billingsley, Jr., to Robert Carter, Nov. 26, 1958, NAACP Papers, part 22, reel 1, frames 296–97; Burns, *Montgomery Bus Boycott*, 42, 125, 287–89; Andrew Michael Manis, *A Fire You Can't Put Out: The Civil Rights Life of Birmingham's Reverend Fred Shuttlesworth* (Tuscaloosa: University of Alabama Press, 1999), 162–63, 232–34; Price, "Violence and Intimidation," 37–84 (frames 374–421).

14. Bartley, *Massive Resistance*, 211; *SSN*, Jan. 1959, 13; Dec. 1963, 10; Apr. 1964, 14; *New York Times*, Dec. 3, 1960, in NAACP Papers, part 20, reel 1, frame 611; "Are You Curious About Mississippi?" Jan. 20, 1961, 2, NAACP Papers, part 20, reel 2, frame 173; Charles M. Payne, *I've Got the Light of Freedom: The Organizing Tradition and the Mississippi Freedom Struggle* (Berkeley: University of California Press, 1995), 7, 36–40, 205, 298–300, 316, 396–97; Robert L. T. Smith, "Visit to Jefferson County (Mississippi)," typescript, NAACP Papers, part 20, reel 2, frame 166; Silver, *Closed Society*, 37–39, 41–42, 65–67, 79–80, 86–87, 92–95, 101–02; Dittmer, *Local People*, 53–60, 107–110, 122, 142; James C. Cobb, *The Most Southern Place on Earth: The Mississippi Delta and the Roots of Regional Identity* (New York: Oxford University Press, 1992), 222–26; Steven F. Lawson, *Black Ballots: Voting Rights in the South 1944–1969* (New York: Columbia University Press, 1976), 130.

15. *SSN*, Jun. 1959, 11; minutes of the NAACP Board of Directors' meeting, May 11, 1959, 3–4, NAACP Papers, part 1, supp. 1956–60, reel 2, frames 100–101; minutes of the NAACP Board of Directors' meeting, Aug. 1959, NAACP Papers, part 1, supp. 1956–60,

reel 2, frame 127. See also Timothy B. Tyson, *Radio Free Dixie: Robert F. Williams and the Roots of Black Power* (Chapel Hill: University of North Carolina Press, 1999), 149–65.

16. *SSN*, Sept. 1957, 6, 7; Nov. 1955, 9; Jun. 1956, 10; "Faubus Silent Again," *Arkansas Faith*, Dec. 1955, 23, in NAACP Papers, part 20, reel 13, frame 318; Peltason, *Fifty-Eight Lonely Men*, 53–54, 163–64; Tony Freyer, *The Little Rock Crisis: A Constitutional Interpretation* (Westport, Conn.: Greenwood Press, 1984), 95, 100; Robert Sherrill, *Gothic Politics in the Deep South: Stars of the New Confederacy* (New York: Grossman, 1968), 98–99, 207–08.

17. *SSN*, Oct. 1955, 3; May 1956, 15; Neil R. McMillen, "Organized Resistance to School Desegregation in Tennessee," *Tennessee Historical Quarterly* 30 (fall 1971): 318–19; *SSN*, Nov. 1958; Mar. 1959, 15; Oscar Handlin, "Civil Rights After Little Rock: The Failure of Moderation," *Commentary* 24 (Nov. 1957): 395; Joseph J. Thorndike, "'The Sometimes Sordid Level of Race and Segregation': James J. Kilpatrick and the Virginia Campaign Against *Brown*," in *The Moderates' Dilemma: Massive Resistance to School Desegregation in Virginia*, ed. Matthew D. Lassiter and Andrew B. Lewis (Charlottesville: University Press of Virginia, 1998), 56–57, 60–61.

18. McCauley, "'Be It Enacted,'" 134–36; Lassiter, "Rise of the Suburban South," 184–88, 192–95, 199; Muse, *Ten Years of Prelude*, 66, 149, 216; Bartley, *Massive Resistance*, 18–19, 42, 94, 144, 278–79, 283; V. O. Key, Jr., *Southern Politics in State and Nation* (New York: Knopf, 1949), 119–22, 666; Helen L. Jacobstein, *The Segregation Factor in the Florida Democratic Gubernatorial Election of 1956* (Gainesville: University of Florida Press, 1972), 14–16, 19, 24.

19. *SSN*, Nov. 1954, 11; Dec. 1954, 6, 8; Feb. 1956, 11; Sept. 1956, 3; Muse, *Virginia's Massive Resistance*, 58, 69–70; David Chappell, "The Divided Mind of Southern Segregationists," *Georgia Historical Quarterly* 82 (spring 1998): 46, 48; Lassiter, "Rise of the Suburban South," 93, 173, 195–200, 216, 222; Matthew D. Lassiter and Andrew B. Lewis, "Massive Resistance Revisited: Virginia's White Moderates and the Byrd Organization," in *Moderates' Dilemma*, 3–4, 14–15; George H. Gallup, *The Gallup Poll: Public Opinion 1935–1971*, 3 vols. (New York: Random House, 1972), 2:1401, 2:1526–27, 3:1616.

20. *SSN*, Dec. 1959, 14; Oct. 1954, 4; Nov. 1954, 6–7, 14; Samuel Lubell, *The Future of American Politics* (New York: Harper, 1952), 93, 96; Peltason, *Fifty-Eight Lonely Men*, 48–49, 95–96; Handlin, "Civil Rights After Little Rock," 393, 395–96; Woodward, "'New Reconstruction,'" 502–3, 507; Bartley, *Massive Resistance*, 127–28, 249; John A. Kirk, "Arkansas, the *Brown* Decision, and the 1957 Little Rock School Crisis," in *Understanding the Little Rock Crisis: An Exercise in Remembrance and Reconciliation*, ed. Elizabeth Jacoway and C. Fred Williams (Fayetteville: University of Arkansas Press, 1999), 73–74, 81.

21. Ely, *Crisis of Conservative Virginia*, 61, 100–102; *SSN*, Jul. 1958, 16; Jul. 1957, 4; Aug. 1956, 9; Tom Brady, *Black Monday* (Winona, Miss.: Association of Citizens' Councils, 1955), 19; Herman E. Talmadge, *You and Segregation* (Birmingham, Ala.: Vulcan Press, 1955), 76, 78; Badger, "Arkansas and the Southern Manifesto," 355, 360; Peltason, *Fifty-Eight Lonely Men*, 95–96, 194.

22. Daniel Broom of White Peoples Association to "All White People," undated, NAACP Papers, part 20, reel 13, frame 483; Dick Mansfield, "Local Report from Norfolk," typescript, May 22, 1958, 3, NAACP Papers, part 22, reel 1, frame 518; Lubell, *White and Black*, 96; Bartley, *Massive Resistance*, 276–77; *SSN*, Mar. 1958, 3.

23. Lubell, *White and Black*, 97–98; Adam Fairclough, *Race and Democracy: The Civil Rights Struggle in Louisiana, 1915–1972* (Athens: University of Georgia Press, 1995), 205; Lassiter, "Rise of the Suburban South," 114–16, 157–60; Muse, *Ten Years of Prelude*, 151, 178–79, 185, 191–92, 215–17; James H. Hershman, Jr., "Massive Resistance Meets Its Match," in Lassiter and Lewis, *Moderates' Dilemma*, 105–13.

24. *SSN*, Dec. 1958, 6; July 1959, 6; Nov. 1959, 9; Dec. 1957, 10–11; Sept. 1958, 1, 6; Feb. 1959, 1, 4–5; *New York Times*, Nov. 16, 1958, 1, 48; "80 Days Without Public Schools," *Newsweek*, Dec. 1, 1958, 23–26; Muse, *Ten Years of Prelude*, 156–57, 178–80, 183–85; Peltason, *Fifty-Eight Lonely Men*, 214–18; Ely, *Crisis of Conservative Virginia*, 83–89.

25. Lubell, *White and Black*, 100; *SSN*, Oct. 1958, 5, 7; Nov. 1958, 8–9; Jan. 1959, 14; Apr. 1959, 10, 12; Jun. 1959, 2, 3; Aug. 1959, 6, 12; Sept. 1959, 15; Muse, *Ten Years of Prelude*, 153–56, 191–97; Peltason, *Fifty-Eight Lonely Men*, 195–205; Freyer, *Little Rock Crisis*, 154–63.

26. *SSN*, Feb. 1961, 1, 8–11; Jun. 1958, 3; Dec. 1958, 15; July 1959, 1, 2; Dec. 1959, 16; Jan. 1960, 1, 16; Feb. 1960, 1, 2; Mar. 1960, 15; May 1961, 14–15; Lassiter, "Rise of the Suburban South," 225–75; Jeff Roche, *Restructured Resistance: The Sibley Commission and the Politics of Desegregation in Georgia* (Athens: University of Georgia Press, 1998), 80–95, 162–88.

27. *SSN*, Mar. 1960, 6; Jun. 1959, 3; Muse, *Ten Years of Prelude*, 156–57, 211, 214; Peltason, *Fifty-Eight Lonely Men*, 193–95; James C. Cobb, "The Lesson of Little Rock: Stability, Growth, and Change in the American South," in Jacoway and Williams, *Little Rock Crisis*, 114–15, 117; Lubell, *White and Black*, 97–102.

28. *SSN*, Feb. 1963, 10; Aug. 1963, 20; Nov. 1963, 6; Lubell, *White and Black*, 106–7; "What of the Law?" *New Republic*, Apr. 2, 1956, 9; Dan T. Carter, *The Politics of Rage: George Wallace, The Origins of the New Conservatism, and the Transformation of American Politics* (New York: Simon and Schuster, 1995), 109.

29. Virginius Dabney, "Virginia's 'Peaceable, Honorable Stand,'" *Life*, Sept. 22, 1958, 55; Bartley, *Massive Resistance*, 270, 277–78, 287; Sherrill, *Gothic Politics in the Deep South*, 107–8; Elizabeth Jacoway, "Taken by Surprise: Little Rock Business Leaders and Desegregation," in *Southern Businessmen and Desegregation*, ed. Elizabeth Jacoway and David R. Colburn (Baton Rouge: Louisiana State University Press, 1982), 24.

30. *SSN*, Oct. 1957, 4, 5, 8, 9, 13, 15, 16; Nov. 1957, 7, 9, 11, 15, 16; Dec. 1957, 2; Tony A. Freyer, "The Little Rock Crisis Reconsidered," *Arkansas Historical Quarterly* 56 (autumn 1997): 369; Stephen E. Ambrose, *Eisenhower*, 2 vols. (New York: Simon and Schuster, 1984), 2:420–21.

TWO

Brown and Backlash

Tony Badger

T he Supreme Court was under no illusions about the danger of a backlash
to the *Brown* decision—which is why the justices took so much trouble
in *Brown II* not to undercut southern moderates and opted for a gradualist solution that placed their faith, as did presidents before and after, in the
role of moderates. Hugo Black forcefully warned the justices about the dangers
of violence in the South, which he believed would eliminate southern moderate politicians like Lister Hill and John Sparkman, but he was rather fatalistic
about the prospect. Felix Frankfurter was more proactive. Frankfurter believed
that any implementation decree for *Brown* would "need to encourage moderate leadership," responsible leaders who would take their communities forward
into compliance with the law of the land—especially southern lawyers whom
he himself had trained at Harvard Law School. Southern friends of Frankfurter
and the other justices, notably their former colleague Jimmy Byrnes, the governor of South Carolina, encouraged this line of thinking. The justices' law
clerks listened to the warnings of moderate southern newspapermen like Harry
Ashmore and Hodding Carter and were almost unanimous that the gradualist
remedy outlined in the implementation decree was the right answer. Why were
these hopes dashed? Why did a backlash lead to mob violence and school clos-
ings, not peaceful compliance? For a new generation of historians, the blame
lies with the *Brown* decision itself.[1]

The lessening of the iconic status of *Brown* is partly the result of skepticism
about the wisdom and success of school desegregation as public policy. There
is, of course, a vigorous debate over whether desegregated schools improved
educational achievement, whether the harm done to historic black colleges was
offset by general educational and social gains, whether school desegregation

led to improved race relations, and whether desegregation itself should have a higher priority than quality education.[2]

But historians of the decision itself and its implementation have analyzed *Brown*'s more immediate relation to the dynamic of racial and political change in the South and have substantially lessened its significance. They argue that the decision itself was not as important as long-term social and economic developments: the growing prosperity, urbanization, and industrialization of the South. The decision itself yielded very little actual school desegregation: legislation and executive action in the 1960s had a much greater impact. Worse, the decision had negative consequences. It halted the "incipient amelioration of Jim Crow practices that had been occurring in much of the South in the late 1940s and early 1950s." The white backlash to *Brown* destroyed the liberal and racially moderate politicians who had flourished in that period in the South. That backlash occurred because African American leaders chose the wrong target in their challenge to white supremacy. In singling out schools, they challenged the area the white South would defend most vigorously. It would have been better and less provocative if they had addressed voting rights or the economic goals of the class-based civil rights movement of the 1940s. The positive effect that the *Brown* decision had was indirect: the backlash and white violence eventually provoked the intervention by the federal government that ended Jim Crow in the 1960s.[3] This essay examines the political dynamic and sequence of change in white southern politics that this interpretation of the backlash to *Brown* lays out.

• • •

Before *Brown*, according to Michael Klarman, "racial moderates generally controlled southern politics." There was, indeed, "a new generation of southerners." Liberal politicians were elected to state legislatures, state houses, and Congress who appealed to a crossrace alliance of lower-income whites, blacks, veterans, women, and labor. They saw themselves as "TVA liberals" who believed that federal government investment in infrastructure and in mass purchasing power would transform the region as the New Deal (in the form of the Tennessee Valley Authority, or TVA) had transformed the Tennessee Valley. They believed that the economic progress that New Deal–style policies could achieve would gradually eliminate racial tensions. They played down the race issue and espoused a policy of gradualism, rarely challenging segregation itself. Their racial caution was in part prudential—they did not want to alienate their lower-income white supporters—and in part ideological: they could rarely conceive of a nonsegregated society, and their faith in the ameliorative effects of economic progress was genuine.[4]

But these racial moderates did not control southern politics. Each state was a battleground between conservatives and moderates, and in most southern states conservatives won. We should not underestimate the difficulties these southern liberal politicians faced in the postwar years. For every GI revolt that elected a racially moderate war hero, there were veterans' campaigns in support of fellow veterans, like Strom Thurmond or Herman Talmadge, who came home determined to install progressive administrations but at the same time to defend the right to segregation as they had defended the right to liberty in the war. For every interracial church women's group, there was an organization like the Mississippi Women for Constitutional Government. For every interracial union, there were white workers resolutely committed to defend the wages of whiteness. The disorganized nature of southern politics also hindered the liberal politicians. Lister Hill, John Sparkman, and Jim Folsom may have been the three leading elected politicians in Alabama, but they could not stop the state from going Dixiecrat in 1947 or from enacting the Boswell amendment to restrict black suffrage. Neither Kerr Scott in North Carolina in 1952 nor Earl Long in Louisiana in 1951 could hand over to a racially moderate successor. Sid McMath of Arkansas was defeated in 1952 attempting to win a third term in the governor's mansion.[5]

How extensive was the gradual racial change these racial moderates espoused? How much "incipient amelioration of Jim Crow practices" occurred in the South before 1954? To Michael Klarman, the economic modernization of the South made racial change "a virtual inevitability." The need to secure outside investment made some southern businessmen accept the need for racial change. In Birmingham, business leaders embarrassed by Bull Connor engineered his downfall. Scandals led him not to seek reelection in November 1953. Anxious to safeguard minor league baseball, the business leaders also revised the ordinance that banned interracial sporting contests. They did so before *Brown*. After *Brown*, Bull Connor was once more reelected and a referendum voted to retain sports segregation. In Baton Rouge before *Brown*, the city authorities settled an African American bus boycott after ten days by reinstating a first-come, first-served seating policy within segregation. In Montgomery, after *Brown*, the city rejected the same black demands for a first-come, first-served policy and defied the year-long bus boycott that followed. The Southern Regional Council carefully documented the appointment of African American policemen and other public officials that black voting in cities like Atlanta and Raleigh secured. African Americans served on southern juries and were admitted to the graduate and professional schools of southern universities. Minor League baseball teams were integrated. Blacks were elected to southern city councils and school boards.[6]

Segregation may have been softening at the edges before 1954, but its core remained intact. A public library in Austin, Catholic schools in St. Louis, some buses, and a hospital in Miami Beach—these institutions were very much at the periphery of southern race relations. Journalists like Ralph McGill said that segregation was crumbling before *Brown*, but their statements were largely wishful thinking designed to reassure northern audiences that change was on its way and southern audiences that *Brown* did not involve a massive adjustment. Much of the evidence of southern businessmen coming to terms with the inevitability of desegregation comes from the 1960s. Most southern businessmen believed through the 1950s that there was no conflict between economic growth and traditional race relations. In some cases, like Atlanta, it was the lesson of Little Rock that made businessmen aware of the unacceptably high economic cost of maintaining segregation. In others, like Alabama, it was the assault on the Freedom Riders in Birmingham in 1961 that first raised doubts. In still others, like South Carolina, it was not until 1962 that textile leaders began to fear for the future, and it was the spectacle of the disastrous confrontation at the University of Mississippi in 1962 that persuaded the state's leadership that resistance was futile.[7]

The Southern Regional Council carefully tabulated the appointment of black policemen and firemen as evidence of postwar progress, but more telling was the evidence the Council provided of the demise of biracial committees set up in towns like Greenville, South Carolina, in the immediate aftermath of war to improve services in black communities. By 1950, most of these committees had disappeared. Robert Corley showed starkly how that interracial dialogue broke down in Birmingham. Connor's downfall in Birmingham before *Brown* had less to do with gradual racial change and more to do with citizen outrage at repeated revelations of corruption. Reform-minded businessmen may have tried to sanction interracial sporting contests in early 1954, but the ordinance banning such contests had only been introduced in 1951. In Baton Rouge, the 1953 compromise ensured that buses did not desegregate until 1962. The admission of African Americans to Louisiana State University graduate schools did not foreshadow either desegregation of the student experience on the campus or the admission of African American undergraduates, which did not take place until 1964. Neither parks nor golf courses in the city were desegregated. African Americans paid for the only black swimming pool in the city despite the fact that their taxpayers' dollars supported white pools. The settlement of the boycott did not lead to segregation crumbling elsewhere in the city: if anything, it intensified the determination of white authorities to make no further concessions. In New Orleans, the trustees of elite, private Tulane University would not countenance desegregation, despite the wishes of the university president, Rufus Harris, and the faculty, and despite the threat of loss of accreditation and the cut-off of foundation grants.[8]

Even in southern cities that prided themselves on their progressive reputations, racial change was limited before *Brown*. In 1979, William Chafe dissected the "progressive mystique" in Greensboro, North Carolina, to show the lack of significant racial progress in employment and public facilities there. John Kirk's study of Little Rock after the war shows that the public libraries were quietly desegregated, as was the zoo on Thursdays. But when it came to building a park for blacks, the city did so, as Lucious Christopher (L. C.) Bates complained, "out of the city in an insect-infested mountain." In Atlanta, where so many gains were meant to have taken place, Whitney Young's *A Second Look* in 1960 demonstrated the lack of black progress. "Atlanta," observed Young, "was comparing itself to Mississippi and saying how enlightened it was." "Nothing," he continued, "was really integrated but the people were beginning to believe their own press clippings—even the Negroes." Ron Cox's forthcoming systematic examination of race relations in South Carolina—looking at schools, colleges, state parks, and cities—shows that in the Deep South, not even that degree of racial change was on the horizon in 1954.[9]

This lack of gradual racial change before *Brown* and the inability of racial moderates to engineer it were highlighted by the failure of the Arkansas Plan—a regional compromise on race designed to forestall the necessity for federal intervention. In the aftermath of the court-ordered admission of an African American to the University of Arkansas Law School, Harry Ashmore, editor of the *Arkansas Gazette*, and the liberal Arkansas congressmen Brooks Hays and James Trimble, attempted to establish the ground rules for this compromise in 1949 with the encouragement of the state's senator, William Fulbright. The South would make good its commitment to gradual racial change by eliminating lynching, by removing the obstacles to full political participation by African Americans, and by striving for genuine equality in the provision of black education. In return, the national government would be patient and back off counterproductive demands for immediate desegregation. The Arkansas Plan received little support in either the North or the South, and the congressional sponsors and Fulbright showed little inclination to revive it. What the failure of the Plan highlighted was that southern liberals may have espoused the necessity for gradual racial change, but they did little in the runup to the *Brown* decision to lay out a strategy for achieving that gradual change. Liberal governors did continue piecemeal to protect black votes, fight for increased appropriations for black institutions, and appoint some African Americans to government office and state Democratic Party positions, but they did not have a coherent policy to secure racial change. When white constituents later blamed Albert Gore, Sr., for failing to sign the Southern Manifesto, he later claimed they should not have been surprised, that he had always been "upfront" on the racial issue. But nothing in Gore's public statements or his private correspondence before 1954 indicated that he envisaged anything less than the segregated status quo. The standard response of liberal politicians was that segregated schooling was the best for both races and that, in any case, the Supreme Court had not ruled yet.[10]

As a result, the most coherent and powerful strategy was that of conservatives who mounted a massive drive genuinely to equalize school facilities in order to shape that Supreme Court ruling. David Robertson's biography of James F. Byrnes shows that the tax-funded equalization drive in South Carolina was not a mere tactical device to deceive the Supreme Court but a genuine attempt by a committed segregationist to acknowledge and remedy the deficiencies of the segregated system in order to ensure its survival. Byrnes took the lead in masterminding the region's resistance to racial change. First, Byrnes and the attorney Robert Figg conceded that the schools in Clarendon County, the subject of the *Briggs v. Elliott* case, were not equal. Then he put before the legislature a massive school equalization program and secured the passage of a three-cents sales tax to fund it. He was helped by the future governor Fritz Hollings, whose own survey had revealed the appalling conditions of the state's schools. The aim was to render separate but equal genuinely equal and to forestall court-ordered desegregation. No other state mounted such a massive program. It was a remarkable achievement and had a short-term success in persuading the local federal court, over Judge J. Waites Waring's passionate objection, to give the state time to make good its commitment to equalization. The second strand of Byrnes's strategy was to take charge of the legal defense in the school desegregation cases: first, to persuade the legendary lawyer John W. Davis to take the case, then to lobby his old Supreme Court colleagues, Fred Vinson and Felix Frankfurter, then to persuade his political ally, Dwight Eisenhower, to prevent the Justice Department from filing an amicus curiae brief on the part of the plaintiffs; and finally to persuade the attorney general of Kansas, a state in which facilities were genuinely equal, to join the case. Equalization was a considered preemptive strategy that Byrnes expected to work and that contrasted with the absence of any public strategy before 1954 on the part of white southern liberals.[11]

Michael Klarman sees the white backlash after World War II in reaction to the increased assertiveness of African Americans as sporadic and of different and far lesser order than the backlash unleashed by *Brown*. He discounts the role of race-baiting in the defeat of ultraliberals like Senator Frank Graham of North Carolina in 1950. In any case, the white backlash in that election was, he pointed out, directed at the Supreme Court decisions that were handed down after the first primary. Similarly, other white violence and reaction was in response to the court-mandated ending of the white primary. I would simply note that politicians like Terry Sanford were in no doubt as to the centrality of race in Graham's defeat. Sanford kept a notebook by his bed in which he jotted down ideas of how to handle racial smears—ideas he would put into play as Kerr Scott's campaign manager in 1954. It seems a little strange to divorce backlash to Supreme Court decisions from general racial backlash when those decisions concerned graduate education, voting, and transport—the very areas in which the gradual racial change he identified is taking place. Stephen Tuck's recent study of Georgia compellingly describes the forces of the reaction led by Herman Talmadge in the state that destroyed the civil rights movement of the 1940s. Racial violence was, after 1948, "unrestrained and unchecked." Violent white supremacy was precipitated by a "reaction to black protest during the Arnall years and the election of 1946." "[T]he acerbic reaction to *Brown* was a predictable continuation of an existing uncompromising stand on segregation."[12]

The extent of this pre-*Brown* white backlash casts doubt on the argument that a strategy that focused on voting rights and economics would have precipitated less backlash. The argument that the civil rights movement tackled the one area that would provoke the most intense white resistance is part of a wider argument that the civil rights movement moved in the wrong direction at the end of the 1940s and that *Brown* was part of that wrong move. Numan Bartley has argued that education was the wrong target: civil rights activists should have concentrated on voting rights. He also believed that national liberals substituted a moralistic concern for symbolic opportunity and the elimination of de jure segregation for the substance of a drive to tackle the problem of black and white disadvantage. Robert Korstad and Nelson Lichtenstein likewise lament opportunity lost for a class-based, union-oriented movement concentrating on economic issues.[13]

These arguments assume that tackling de jure segregation was somehow a goal that had nothing to do with the aspirations of southern blacks active in the voter registration and union organizing drive of the 1940s. Second, they assume that a concentration on extending the franchise would not have aroused the same powerful opposition that desegregating the schools provoked. The violent resistance to extending voting rights in Mississippi throughout this period rather belies that assumption. What Jeff Norrell showed in Alabama was that black-belt leaders like Sam Engelhardt feared black voting and black tax assessors far more than school desegregation. The unrestrained mob violence that finally provoked federal intervention in the 1960s was, of course, not about schools but about transport and public accommodations.[14]

· · ·

What was the impact of *Brown*? Certainly, after *Brown*, racially moderate politicians ran for cover, became closet moderates, or were sometimes defeated. Candidates were elected instead who most vigorously pronounced their loyalty to segregation. A key factor was the intensity of commitment—conservatives were intensely committed to segregation, and moderates had nothing like the same commitment, indeed if any, to desegregation. The moderate cause was handicapped as long as it appeared that there was an alternative to compliance with the Supreme Court. Partly in order to protect southern white moderates, neither the Court nor the executive nor the legislature in the 1950s made it clear that the Court could not be defied. But I do not believe that *Brown* released an uncontrollable white backlash that inevitably swept the moderates aside. After all, Earl Long could get elected in 1955; Jim Folsom would have his greatest success with a state legislature in 1955. Tennessee managed to sustain moderate senators and a governor. Conservative success after 1954 owed as much, I would argue, to moderate failings as it did to the misconceived logic of *Brown*.

Both conservatives and moderates believed that public opinion was on the other side. Most liberal politicians believed that whites were so stirred up on the race issue that politicians had either to retreat and become "closet moderates" or adopt a stealth-like approach to racial change. Conservative leaders, by contrast, feared that public opinion was insufficiently aroused on the race issue and that most southerners were too likely to accept the inevitability of compliance with the Supreme Court. The difference was that conservatives, passionately committed to segregation, in the 1950s were prepared to mount a righteous crusade to convince white southerners that desegregation was not inevitable, that white supremacy could be protected. I do not wish to underestimate the popular white backlash to *Brown*, but massive resistance was not a knee-jerk response by white leaders in the South to overwhelming mass white racism. As Numan V. Bartley demonstrated over thirty years ago, it was a top-down policy shaped by black-belt elites and conservative economic leaders, whether in the state legislatures or at the local level in the Citizens' Councils. In Virginia it was not the need to placate Southside mass white sentiment that drove Harry Byrd to drive forward mandatory school closing legislation and to sponsor the Southern Manifesto; it was his personal opposition to even the token integration that the segregationist Gray Commission was prepared to tolerate. In South Carolina, the conservative journalist W. D. Workman bemoaned a "blight of submissiveness," the "cry of surrender." The Citizens' Council leader Farley Smith complained of "the apathy of the average white citizen." Alice Spearman described the Committee of 52—leading clergy, businessmen, and professionals who called for maintaining segregation and interposition—as a "revolt in high places." When the South Carolina Association of Citizens' Councils gathered to hear Senator James Eastland of Mississippi in early 1956, the entire political leadership of the state was on the platform. When Strom Thurmond drafted the Southern Manifesto, his aim was not to assuage popular racism but to stir up popular segregationist feeling by convincing wavering politicians and their constituents that the Supreme Court could, and should, be defied. Even in North Carolina, as Anders Walker has recently shown, Luther Hodges and the Pearsall Commission modeled their pupil placement legislation directly on the Mississippi model. What distinguished segregationist leaders was, on the one hand, how much they perceived that white violence might harm their cause, in terms both of provoking federal intervention or frightening outside investors and of the tactical question of whether some token integration had to be accepted in progressive urban areas in order to preserve segregation for the overwhelming majority of white students. "Masked" or "sly" resistance was arguably more effective than massive resistance.[15]

Liberal and moderate politicians, personally much less passionate about the issue of desegregation, were not prepared to put their position to the people. In a battle between politicians prepared to take their case for massive resistance to the people and politicians who were reluctant to campaign for gradualism, there could only be one winner. The moderates never campaigned or offered a coherent strategy for effective gradual change. For example, in Arkansas, Sid McMath recalled that "there were people, intelligent and educated people, and people in positions of leadership that knew it [desegregation] was inevitable." He blamed Governor Orval Faubus for undercutting the Blossom Plan for school desegregation in 1957. Yet those "intelligent and educated people" had devised a plan that enabled their own children to go to a new segregated school and put the burden of school desegregation at Central High on white working-class families. They helped Blossom win over elite opinion in Little Rock; they made no effort to prepare or win over working-class parents at Central High for token compliance. McMath himself admits that he and Winthrop Rockefeller, powerful community and business leaders, ignored the looming crisis, and by the time they went to plead with Faubus to support the school board, it was too late. McMath's most notable contribution to the crisis was to plead belatedly with Vice-President Richard Nixon to send marshals, not the troops that Eisenhower planned to deploy, to enforce the court order. Faubus had no reason to bail out a Little Rock community leadership that had failed to build up the political support that would have enabled him to avoid confrontation with the courts. Not that the former McMath protégé was without his own responsibility. He might claim that he was the victim of popular segregationist sentiment. Yet he himself had helped create that segregationist sentiment. In 1956 he persuaded the reluctant Arkansas congressmen James Trimble and Brooks Hays to sign the Southern Manifesto in order to defuse segregationist protest. Then he claimed that the signing of the Manifesto by two known moderates illustrated just how powerful that segregationist sentiment was and how he had no alternative but to go along with it.[16]

In Alabama, Jim Folsom in 1956 realized that interposition resolutions being passed by the legislature were futile, that Montgomery black leaders should push for the ending of segregation on the buses, rather than the first-come, first-served solution they had initially demanded, and that black plaintiff Autherine Lucy would have to be admitted by the University of Alabama. Yet he persisted publicly in claiming that it was possible to maintain segregation and uphold the Supreme Court decision. As a result, the legislature passed a barrage of antidesegregation measures, white leaders refused to negotiate meaningfully with the Montgomery Improvement Association during the city's bus boycott, and university leaders caved in to the mob at Tuscaloosa while Folsom was incommunicado on a drunken fishing expedition. At the local level, governors like Folsom and moderate community leaders in Little Rock seemed to believe that a stealth-like approach might bring token desegregation without alerting or alarming ordinary whites. Similarly in Congress, moderates like Lyndon Johnson, Albert Gore, and Estes Kefauver upheld the Court but argued that it was best to leave matters to local communities rather than hamstring them with massive resistance state legislation or provocative Senate manifestos. But they made no effort to indicate what would happen if local white men and women of goodwill would not agree to desegregate, because the liberals had also set their face firmly against what they called "forced integration."[17]

Did moderate politicians who were so cautious and moderate politicians who ran for cover need to be so fatalistic and supine? I have argued at length elsewhere that, while it is easy to second-guess courageous white politicians like congressmen Frank E. Smith of Mississippi or Carl Elliott of Arkansas, who made reluctant decisions that constituency sentiment allowed them no leeway on the desegregation issue, there was nevertheless more room for maneuver than they acknowledged. In particular, William Fulbright, Lister Hill, and John Sparkman in the U.S. Senate operated from virtually impregnable positions in their states in the mid 1950s. They had a proven electoral base, they had secured powerful financial support, and they faced only token opposition. Their willingness to sign the Southern Manifesto or support the 1957 Civil Rights Act or intervene in their states' racial crises strongly suggests a reluctance personally to envisage the end of segregation and what, in the long run, turned out to be a misguided attempt to preserve their political influence on nonracial matters. In the 1950s they had room to maneuver that had disappeared by the 1960s.[18]

•   •   •

One consequence of this moderate paralysis was that conventional biracial politics failed to deliver substantive racial change for African Americans. Since 1945, black politicians at the local level had been able to lever some concessions from white politicians in return for the support of the small, but increasing, black electorate, an electorate that was worth cultivating by white factions in cities like Baton Rouge, Montgomery, and Atlanta. The politics of local negotiation and occasional legal challenge were the dominant political mode of most African Americans during the 1950s. But increasingly this system of biracial politics failed to deliver the changes that a younger generation of African Americans expected. As a result, they turned to direct action from 1960 onward.

One reason why southern moderates were so resigned was they were much more attuned to the passions of their white constituents than to the impatience of their black supporters. Traditionally, relationships between white moderates and black leaders in the South were conducted through an elaborate ritual of condescension and deference. That pattern continued for many in the 1950s. We do not yet know enough about how politicians secured black support in the politics of the 1940s and 1950s, but we know they rarely campaigned directly for black support. Instead, they approached local leaders in the black community who delivered their community's vote as a bloc. It might be a local funeral director, a university janitor, or the governor's chauffeur. When one of the most liberal southern congressmen, Charles Deane of North Carolina, faced a tough primary battle after refusing to sign the Southern Manifesto, he did not have any close black contacts in his constituency; he had to write to a professor at North Carolina Central outside his constituency to find the names of local African Americans he should contact. Despite Deane's racial moderation, the black vote was delivered to his segregationist opponent by the sheriff's local contacts. Dante Fascell recalled this old style of securing black support. When he first ran for the Florida state legislature in Miami, he approached the former sheriff, who said he had little chance of winning but that he could do something for Fascell with the black vote. The former sheriff drove Fascell out to a black church in the country after dark to meet local black leaders, but Fascell could not offer them any money. When he ran for Congress in 1954, he recalled that he was the first candidate in Miami to campaign for the black vote "in daylight" alongside a local black high school principal. Such a direct appeal was a rarity. There is little evidence, for example, that Albert Gore, Sr., despite his racial moderation and despite his overwhelming African American support, ever campaigned directly for the black vote, aside from a few meetings in black churches in his later campaigns.[19]

Prudent black leaders, described by Numan Bartley as racial diplomats, often told white politicians what they thought the white politicians wanted to hear. They often made allowances for the need of politicians they regarded as sympathetic to cater to white constituents. I. S. McLinton in Arkansas assured Fulbright that the black community recognized that the senator had no alternative but to sign the Southern Manifesto. They also supported candidates whom they believed to be racial moderates, perhaps despite their public posture, in opposition to vocal segregationists. I. DeQuincy Newman in South Carolina supported Olin Johnston against Strom Thurmond in 1950 and Fritz Hollings against Donald Russell in 1966, despite the absence of civil rights rhetoric on the part of Johnston and Hollings. In 1966, Hollings's supporters were race-baited, distributing among textile mill workers photographs of Russell shaking hands with the black civil rights leader Newman at his integrated inaugural. But the Hollings supporters had the photograph because the black leader Newman himself had given it to them, anxious to help Hollings win.[20]

Most white politicians were shielded from the growing sense of grievance in the black community: they did not have the same personal feel for the humiliations and impatience of the black community that they had for the fears of the white community. As a result, this first postwar system of bira-cial politics simply could not satisfy the demands of black voters. As J. Mills Thornton clearly demonstrated, Montgomery provided an early example of how politics and traditional negotiations with the city commission for better treatment on the buses failed to yield results and pushed African Americans into direct action. The boycott started out as simply a modest, temporary stepping-up of the bargaining process that had bought Montgomery blacks a modicum of change before 1955. The refusal of the city commission and the bus company to negotiate pushed the black leaders to demand the end of segregation and mount a different kind of year-long boycott. By contrast, in Mobile the white politician Joseph Langan actively solicited black support in his race for the state legislature in 1946 and worked closely with the NAACP leader John LeFlore, protected black voters, and worked to equalize teachers' salaries. In 1953, Langan was elected to the city commission with black support, which he publicly welcomed. In office he worked with LeFlore and the Non-Partisan Voters' League to secure urban renewal and to desegregate public accommodations, schools, and the University of South Alabama. Because the system was responsive, African Americans in Mobile eschewed direct-action protest.[21]

But in many southern cities, white leaders had all too easily patronized the older generation of racial diplomats. Younger, more assertive leaders grew impatient with the lack of change. In Atlanta, where black voters provided one-third of the overall total voting population, T. M. Alexander recalled that the system allowed "a minority of the white voters to dictate to all of the black voters, a subtle kind of racial 'whitemail' that worked for more than 25 years." In 1960, the students of Atlanta University would make it clear that the cautious, deferential alliance of the Auburn Avenue business elite with the white power structure simply had not delivered the changes to de jure segregation that they wanted, and started direct action protests. Similarly, in Baton Rouge, the city made few concessions, and the black leader T. J. Jemison made few demands, in the years after the 1953 boycott. In 1960–61, World War II activists like Johnnie Jones, who had been opposed to what they considered to be Jemison's premature settlement of the boycott within the parameters of segregation, supported students and activists from the Congress of Racial Equality who sat in in downtown Baton Rouge in defiance of the president of Southern University, Felton Clark. Clark closed the campus and expelled students. Jemison remained silent throughout the confrontation.[22]

In community after community, biracial politics of the 1950s variant increasingly could not deliver the changes in segregation that black community leaders and their supporters wanted. Rising black expectations came up against white intransigence. Direct action, rather than electoral politics and negotiation, and demands for the immediate, rather than gradual, end of segregation increasingly became the tactics of the black community.

It was these direct action protests of the 1960s that provoked violent white repression—against the Freedom Rides, against schoolchildren at Birmingham, and against peaceful marchers at Selma. In turn, this well-publicized violence produced the civil rights legislation that brought institutionalized white supremacy to an end in the South. As Anders Walker has recently observed, the civil rights protesters between 1960 and 1965 successfully waged "cultural wars." Studious, middle-class, peaceful black protesters reversed the elaborate segregationist portrayal of the 1950s of blacks as culturally stunted, illegitimate, and criminal.[23]

Why was the white backlash in the 1960s so much more intense and violent than the reaction to black assertiveness after World War II? It was not because the *Brown* decision affected schools, the institutions white southerners most wanted to defend. The protests of the 1960s had little to do with schools. What whites reacted so violently against was the notion of African Americans dictating the timetable of racial change, and what they perceived as black aggressive intrusion into white-controlled public space.

• • •

Brown and the backlash to it neither halted gradual racial change in the South nor destroyed racial moderation. Liberal fatalism, rather than the *Brown* decision, caused the downfall of racial moderation in southern politics. The fatalism and the lack of sensitivity to the urgency of black demands meant that conventional electoral politics after the *Brown* decision failed to deliver the racial changes that African Americans wanted. Their shift to direct action protest, rather than the *Brown* decision and the backlash to it, caused the well-publicized white violence of the 1960s and the federal intervention that brought down segregation.

As the fortieth and fiftieth anniversaries of so many of the great civil rights struggles come thick and fast, southerners and historians naturally remark on the immense changes that have taken place in what was not so long ago the poorest region in the country and the bastion of white supremacy. There is a tendency to assert a "self-exculpatory" model of massive resistance. The responsibility for massive resistance in this interpretation lies with everybody *except* the white political leaders of the South. The blame is placed on racist white workers, the misplaced strategy of the NAACP, the insensitive decisions of the Supreme Court, and northern liberals. The fact that the South after a decade eventually complied with school desegregation and, despite the dire warnings of the 1950s, did so largely peacefully is an occasion for "self-congratulation."

But massive resistance to *Brown* was not a restrained response by a white leadership anxious to channel white supremacist sentiment into safe channels until an accommodation with inevitable change could be worked out. If there were politicians who saw the writing on the wall and saw inevitable racial change, they were silent. Southern leaders had the opportunity to go in another direction, but instead they worked to convince white southerners that the Supreme Court could be defied. White southerners, like their leaders, saw no reason voluntarily to give up the privileges of whiteness, even if they had doubts about segregation, if they did not have to, and the South's leaders were telling them they did not have to.

Racial change came eventually. Southern leaders marched their followers to the brink. It is to their credit that, having got to the brink, they looked into the abyss and turned back. But how much congratulation is due to a white leadership for eventually and belatedly complying with the law of the land? How much credit is due to that leadership for averting the threat of violence, a threat that the leadership had unleashed in the first place?

It is right to question the glib celebrations of the *Brown* decision, but there is a danger in downplaying the significance of *Brown*. Racial change did not come about in the South as the inevitable result of long-term economic and demographic changes. It did not come about simply as a result of economic modernization. Racial change did not come about because southern white leaders voluntarily came to terms with issues of morality and justices. Racial change was imposed on the South as a result of pressure from within, from the civil rights movement of African Americans, and from without, from the federal government. In creating that pincer movement on the white South, the *Brown* decision, for all its limitations and for all its misplaced confidence in white southern liberals, was crucial.

Notes

1. Michael J. Klarman, *From Jim Crow to Civil Rights: The Supreme Court and the Struggle for Racial Equality* (New York: Oxford University Press, 2004), 315–16.

2. For a vigorous, hostile analysis of the way school desegregation was implemented from 1970 onward, see David Armor, *Forced Justice: School Desegregation and the Law* (New York: Oxford University Press, 1994). For a judicious summing-up of the successes and failures of school desegregation see James T. Patterson, *Brown v. Board of Education: A Civil Rights Milestone and Its Troubled Legacy* (New York: Oxford University Press, 2001), 170–223.

3. Michael J. Klarman, "*Brown*, Racial Change and the Civil Rights Movement," *Virginia Law Review* 80 (1994): 7–150; Michael J. Klarman, "How *Brown* Changed Race Relations: The Backlash Thesis," *Journal of American History* 80 (1994): 81–118, Klarman, *From Jim Crow to Civil Rights*, 290–442; Numan V. Bartley, *The New South, 1945–1980: The Story of the South's Modernization* (Baton Rouge: Louisiana State University Press: Baton Rouge, 1995), 70, 73; Numan V. Bartley, comment, fortieth anniversary of Little Rock conference, University of Arkansas at Little Rock, Sept. 27, 1997; Robert Korstad and Nelson Lichtenstein, "Opportunities Found and Lost: Labor, Radicals and the Early Civil Rights Movement," *Journal of American History* 75 (1988): 786–811.

4. Klarman, *From Jim Crow to Civil Rights*, 385; Tony Badger, "Whatever Happened to Roosevelt's New Generation of Southerners?" in *The Roosevelt Years: New Essays on the United States, 1933–1945*, ed. Robert A. Garson and Stuart Kidd (Edinburgh: Edinburgh University Press, 1999), 122–38.

5. James C. Cobb, "World War II and the Mind of the Modern South," in *Remaking Dixie: The Impact of World War II on the American South*, ed. Neil R. McMillen (Jackson: University Press of Mississippi, 1997) 6–9; Jennifer Brooks, "From Fighting Nazism to Fighting Bossism: Southern World War II Veterans and the Assault on Southern Political Tradition," unpublished paper in my possession; Bryant Simon, *A Fabric of Defeat: The Politics of South Carolina Millhands, 1910–1948* (Chapel Hill: University of North Carolina Press, 1998), 221; Bruce Nelson, *Divided We Stand: American Workers and the Struggle for Black Equality* (Princeton, N.J.: Princeton University Press, 2001) xix–xliv; Bruce Nelson, "Organized Labor and the Struggle for Black Equality in Mobile During World War II," *Journal of American History* 80 (1993): 952–88; Tony Badger, "Fatalism Not Gradualism: Race and the Crisis of Southern Liberalism, 1945–1965," in *The Making of Martin Luther King and the Civil Rights Movement*, ed. Brian Ward and Tony Badger (London: Macmillan, 1996).

6. Klarman, *From Jim Crow to Civil Rights*, 189–90, 371–72.

7. Ralph McGill, *The South and the Southerner* (Boston: Little, Brown, 1963); James C. Cobb, *The Selling of the South: The Southern Crusade for Industrial Development, 1936–1980* (Urbana: University of Illinois Press, 1982), 122–50; Glenn T. Eskew, *But for Birmingham: The Local and National Movements in the Civil Rights Struggle* (Chapel Hill: University of North Carolina Press, 1997) 153–79; Maxie Myron Cox, Jr., "1963: The Year of Decision: Desegregation in South Carolina" (Ph.D. diss., University of South Carolina, 1996), 1–71.

8. Robert Gaines Corley, "The Quest for Racial Harmony: Race Relations in Birmingham, Alabama, 1947–1963" (Ph.D. diss., University of Virginia, 1979); Eskew, *But*

for Birmingham, 91–106; Mary Jacqueline Herbert, "Beyond Black and White: The Civil Rights Movement in Baton Rouge, Louisiana, 1945–1972" (Ph.D. diss., Louisiana State University, 1999), 42–45, 52–70, 97. Herbert noted that, while African Americans in Baton Rouge remembered the boycott as a landmark, white leaders in the city considered it of little import. Tulane trustees were not even prepared to consider merit-based admission in the 1950s: rather than attract nationally talented students, they preferred to retain the university as the preserve of their uptown offspring.

9. William H. Chafe, *Civilities and Civil Rights: Greensboro, North Carolina, and the Black Struggle for Freedom* (New York: Oxford University Press, 1980); John A. Kirk, *Redefining the Color Line: Black Activism in Little Rock, Arkansas, 1940–1970* (Gainesville: University Press of Florida: Gainesville, 2002) 63–68; Stephen G. N. Tuck, *Beyond Atlanta: The Struggle for Racial Equality in Georgia, 1940–1980* (Athens: University of Georgia Press, 2001), 94; Cox, "1963."

10. Brooks Hays, interview, Columbia Oral History Program, Lawrence Brooks Hays Papers, Special Collections Division, University of Arkansas Libraries, Fayetteville; J. William Fulbright to Mrs. Walter Bell, Aug. 31, 1948, Papers of J. William Fulbright, Special Collections Division, University of Arkansas Libraries, Fayetteville; Randall B. Woods, *Fulbright: A Biography* (Cambridge: Cambridge University Press, 1995), 114–19, 152; Albert Gore, Sr., and Mrs. Pauline Gore, interview with the author, Dec. 1, 1990; Tony Badger, "Southerners Who Refused to Sign the Southern Manifesto," *Historical Journal* 42 (1999): 525–26.

11. David W. Robertson, *Sly and Able: A Political Biography of James F. Byrnes* (New York: Norton, 1994), 507–10; Marcia G. Synott, "Federalism Vindicated: University Desegregation in South Carolina and Alabama, 1962–63," *Journal of Policy History* 1 (1989): 299.

12. Klarman, "How *Brown* Changed Race Relations," 92, 94–97; Klarman, *From Jim Crow to Civil Rights*, 186, 260–61; Terry Sanford, interview, May 14, 1976, Southern Oral History Program, Southern Historical Collection, University of North Carolina, Chapel Hill; Tuck, *Beyond Atlanta*, 101.

13. Bartley, *New South*, 69–73; Korstad and Lichtenstein, "Opportunities Found," 786–811.

14. Robert J. Norrell, *Reaping the Whirlwind: The Civil Rights Movement in Tuskegee* (New York: Knopf, 1985), 85.

15. Numan V. Bartley, *The Rise of Massive Resistance: Race and Politics in the South During the 1950s* (Baton Rouge: Louisiana State University Press, 1969); Tony Badger, "The Southern Manifesto," paper delivered at the annual meeting of the Southern Historical Association, Orlando, Florida, November 1993, copy in my possession; Howard Quint, *Profile in Black and White* (Washington, D.C.: Public Affairs Press, 1958), 35, 46; Marcia G. Synnott, "Alice Norwood Spearman: Civil Rights Apostle to South Carolinians," in *Beyond Image and Convention: Explorations in Southern Women's History*, ed. Janet L. Coryell, Martha H. Swain, Sandra Gioia Treadway, and Elizabeth Hayes Turner (Columbia: University of Missouri Press, 1998), 184; Anders Walker, "The Ghost of Jim Crow: Law, Culture and the Subversion of Civil Rights, 1954–1965" (Ph.D. diss., Yale University, 2004).

16. Sidney McMath, interview by John Egerton, Sept. 8, 1990, Southern Oral History Program; Jim Lester, *A Man for Arkansas: Sid McMath and the Southern Reform*

Tradition (Little Rock: Rose, 1976); 233–35; Sidney S. McMath, *Promises Kept: A Memoir* (Fayetteville: University of Arkansas Press, 2003), 301–6; Tony Badger, "The Forerunner of Our Opposition: Arkansas and the Southern Manifesto of 1956," *Arkansas Historical Quarterly* 56 (1997): 353–60; Tony Badger, "The White Reaction to *Brown*: Arkansas, the Southern Manifesto and Massive Resistance," in *Understanding the Little Rock Crisis,* ed. Elizabeth Jacoway and C. Fred Williams (Fayetteville: University of Arkansas Press, 1999) 83–97.

17. George Sims, *The Little Man's Big Friend: James E. Folsom in Alabama Politics, 1946–58* (Tuscaloosa: University of Alabama Press, 1985), 175–88; Badger, "Southerners Who Refused to Sign," 517–34.

18. Badger, "Fatalism Not Gradualism"; Tony Badger, "'Closet Moderates': Why White Liberals Failed, 1940–1970," in *The Role of Ideas in the Civil Rights South,* ed. Ted Ownby (Jackson: University Press of Mississippi, 2002), 103–5; Tony Badger, *Race and War: Lyndon Johnson and William Fulbright* (Reading, England: University of Reading Press, 2000).

19. Dante Fascell, interview with the author, Feb. 27, 1997; James Sasser, interview with the author, Dec. 11, 2003.

20. Bartley, *New South,* 174; Woods, *Fulbright,* 211; John Carl West, interview by Herbert J. Hartsook, 1997, Modern Political Collections: Oral History Project, South Caroliniana Library, University of South Carolina, Columbia. I am extremely grateful to Governor West for allowing me to consult this interview.

21. J. Mills Thornton, *Dividing Lines: Municipal Politics and the Struggle for Civil Rights in Montgomery, Birmingham and Selma* (Tuscaloosa: University of Alabama Press, 2002), 21–88; Nahfiza Ahmed, "Race, Class and Citizenship: The Civil Rights Struggle in Mobile, Alabama, 1925–1985" (Ph.D. diss., University of Leicester, 1999), chapters 4 to 5.

22. Tuck, *Beyond Atlanta,* 93; Herbert, "Beyond Black and White," 170–221.

23. Walker, "Ghost of Jim Crow," 275, 361.

[55]

THREE

A Political *Coup d'État*:
How the Enemies of Earl Long Overwhelmed
Racial Moderation in Louisiana

Adam Fairclough

In *Origins of the New South*, C. Vann Woodward famously asserted that the politics of white supremacy was as much about "*which whites* should be supreme" as it was about the supremacy of whites over blacks. The course of massive resistance in Louisiana confirms the truth of Woodward's insight. If the term "Solid South" is of limited utility in understanding southern politics after Reconstruction, it is practically useless when it comes to examining the 1950s. Although few whites had any stomach for school integration, the political warfare precipitated by *Brown* pitted one set of whites against another set of whites, each faction holding very different attitudes toward blacks. In presidential elections, Louisiana was up for grabs. In 1948 its Electoral College votes went to Strom Thurmond (States' Rights Party), in 1952 to Adlai Stevenson (Democrat), in 1956 to Dwight Eisenhower (Republican), and in 1960 to John F. Kennedy (Democrat).[1]

Numan V. Bartley's classic analysis of massive resistance depicted a political conflict among whites that echoed the longstanding division between the whites of the black belt and those in the "white" counties of the Piedmont and hill country—a strong historical echo of the New South conflicts sketched by Woodward. The white planters, lawyers, and merchants of the black belt, who still enjoyed disproportionate political power through the combined effects of disfranchisement and malapportionment, led the various organizations, notably the White Citizens' Councils, that spearheaded the massive resistance movement. Sometimes, Bartley added, these "neo-Bourbons" were joined by wealthy urbanites. For example, massive resistance found strong support among whites in older cities like Jackson and New Orleans, as well as in modern cities such as Shreveport and Birmingham. Pitted against the neo-Bourbons of the black belt were the "neopopulists," who drew their support from white voters in the hill country and from the emerging black electorate. That division was most evident, perhaps, in Alabama and Louisiana, where governors Jim Folsom and Earl Long emphasized bread-and-butter issues, downplayed race, encouraged black voter registration, and forged political alliances with black leaders.[2]

Louisiana's political and cultural peculiarities require some modification of the Woodward-Bartley model. Support for massive resistance did not always increase in proportion to the black population. The black-majority cotton parishes of northern Louisiana—especially the tier along the west bank of the Mississippi River—were *the* most hostile to black voting. In the parishes of southern Louisiana, on the other hand, Catholicism and Creole-Cajun culture, as well as a lingering tradition of Republicanism in the sugar parishes, muted white opposition to black voting, even where blacks constituted a substantial percentage of the overall population.[3]

In addition, Louisiana, which had a large urban population, did not practice the kind of gross malapportionment that in other southern states hugely inflated rural representation at the expense of the cities. True, a candidate could still be elected governor without carrying New Orleans. Once in the statehouse, however, he could scarcely ignore the Crescent City, as it supplied a quarter of the members of the state legislature. The high level of urbanization in Louisiana not only reduced the political influence of the black belt but also encouraged black voter registration. In 1952, Louisiana's three biggest cities, New Orleans, Shreveport, and Baton Rouge, contained 38 percent of the state's 95,000 black voters.[4]

One final peculiarity is worth noting. The electoral behavior of St. Bernard and Plaquemines parishes was unpredictable, eccentric, and often totally at odds with how the rest of south Louisiana voted. The political idiosyncrasies of these adjacent parishes owed everything to their political boss, Leander Perez. Louisiana had other "bossed" parishes, of course, but Perez's manipulation of the ballot box was in a class of its own: it would put even Robert Mugabe or the late Ngo Dinh Diem to shame. In 1950, for example, Russell Long, running for U.S. Senate, carried every parish in the state except Plaquemines—which delivered 93 percent of its votes to his opponent. Moreover, when wedded to Perez's brilliant cunning and enormous wealth—he was a corruptionist of epic proportions—this dictatorial rule gave him a degree of political influence in state and regional politics that was disproportionate to the number of voters he controlled.[5]

Nevertheless, Louisiana's distinctiveness warranted a degree of optimism about the implementation of the *Brown* ruling. Louisiana State University had already admitted black students, and in 1954 its first black law graduate,

Ernest N. Morial—a future mayor of New Orleans—joined the state bar. In 1954–55, blacks also enrolled peacefully in state colleges in Lake Charles, Lafayette, and Hammond. The influence of the Catholic Church also augured well for integration. Under Archbishop Joseph Rummel, the archdiocese of New Orleans had admitted blacks to Holy Name Seminary and Loyola University. It had also ordained its first black priest. Rummel publicly endorsed *Brown* and implied that the Church would start to integrate its parochial schools in 1956. Influential newspapers such as the *New Orleans Time-Picayune* urged people to calmly accept *Brown* and do nothing to foment racial friction. No wonder the NAACP believed that Louisiana would gain a head start in the integration stakes.[6]

Yet the reaction to *Brown* from Louisiana's white politicians seemed unequivocally negative. With only three dissenting votes in the house and one in the senate, the state legislature condemned *Brown* as an "unwarranted and unprecedented abuse of power" and branded integration as "intolerable, impractical, and in the ultimate sense unenforceable." Two bills to circumvent *Brown* swiftly became laws. The legislature also created a Joint Legislative Committee to Maintain Segregation (JLC), chaired by State Senator William Rainach of Claiborne Parish. Advised by the wily and indefatigable Leander Perez, Rainach and the JLC engaged in a frenzy of activity to fend off the threat of integration. They coordinated the burgeoning Citizens' Council movement, which by 1956 claimed 80,000 members in Louisiana. They swapped ideas with ultrasegregationists in Mississippi, Georgia, and Alabama on how to thwart the NAACP. They excavated "footnote 11" of the *Brown* decision to expose the influence of "communist" social scientists. Finally, they began devising a legalistic and political strategy to block integration. In a statewide referendum, voters by a five-to-one margin endorsed a constitutional amendment assigning the enforcement of segregation to the "inherent police power of the state."[7]

Still, the public mood was not one of alarm and panic over *Brown*. Rainach and his allies were well aware that they lacked political support for an all-out defense of segregation. The five-to-one vote in favor of their "police power" amendment did not fool them. In south Louisiana, support for segregation was "soft," with a third of the voters opposing the amendment. In any case, the measure lacked teeth and would never survive judicial scrutiny. "We face ultimate defeat in the federal courts," Rainach admitted, "and all legal action is merely a delaying tactic." Moreover, the threat of closing public schools rather than accepting integration was rather like Secretary of State John Foster Dulles's policy of nuclear "brinkmanship": it was a threat that could never be carried out. "Our whole cause will be lost if we are forced to abandon our public school system." Given a choice between integration and no public schools, Rainach knew that white voters would reluctantly accept integration.[8]

The ultrasegregationists received minimal cooperation from Governor Robert F. Kennon. Although a segregationist and a conservative from north Louisiana, Kennon did not wish to agitate the race issue. He had good relations with President Eisenhower and considered himself a future federal judge. When Rainach devised an ambitious proposal for the state to devote $33.5 million of tidelands oil revenues to equalizing black schools, the governor watered down the plan. Kennon preferred to spend money on building highways.[9]

Two racial moderates dominated the 1955–56 governor's race: Chep Morrison, mayor of New Orleans, and former governor Earl K. Long. Both of them made strong appeals for black votes. All five candidates affirmed their support for segregation, but other issues—gambling, state spending, and the antiunion "right-to-work" law—drew more attention. Only one candidate ran solely on the race issue, proclaiming himself the "white man's candidate," but he finished last with a paltry 13,000 votes. (Rumour had it that Earl Long secretly subsidized the white supremacist in order to damage Chep Morrison in north Louisiana.)[10] The final outcome was a resounding triumph of neopopulism over neo-Bourbonism. Earl Long won 51 percent of the first primary votes. Having won a clear majority, Long did not have to face a runoff election. He then pulled off a remarkable piece of political legerdemain by persuading the Democratic State Central Committee to cancel *all* the other runoff elections for statewide offices. The entire Long ticket was elected. The defeated anti-Long candidates included Attorney General Fred S. LeBlanc, who had been plotting with Rainach and Perez to attack the NAACP in the law courts.[11]

The ultrasegregationists had suffered a serious political reverse. They stumbled again in November 1956, when voters rejected a proposal to make voter registration more difficult. And to make matters worse, once in office Long attacked Leander Perez's power base, passing eleven bills that transferred control of local government in Plaquemines Parish to Long partisans. The *Louisiana Weekly*, the state's leading black newspaper, crowed over the plight of the once mighty Dixiecrat: "The political power of Leander Perez is broken."[12]

Such triumphalism was premature, however. Perez and his allies were down, but not yet out. Throughout 1955 they had been hatching an elaborate plot to smash the NAACP, decimate the black electorate, and destroy the Long machine. This ambitious project required, in Willie Rainach's words, "unusually deliberate" and "carefully planned action." Crucial details of the plot were confirmed at a series of secret meetings between Rainach, Governor Kennon, and State Attorney General Fred LeBlanc. Rainach, a meticulous record-keeper, made careful, hand-written notes of what transpired. The most important point was that the governor and the attorney general agreed to prosecute the NAACP for violating the Fuqua Law—a measure passed in 1924, designed to embarrass the Ku Klux Klan, which required all organizations to file their membership lists with the secretary of state. It is inconceivable that Earl Long would have committed such an agreement to paper. Summarizing his philosophy of political communication, Long once said, "Don't write anything you can phone. Don't phone anything you can talk. Don't talk anything you can whisper. Don't whisper anything you can smile. Don't smile anything you can nod. Don't nod anything you can wink."[13]

Although Earl Long's election placed a political foe in the statehouse, it did not derail the ultrasegregationists' plans. LeBlanc launched the prosecution of the NAACP before he relinquished the office of attorney general, and before Long's inauguration as governor. The state judge J. Coleman Lindsey stuck to his part of the plotters' script by enjoining the NAACP from operating in Louisiana until it filed its membership lists with the secretary of state. Moreover, the incoming attorney general, Jack Gremillion, took over the prosecution and continued to harass the NAACP in collaboration with Rainach's JLC. The effect of the injunction crippled the NAACP. For a time, NAACP leaders had to travel to Texas in order to hold meetings. When the NAACP agreed to comply with the injunction, most of its members left, and all but three of its branches—New Orleans, Shreveport, and Lake Charles—folded.

The attack on the NAACP revealed two important facts about Long's relationship to massive resistance. The first has to do with the character of his political organization. Earl's brother, Huey P. Long, had ruled Louisiana with a rod of iron between 1927 and 1935, first as governor and then as a U.S. senator, creating a centralized political machine of formidable, indeed frightening, power. Earl Long's political methods were more avuncular and informal. He never built the kind of political organization that Huey had operated, relying instead upon myriad informal agreements with individual politicians: "Earl had more alliances in Louisiana than Solomon had wives," quipped one insider. However, the factional alignments constantly shifted, and Long exercised only weak control over his allies. Hence Jack P. F. Gremillion, the successful Longite candidate for attorney general, pursued a policy of cooperation with Rainach that ran counter to Long's own instinct for racial moderation. Although Long had no great respect for Gremillion—once quipping that the best way to hide something from the attorney general was to put it inside a law book—he could do little to impede Gremillion's harrying of the NAACP.[14]

In the second place, Long, like other southern liberals, had to tread exceedingly cautiously in opposing massive resistance. He tried to situate himself in the political center, criticizing both the NAACP and the Citizens' Councils as extremists. But the nearly universal unpopularity of school integration among southern white voters—who were far more numerous than black voters—posed an enormous problem for racial moderates. Long would not defend the NAACP, and he would not campaign for integration. Instead, he underlined his segregationist credentials in an effort to protect his right flank. "Mr Rainach is not a bit more for segregation than I am," he insisted. "I'm for it 1,000 percent."[15]

In signing Rainach's segregation bills, however, Long did not buy political protection from the ultrasegregationists. As they attacked the NAACP and stoked the fires of massive resistance bills, Rainach and his cohorts tried to halt, and then reverse, the growth of the black electorate. Their reasoning was simple: whites would be unable to unite behind segregation if their political leaders listened to black voters. With black registration at 160,000—about 15 percent of Louisiana's electorate—rival candidates were inexorably pulled toward "moderate" racial positions that weakened segregation. Moreover, the black vote had the potential to grow much larger, for blacks constituted about a third of Louisiana's total population. The ultras, on the other hand, did not have to woo black voters. In Claiborne and Plaquemines parishes, the political bases of Rainach and Perez, blacks constituted less than 1 percent of the voters. In the three parishes that elected the district attorney Thompson Clarke, another Rainach ally, no blacks voted at all. "We are going all out to eliminate low white trash who desire to get elected with the help of the Negro vote," vowed one ultrasegregationist.[16]

In April 1956, beginning in Monroe in Ouchita Parish, Citizens' Council members began to systematically "challenge" voters whose registration cards contained misspellings and other errors. Mrs. Mae Lucky, the registrar of voters, notified those challenged that in order to retain their vote they must personally appear at her office and supply an affidavit signed by three registered voters. The 4,084 challenges included only thirty-seven whites.

The Citizens' Council justified the challenges on the grounds of "good government." It aimed to remove "unqualified" voters and to eliminate "bloc voting." One council member explained the political arithmetic thus: "an individual could still receive 65 percent of the 'non-block' votes in the City of Monroe and still be defeated by the 'block votes.'" He further complained that "these so-called bloc-voting individuals were merely voting by number and giving no consideration to the qualifications of the candidate or even the name of the candidate." The purge was "nonpolitical," another man affirmed, and it was not directed "against the Negroes." These explanations were disingenuous. As one anti-Long politician put it, black voters had been registered by the Long faction "through force, cajolery, unkept promises, and, in general, political skullduggery." Thus the elimination of black voters represented a direct attack upon supporters of Earl Long and, by extension, upon Long himself. The Citizens' Council's immediate goal was to oust the incumbent mayor, Long's political ally John E. Coon.[17]

The larger significance of the Citizens' Council's intervention becomes apparent when one considers the history of race relations in Monroe. John Coon had governed Monroe, a city of 45,000 people, of whom almost half were black, in the tradition of racial moderation practiced by his predecessors, Arnold Bernstein and Harvey H. Benoit. Like previous mayors, he discouraged police brutality. In 1950, for example, when a black man was beaten up while in custody, he called a special meeting of the police force and warned that he would press charges against anyone who abused prisoners. "This practice must stop." The effects of such policies were palpable. Local blacks displayed a "lack of fear" and "buoyancy of spirit," noted one observer, "born of the fact that 'the white people here are not nearly as mean as they are in other southern cities.'" By the early 1950s Monroe boasted a new black high school, an integrated police force, and a high level of black voter registration. Black voters enthusiastically supported John Coon.[18]

Henry Carroll, the most influential black citizen in Monroe, exemplified the way in which the accommodationist leaders of the Jim Crow era often became political go-betweens after white leaders decided to encourage black voter registration. Like many of the "racial diplomats" who mediated between the white and black communities under segregation, Carroll was a public school teacher whose position depended upon white favor. His career and influence flourished under the patronage of white business progressives who, ever since Arnold Bernstein was first elected mayor in 1919, had steered Monroe in the direction of "excellent race relations." Bernstein helped pay for Carroll's education at Southern University. After Bernstein's death in 1937, Carroll found another powerful sponsor in James A. Noe. A former governor, wealthy oilman, plantation owner, and proprietor of the radio station KNOE, Noe had close links to the Long organization.

In the late 1940s, through the intercession of Noe's wife, Anna, a member of the school board, Henry Carroll was selected to be principal of Monroe Colored High School, a position he held for more than twenty years. The Noes then helped Carroll to secure a new building, which the school board named "Carroll High School." When Noe's radio station, KNOE, began broadcasting "The Voice of the South," a weekly program devoted to the black community, Carroll served as the commentator. Later, he hosted a children's show on Noe's television station. Carroll became one of Noe's closest political allies. "His endorsement of a candidate was almost tantamount to full Negro support at the polls, and Carroll never backed a candidate not supported by his friend and backer James A. Noe."[19]

The black voters of Monroe, backed by Carroll and Noe, formed the first line of resistance to the Citizens' Council. Hundreds of challenged voters flocked to the courthouse in an effort to save their registration. Many stood in line for days, arriving before dawn and staying until the office closed at five. "Frozen in my imagination is the picture of determination I saw on the faces of crippled men, sick and pregnant women," recalled Carroll.

But the odds were stacked against them. The registrars could process no more than a hundred cases a day, and often fell far short of that target. Moreover, they refused to accept counteraffidavits unless the three signatories were voters who had not themselves been challenged. They even insisted that the signatories reside in the same ward and precinct as the challenged voter. The obstacle course did not stop there: challenged voters then had to fill out new registration cards, unassisted, and then read and understand, to the registrar's satisfaction, a portion of the United States or Louisiana constitutions. Even if they saved their registration, Mrs. Lucky treated them as new voters, rendering them ineligible to cast ballots in the May 22 election.[20]

Carroll called upon his friend and ally, James A. Noe, to stop the wholesale purge of black voters by avowed enemies of Earl Long who were acting under cover of the Citizens' Councils. Noe, outraged to discover that the challenged voters included his own cook, maid, and gardener, went to the courthouse to see the situation for himself. The misapplication of the rules by Mrs. Lucky's office appalled him. Discovering that the registrar's office had run out of affidavit forms, he borrowed a blank and ran off one thousand copies at his own expense. He also asked the state attorney general to send an official to Monroe to clarify the law. When the official turned out to be William Shaw, an architect of the Citizens' Council movement and a close associate of Willie Rainach, Noe could hardly believe what was happening. Incandescent with anger, he demanded to know if Shaw belonged to the Citizens' Council. "Yes," Shaw replied, adding, "Now I want to ask you something. Are you a member of the NAACP?" The sixty-five-year-old Noe, a self-styled "roughneck," moved to punch Shaw; Henry Carroll restrained him and sheriff's deputies were hurriedly summoned to prevent a fracas. Later, after he regained his composure, Noe warned that if the Citizens' Council eliminated the black vote, "they will, as well, disfranchise our Italians, our Jews, our Catholics, or even our Protestants." Referring to the prosecution of the NAACP, he complained that "laws once established for the protection of minority groups from campaigns of racial hate . . . seem to have been perverted to attack and strangle a helpless segment of our people."[21]

Noe, an on-again, off-again, on-again political ally of Long, poured scorn on the argument that "bloc voting" was somehow undemocratic. He noted that bloc voting by various groups, including at times Catholics, had been a consistent feature of Louisiana politics. When he himself ran for office "he earnestly endeavored to obtain as many blocks of voters as possible." Noe showed FBI agents some of the hate mail he had subsequently received. "Why don't You and Erl Long, Koon and the other nigger lovers in Louisiana move to Independence with the 'Great Nigger Lover' old harry truman." According to Noe, the Citizens' Council was organizing a quiet boycott of his television station, costing him $5,000 a month in lost revenue.[22]

Noe's intervention proved unavailing. Of the 4,000 blacks who were challenged, only 917 succeeded in staying on the registration rolls. Between the primary election in January and the runoff in May, the Citizens' Council succeeded in reducing the number of black voters in Monroe from about 4,000 to 921. The purge tipped the election from the pro-Long incumbent, John Coon, to the anti-Long challenger, W. L. Howard.[23]

The stage was now set for a three-year struggle between Long and Rainach over voting. Neither Earl nor Huey Long were paragons of democracy. Yet in a very broad sense, the Longite political tradition was to expand the electorate rather than restrict it. In 1934, Huey Long abolished the poll tax, doubling the size of the electorate. After 1948, Earl Long encouraged black registration and was extraordinarily successful in winning black votes. His first reaction to the voter purge in Monroe, therefore, was to propose loosening, not tightening, the registration procedures. "It's far fetched to ask a man to interpret the Constitution. Why, if you turn around and asked the man who asked you the same question, chances are he couldn't answer it." Long promised a bill to abolish the constitutional interpretation test. He promised another bill to allow elderly voters to receive assistance in casting their ballots—a measure designed to help those who were illiterate.[24]

In the event, neither Long nor Rainach got their way. Their respective proposals to expand and restrict the franchise both failed, producing no change in the existing law. And the Citizens' Council bandwagon moved on. Purges were instituted in nine other north Louisiana parishes, eliminating as many as nine thousand black voters. That Rainach was taking dead aim at Earl Long became unmistakably clear when, on September 4, 1958, he and William Shaw turned up at Winnfield in Winn Parish, Earl Long's home town. With members of the local Citizens' Council, they trawled through the registration cards of black voters.[25]

At the end of 1958, Rainach announced his intention of extending the purge to south Louisiana. He sent every voter registrar in the state a Citizens' Council pamphlet outlining the procedure, based on a law of 1940, for challenging and removing "illegally registered voters." And the JLC organized meetings in each congressional district for the purpose of instructing registrars, sheriffs, district attorneys, and other officials on the most effective techniques for disfranchising blacks. The presence of Jack Gremillion, the state attorney general, and Douglas Fowler, director of the State Board of Registration, implied that it was now official state policy to reduce the black electorate.

At these meetings, held throughout Louisiana, registrars were also told to prevent blacks from reregistering. They should administer a constitutional interpretation test, using a set of twenty-four "model" questions devised by Leander Perez. Applicants might be asked to identify the Articles of Confederation, name the exact number of presidential electors to which Louisiana was entitled, or explain the constitutional provision for impeaching a president. Questions were deviously framed with "multiple choice" answers that invited error. One asked, "Our form of government in which we elect officials to act for us is called a [blank]," and offered the following alternatives: "representative form of government," "limited form of government," and "congressional form of government."

The meetings urged two other procedures upon the officials. One was a requirement that applicants should be identified by two existing voters. (They ignored the fact that the federal district judge Gaston L. Porterie had declared such a rule illegal six years earlier.) The other defined "good character" to exclude people who lived in common-law marriages, parents of illegitimate children, and those with criminal records.[26]

But white opposition to the purge began to stiffen. Even in north Louisiana, some registrars proved recalcitrant. In Webster Parish, Winnice Clement tried to frustrate the Citizens' Council by enforcing the law impartially, which meant rejecting whites as well. "[I]f the Negroes have to do it, so do the white people, that's only being fair." Pressured by the police jury to resign, she was immediately reappointed by Earl Long. In 1957, when all voters had to reregister, she began applying the constitutional interpretation test. While the number of black voters fell from 1,700 to 70 white voters declined by over 6,000.[27]

In Winn Parish, Mary C. Flournoy flatly refused to cooperate with the Citizens' Council, telling them: "if you don't leave me alone, I'm going to call Earl Long." Even when Rainach and Shaw showed up, she refused to be intimidated. Angry that the purgers were only scrutinizing the registration cards of black voters, she locked her office during the lunch break and refused to reopen it. Rainach had to get a court order to get back into the office. He then summoned Flournoy before his committee and tried to bully her into adopting the constitutional interpretation test. But Flournoy still resisted. "One thing, especially, I need advice on," she wrote Rainach. "How to cope with a fine Old Timer who has voted all his life and now finds the 'Younger Generation' refuses him the privileges he prizes most; the right to help or reject any local politician. Believe me. There's plenty of bitterness among them."[28]

Registrars in south Louisiana proved even more obdurate. In East Feliciana Parish, the registrar Charles Kilbourne refused to employ the interpretation test and had a policy of assisting applicants in filling out the form. The police jury replaced him with a more pliant official, whereupon black registration plummeted from 1,276 to 50. In Washington Parish, the registrar Curtis Thomas asked a state district judge to enjoin the Citizens' Council from making challenges on the grounds that they interfered with his job, created a nuisance, and served "no useful purpose." But the judge ordered Thomas to accept the challenges: 1,377 black voters were expunged. In St. Landry Parish, however, the Council ran into a brick wall in the person of Sheriff D. J. Doucet. Known as "the Cat"—apparently because he tolerated so many "cat-houses" (brothels)—Doucet had registered blacks en masse after his election as sheriff in 1952. Grateful blacks returned the favor by voting for Doucet. "If you knock them off the rolls," Doucet promised Rainach, "I'll put them back on." When the registrar accepted only twelve challenges a day, the Council members gave up.[29]

During the three years that Rainach and Perez hacked away at the black vote, Long avoided directly challenging them over the race issue. He made little effort to oppose the stream of segregationist bills (many of them drafted by Leander Perez) that issued from the JLC. According to the historian Glen Jeansonne, the fertility of Perez's legal brain ensured that Louisiana passed more "anti-Negro measures" than any other state. They sailed through the legislature with little or no opposition. In July 1956, for example, the state senate passed bills to prohibit interracial athletic events, entertainments, and social gatherings—without a single dissenting vote. With one exception, Long signed them into law.

Long's failure to oppose Rainach's legislative onslaught might be attributed to a failure of nerve. But a more likely explanation would be shrewd political calculation. Given the probability that segregationist measures would be struck down by federal judges in due course, why should Long waste political capital, and imperil his legislative program, by opposing them? Declining to pick a fight over segregation, Long passed all the measures most important to him: increases in old age pensions, pay increases for teachers, expansion of the state university system, and repeal of the antiunion right-to-work law. In pressing for another of his goals, a constitutional convention to rewrite the state's antiquated constitution, he dismissed segregation as irrelevant. "I'm tired of that colored bugaboo coming up every time that something worthwhile comes up."[30]

Like Chep Morrison, his political arch rival, Long may also have simply underestimated the capacity of the segregation question to arouse political passions. Despite his own proclamations of fealty to segregation, he came to the conclusion that defending Jim Crow was a lost cause. After Eisenhower intervened in the Little Rock crisis, he reportedly commented: "Well, that's it. The feds are behind the niggers. I'll be damned if I'll make a fool of myself like Faubus." Another story, possibly apocryphal, had Long taunting his archenemy Perez: "What are you gonna do now, Leander? The feds have the atom bomb." Not only did Long refuse to man the barricades; he also took steps to ease the transition to integration. In 1958, Louisiana State University in New Orleans opened as an integrated university. State colleges in Hammond, Lafayette, and

Lake Charles already admitted black students. In New Orleans, buses and street-cars abandoned segregated seating, and Long cooperated with Chep Morrison, the city's mayor, to see that the change went smoothly. "It's easy to say 'nigger' and scare everybody in the state," Long explained. "I think you should have a kindly feeling toward the Negro."[31]

Long also calculated that he should take a stand on the issue of voting, not segregation. To support blacks over integration, he explained, would get "all the whites aroused" and "you'd get beat bad." In fighting the Citizens' Councils' efforts to restrict the franchise, on the other hand, Long could rely upon considerable white support. The purge in Monroe not only outraged Jimmy Noe but also aroused opposition from white ministers, labor leaders, and the League of Women Voters. Along with aggrieved blacks, they complained to the FBI. Senator Russell Long, Earl's nephew, also asked—privately—for a federal investigation. Publicly, Long told the Baton Rouge Chamber of Commerce that the voter purges had damaged Louisiana's public image and were indefensible.[32]

In May 1959, Earl Long finally hit back at Rainach over the purge of black voters. He tried to stiffen the spines of local registrars by assuring them that they would not be dismissed if they stood up to the Citizens' Councils. Then he introduced two bills designed to halt the purges. One would make it illegal to challenge voters for minor errors on their application forms; the other would make it illegal to challenge voters who had been registered for a year or more.

At that precise moment, however, Long suffered a spectacular public mental breakdown. Testifying before the House Judiciary Committee at the state capitol in Baton Rouge, he delivered what his biographers described as a "torrent of graphic obscenity." The next day he compounded the offense by haranguing the legislature for ninety minutes. He directed his most graphic abuse at Rainach, implying that fanatical segregationists of his ilk damned the Negro by day but slept with black women by night. "After all this is over," he predicted, Rainach would "probably go back there to Summerfield, get up on his front porch, take off his shoes, wash his feet, look at the moon, and get close to God." After a dramatic pause, the governor pointed at Rainach: "And when you do, you got to recognize that niggers is human beings!" Four days later, Long was admitted to a mental hospital in Galveston, Texas. The legislature rejected his proposed bills. Rainach, crowing about the "drubbing" he had administered to Long, laid plans to run for governor.[33]

By late 1959 Long had recovered sufficiently to run for the post of lieutenant governor. Because state law barred him from a second consecutive term, he campaigned alongside James A. Noe, who ran for governor. But the Noe-Long ticket finished a poor fourth. Rainach also failed to qualify for the runoff, but his strong showing in third place enabled him to influence the outcome. He threw his support to Jimmie H. Davis, and the country singer became governor just as the civil rights movement reached its height. For devious reasons of his own, Earl Long also endorsed Davis. A few months later, Long astonished everyone by coming back from the political grave. He won election to Congress, only to drop dead a week later.[34]

For all its cultural and political distinctiveness, it appeared that Louisiana not only joined the ranks of massive resistance but also, in its own sly way, resisted integration more effectively than some other states. With his toothy smile and easy charm, Jimmie Davis lacked the aggressiveness or demagogy of an Orval Faubus or George Wallace; some credited him with keeping the racial temperature low, avoiding an open state–federal clash over integration. Yet Davis gave free rein to the ultrasegregationists. At Rainach's insistence, he created a state sovereignty commission, albeit a weak one. He supported the legislature's financial blockade of the Orleans Parish School Board when the latter began school integration in November 1960. He said nothing when Leander Perez whipped up a frenzy of racial hatred among white parents and, by opening private schools in St. Bernard Parish, which abutted New Orleans, orchestrated a crippling boycott of the first two integrated schools.[35]

School integration in New Orleans was probably doomed from the start. As Superintendent of Schools James F. Redmond noted, the inaction of the moderates did as much damage as the actions of the extremists.

> When the churches don't do a thing, when they sit down and ignore the situation and more yet, tuck in their tails and run; when civic groups won't touch this issue because it's "too hot"; when business associations and chambers of commerce turn their backs and say, "Well, this hurts our pocketbooks, we can't afford to take a side in this," then you're subjecting your school system to destruction.

Still, Redmond allowed himself the thought that things might have turned out better: "I'm convinced that Earl Long would have handled this differently."[36]

Under Jimmie Davis's governorship, the ultrasegregationists finally achieved the voter restrictions that Earl Long had resisted. Between 1960 and 1962 the legislature made the voter application form even more complicated, nonsensical, and confusing. It added six definitions of "bad character" that would bar a person from voting, and it adopted the "citizenship test" devised by Leander Perez. Prospective voters now faced such imponderable questions as: Did the votes of "the few," "the majority," or "male citizens" "usually decide public questions in the "U.S.A."? In New Orleans, the registrar of voters printed six versions of the application form, each subtly different from the others. Black registration was stuck at about 160,000. In 1956 blacks constituted 15 percent of the electorate, one the highest levels in the South; in 1964 they constituted 14 percent, one of the lowest.[37]

Interviewed in 1977, shortly before he died, Rainach claimed that the Citizens' Councils "completely threw the civil rights revolution off its timetable." Yet their political strategy of eliminating the black vote failed, and their antidemocratic tactics rebounded against them. The purge of black voters in Monroe evoked widespread national condemnation. It prompted the Department of Justice to launch a full-scale FBI investigation, followed by probes in several other parishes. Although the FBI found it politically embarrassing to investigate the Citizens' Councils—whose members were the Bureau's natural supporters—Hoover's men amassed reams of evidence about the Councils' purge activities. Assistant Attorney General Warren Olney III presented that evidence to both houses of Congress. When Jack Gremillion appeared before the House Judiciary Committee to deny any concerted effort to disfranchise black voters, Olney refuted his testimony point by point. When the Monroe purge took place, the Eisenhower administration was already considering civil rights legislation. The evidence from Louisiana strengthened its hand and made voting rights the core of the Civil Rights Bill it proposed in 1956.[38]

The 1957 Civil Rights Act, although often derided as ineffective, helped to blunt the voter purge. Its hand strengthened, the Justice Department ordered further FBI investigations. The first case under the Act involved Webster Parish. The litigation dragged on and failed to produce results. But in 1960, after the federal government invoked the Act to sue the registrar of Washington Parish, Federal District Judge J. Skelly Wright ordered the registrar Curtis Thomas to restore all 1,377 purged voters. Federal lawyers reversed the purges in three other parishes. Meanwhile, the Civil Rights Commission, a body created by the 1957 Act, gathered its own evidence of discrimination—most of it supplied by blacks, but some of it passed on by Earl Long. In public hearings in New Orleans, the Commission questioned a parade of defensive registrars and aggrieved blacks—including Henry Carroll and Mae Lucky—adding to the documentary record of democracy, Louisiana-style. It took Selma to end the scandal of black disfranchisement. Yet the Justice Department could not have drafted the 1965 Voting Rights Act unless it had first tried the laborious and far-too-slow litigation route, accumulating a mountain of evidence along the way.[39]

Massive resistance did, it is true, delay school integration and make a shambles of it in New Orleans. Yet the ultrasegregationists saw the New Orleans integration crisis as a humiliating defeat for them, which indeed it was. The legislature huffed and puffed, but Judge J. Skelly Wright struck down every effort to halt integration. School closing was exposed as an empty threat when state officials, faced with the prospect of going to jail for contempt of court, caved in.

The state superintendent of education, Shelby Jackson, meekly answered "No" when Judge Wright asked if he intended interfering with the schools in New Orleans. State Attorney General Gremillion burst into tears when Wright let him off with a suspended sentence.[40]

In 1961, Willie Rainach retired from politics. By 1963, the Citizens' Council movement had disintegrated as a statewide force. Some of its surviving fragments, however, became bastions of the radical right. In New Orleans, the Citizens' Council reflected the anti-Semitic views of Leander Perez—now excommunicated from the Catholic Church—whose subsidies kept it alive. In Shreveport, too, the Citizens' Council became increasingly anti-Semitic, and stood somewhere between the John Birch Society and the Ku Klux Klan. Nevertheless, it continued to enjoy the approval of the city's leading newspapers, the *Shreveport Journal* and the *Shreveport Times*. President Johnson was enraged by the torrent of abuse those papers directed at him over his support for the Civil Rights Bill. He would never set foot in Shreveport again, Johnson told Senator Russell Long, until he received an apology. "Those are the meanest, most vicious people in the United States. . . . God Al-*mighty!* . . . Called me a *crook!* Called me a *rapist!* Called me everything under the sun!"[41]

The 1963–64 governor's race looked like a carbon copy of 1959–60. Chep Morrison faced another Protestant from north Louisiana, John J. McKeithen. Once again, Morrison's strategy of playing down the race issue was thwarted by his opponent's loud defense of racial segregation. Now, to make matters worse, Morrison suffered for his association with the Kennedy administration, having served as U.S. ambassador to the Organization of American States. As in 1960, Morrison carried most of south Louisiana, and won virtually all the black vote, but lost to an opponent who piled up huge white majorities in north Louisiana.[42]

What was the meaning of massive resistance in Louisiana? The state's political, religious, and cultural differences did not prevent it from joining the rest of the South in vigorously opposing school integration and viciously attacking the NAACP. The failure of the Catholic Church to back its approval of *Brown* with appropriate action—it did not integrate its parochial schools until 1962—was particularly disappointing.

On the other hand, the extremism of the Shreveport–Bossier City corner of northwestern Louisiana—part of a geographic subregion known as the "Ark-La-Tex"—was not typical of Louisiana as a whole. Nor was the extremism of the state's southern tip, Plaquemines Parish, whose immense mineral wealth, corruptly exploited, grossly magnified Leander Perez's political influence. It is significant that the anti-Semitism espoused by Leader Perez and Ned Touchstone (who led the Shreveport Citizens' Council in the 1960s) was not characteristic of the Citizens' Councils during their late 1950s heyday. "Although I thoroughly realize that some Jews are a dominant factor in the NAACP," Rainach told one anti-Semite, "I am unable to bring myself to condemn the whole Jewish people because of this." The growth of anti-Semitism in the Citizens' Councils was directly related to their diminishing influence and popular support.[43]

Generalizing about a state, it is true, can be as difficult as generalizing about the South as a whole. If Shreveport and Plaquemines Parish were not typical of Louisiana, what parts of the state were? New Orleans was *sui generis*, but then so was the tough paper mill town of Bogalusa, a Ku Klux Klan stronghold adjacent to Mississippi. Washington Parish, where Bogalusa can be found, forms one of Louisiana's eight "Florida Parishes," which, while constituting a distinctive subregion, exhibited enormous variety in their race relations in the 1950s and 1960s. One could go on. A search for typicality is self-defeating.

Still, civil rights activists always believed that the Pelican State handled racial issues in its own distinctive way. That difference had long been the case. The racist "demagogues" of the period 1890–1920 all came from other states. On the other hand, the one demagogue that Louisiana did produce, Huey Long, sidestepped race and preached class warfare instead. Earl Long adopted the same political strategy. Many blacks idolized both men.[44]

According to Glen Jeansonne, whenever race constituted the main campaign issue in a gubernatorial election, most of Louisiana's white voters supported segregation rather than change. But although the Citizens' Councils disrupted the Longite tradition, supplanting the politics of class with the politics of race, their success was short-lived. Before he died in 1961, Earl Long had made a spectacular political recovery. And McKeithen, after his installation as governor in 1964, behaved as a racial moderate, creating a biracial commission and seeking black support. In 1967, faced with a Klan-backed candidate of the far right, McKeithen romped home to reelection with 82 percent of the total vote and an even greater percentage of black votes. As a protégé of Earl Long, McKeithen knew that oil and water do sometimes mix in Louisiana politics. Perhaps the Louisiana difference was style rather than substance. But style and substance are not entirely separable. As one NAACP official put it: "There was always an underlying feeling in Louisiana of some kind of comradeship between blacks and whites. . . . We had worked out our own pace, and things were generally going to get better, but it was not on a national time schedule, it was on Louisiana's time schedule."[45]

Notes

1. C. Vann Woodward, *Origins of the New South, 1877–1913* (Baton Rouge: Louisiana State University Press, 1951), 328.

2. Numan V. Bartley, *The Rise of Massive Resistance* (Baton Rouge: Louisiana State University Press, 1969), 17–21.

3. John H. Fenton and Kenneth N. Vines, "Negro Registration in Louisiana," *American Political Science Review* 51 (Sept. 1957): 704–13.

4. "Registered Voters in Louisiana, Oct. 4, 1952," in *Louisiana Almanac and Fact Book, 1953–54*, ed. Stuart O. Landry (New Orleans: Pelican, 1954), 466–67.

5. Glen Jeansonne, *Leander Perez: Boss of the Delta* (Baton Rouge: Louisiana State University Press, 1977).

6. *Louisiana Weekly*, Oct. 10, 1949; Feb. 27, 1954; Jun. 5, 1954; Sept. 3, 1955; Joe Gray Taylor, *McNeese State University, 1939–1987: A Chronicle* (Lake Charles, La.: McNeese State University), 82–84; William M. Rainach to Leander Perez, Nov. 30, 1954, Leander H. Perez Papers, New Orleans Public Library; Daniel E. Byrd, "Activity Report," typescript, Aug. 23, 1955, folder 2, box 4, Daniel E. Byrd Papers, Amistad Research Center, Tulane University; Joseph H. Fichter, *One-Man Research: Reminiscences of a Catholic Sociologist* (New York: Wiley, 1973), 77; Stephen J. Ochs, *Desegregating the Altar: The Josephites and the Struggle for Black Priests, 1871–1960* (Baton Rouge: Louisiana State University Press, 1990), 404–5; John Robert Payne, "A Jesuit Search for Social Justice: The Public Career of Louis J. Twomey, S.J., 1947–1969" (Ph.D. diss., University of Texas at Austin, 1976), 204–5; Joseph T. Taylor, "Desegregation in Louisiana: One Year Later," *Journal of Negro Education* 24 (summer 1955): 264–67. For the NAACP's initial optimism, see Daniel E. Byrd to Thurgood Marshall, Apr. 9, 1953, folder 3, box 1, Byrd Papers; E. A. Johnson, "Report on Atlanta Meeting," in minutes of Executive Board and Regional Board, folder 15, box 12, A. P. Tureaud Papers, Amistad Research Center; "Suggested Program for Southern Branches, 1954–1955," folder 7, box 4, Byrd Papers.

7. Earleen May McCarrick, "Louisiana's Official Resistance to Desegregation" (Ph.D. diss., Vanderbilt University, 1964), 26–34; clerk, U.S. Supreme Court, to Rainach, Jan. 24, Feb. 9, 1955; Charles Wallace Collins to Perez, Jan. 30, 1955; Perez to Collins, Feb. 17, 1955; Perez, "Re: May 17, 1954 Decision," typescript, Feb. 17, 1955, all in Perez Papers; William McFerrin Stowe, "William Rainach and the Defense of Segregation in Louisiana, 1954–1959" (Ph.D. diss., Texas Christian University, 1989), 38–43; "Minutes, Convention of Delegates Organizing the Citizens Councils of America," typescript, Apr. 7, 1956, box 5, William M. Rainach Papers, Louisiana State University, Shreveport.

8. William Rainach to Gervaise and Rex, Nov. 24, 1954; Ranaich to Paul G. Borron, Nov. 26, 1954; Rainach to Jay Murphy, Oct. 7, 1954, all in box 2, Rainach Papers; Stowe, "William Rainach," 62–63.

9. William Rainach, interview by Hubert Humphreys, 1977, 24, Rainach Papers, Archives and Special Collections, Noel Memorial Library, Louisiana State University, Shreveport; *Richmond Times-Dispatch*, May 17, 1955, Nov. 15, 1956; *New Orleans Times-Picayune*, May 22, 24, 26, 1955; Donald Ewing to Rainach, Jun. 15, 1955, box 2, Rainach Papers.

10. Dave McGuire to Alex George, Mar. 30, 1956, Dave McGuire Papers, Howard-Tilton Library, Tulane University.

11. *New Orleans Times-Picayune*, Dec. 11, 1955; Hunter O'Dell, "The Political Scene in Louisiana," *Political Affairs*, Aug. 1956, 12–23; John H. Fenton, "The Negro Voter in Louisiana," *Journal of Negro Education* 26 (summer 1957): 288–90.

12. Jeansonne, *Leander Perez*, 199–203; *Louisiana Weekly*, Jan. 28, 1956.

13. Rainach to Wade O. Martin, Apr. 18, 1955; Rainach, "$100,000 Segregation Suit, etc.," Nov. 3, 1955; "Action Against the NAACP by State of Louisiana for Violation of Louisiana Laws," Nov. 29, 1955, Rainach Papers; Stowe, "William Rainach," 53–54; Michael L. Kurtz and Morgan D. Peoples, *Earl K. Long: The Saga of Uncle Earl and Louisiana Politics* (Baton Rouge: Louisiana State University Press, 1990), xiii.

14. *Newsweek*, Jun. 15, 1959, 3.

15. *St. Petersburg Times*, Jun. 27, 1958.

16. Rainach to Walter M. Hester, Dec. 5, 1955, Rainach Papers; William C. Havard, Rudolf Heberle, and Perry H. Howard, *The Louisiana Elections of 1960* (Baton Rouge: Louisiana State University Press, 1963), 116–17; Jeansonne, *Leander Perez*, 148; *Baton Rouge Morning-Advocate*, Oct. 24, 1955.

17. Special Agent in Charge (SAC), New Orleans, to Director, "Mae Lucky et al.," Jun. 15, 1956, FBI file 56–1553-27, 40–43; Kenneth N. Vines, "A Louisiana Parish: Wholesale Purge," in *The Negro and the Ballot in the South*, ed. Margaret Price (Atlanta: Southern Regional Council, 1959), 39; "Statement of Albin P. Lassiter," Apr. 27, 1961, U.S. Commission on Civil Rights, *Hearings Held in New Orleans, 1960–1961*, 2 vols. (Washington, D.C.: Government Printing Office, 1961), 2:745–46.

18. Philip S. Johnson, "The Limits of Interracial Compromise: Louisiana, 1941," *Journal of Southern History* 69 (May 2003): 330–31; *Baton Rouge Morning-Advocate*, Jun. 4, 1950; "Ouchita Parish," [1941–42], folder 3, box 225, Charles S. Johnson Papers, Fisk University, Nashville, Tennessee.

19. "Morris Henry Carroll," available online at: http://monroefreepress.com/history/blkhis11.htm. Consulted Mar. 19, 2004. Monroe Colored High School was renamed "Carroll High School," ostensibly in honor of Carroll's father. It is worth noting that Carroll also developed business interests that made him a wealthy man.

20. SAC, New Orleans, to Director, "Mae Lucky et al.," May 11, 1956, FBI file 56-1553-16, 1–8.

21. *Monroe Morning World*, Apr. 30, May 2, 1956; *Monroe News-Star*, May 4, 1956.

22. SAC, New Orleans, to Director, "Mae Lucky et al.," Jun. 15, 1956, FBI file 56-1553-27, 126–29.

23. SAC, New Orleans, to Director, "Mae Lucky et al.," Jun. 15, 1956, FBI file 56-1553-27, 2; Ben C. Dawkins, draft opinion, *U.S. v. Lucky*, Civil Action 8366, Mar. 1965, in FBI file 56–1553-199, 4–7; *Louisiana Weekly*, May 26, 1956. Howard defeated Coon by 5,269 votes to 4,230.

24. *Monroe News-Star*, May 3, 1956; *Monroe Morning World*, May 9, 1956.

25. Stowe, "William Rainach," 130–31.

26. Stowe, "William Rainach," 116–17, 135–39; "Minutes of First and Second Congressional Districts Conference on Uniform Enforcement of Louisiana Voter Qualification Laws," Feb. 12, 1959, exhibit J, U.S. Commission on Civil Rights, *Hearings Held in New Orleans*, 2:484–90. Seven such meetings took place, between December 17, 1958, and February 12, 1959.

27. Stowe, "William Rainach," 109–10; A. Rosen to Mr. Boardman, "Winnice P. Clement, Registrar of Voters, Webster Parish, Minden, Louisiana," Mar. 14, 1958, FBI file 44-12469-27.

28. Stowe, "William Rainach," 109–10, 121; Mary C. Flournoy to Rainach, Jan. 10, 1959, box 6, Rainach Papers.

29. Plaintiff's Trial Brief, *U.S. v. Louisiana*, 37–39; "Statement of Charles S. Kilbourne, appendix B, *U.S. v. Louisiana*, Burke Marshall Papers (microfilm), Alderman Library, University of Virginia; Rainach to Saxon Farmer, Nov. 8, 1958, and handwritten annotation of Mar. 2, 1959; Rainach to Bob Angers, Jul. 9, 1959; Rainach to Jules Ashlock, Jul. 11, 1959, all in Rainach Papers; *Louisiana Weekly*, Jul. 18, 1959; U.S. Commission on Civil Rights, *Hearings Held in New Orleans*, 1:327–32; Stowe, "William Rainach," 142, 146–47.

30. *New York Times*, Jul. 22, 1956; McCarrick, "Louisiana's Official Resistance to Desegregation," 45; Stowe, "William Rainach," 58–59; Jeansonne, *Leander Perez*, 234–35; *Times-Picayune*, Jun. 2, 1956. The bill that Long vetoed would have required couples to produce birth certificates in order to obtain a marriage license.

31. Kurtz and Peoples, *Earl K. Long*, 199–202; Stowe, "William Rainach," 129.

32. *New Orleans States*, Feb. 26, 1957; *New Orleans Item*, May 7, 1956; *Washington Post*, May 29, 1956; L. B. Nichols to C. Tolson, "Mae Lucky, Registrar of Voters, et al.," May 10, 1956, FBI file 56–1553-13; *Councillor*, Nov. 1957, reel 34/C57, Right-Wing Collection, University of Iowa (microfilm).

33. Stowe, "William Rainach," 143–45; A. J. Liebling, *The Earl of Louisiana: Profile of an Eccentric* (London: Allen, 1962), 28–32; Kurtz and Peoples, *Earl K. Long*, 207–8, 216–18.

34. Havard, Heberle, and Howard, *Louisiana Elections of 1960*, 38–54; Perry H. Howard, *Political Tendencies in Louisiana* (Baton Rouge: Louisiana State University Press, 1971), 341–53; Glen S. Jeansonne, *Race, Religion, and Politics: The Louisiana Gubernatorial Elections of 1959–60*, University of Southwestern Louisiana History Series, no. 10 (Lafayette: University of Southwestern Louisiana, 1977), 56–69, 95–105; Kurtz and Peoples, *Earl K. Long*, 204–6, 243–47.

35. Howard, *Political Tendencies in Louisiana*, 360; Jason Berry, "The Legacies of Jimmie Davis," *Gambit Weekly*, Nov. 28, 2000, 21–29; *Times-Picayune*, Nov. 16, 17, 1960; *States-Item*, Nov. 16, 1960.

36. "Integration in New Orleans: An Interview with James F. Redmond," *Cambridge* 38 (Apr. 1961): 26.

37. Act no. 613 (1960); act no. 61 (1962); act no. 63 (1962), *Louisiana Revised Statutes*; Plaintiff's Trial Brief, *U.S. v. Louisiana*, 53–54, 106–7, appendix A, table C, reel 1, Burke Marshall Papers; "Louisiana Citizenship Test," folder 109, series 6, Southern Regional Council Papers (microfilm), Alderman Library, University of Virginia; "final Voter Education Project report" [draft, 1964], folder 36, series 6, Southern Regional Council Papers.

38. *Monroe News-Star*, Oct. 10, 1956; *Washington Post*, Oct. 11, 1956; *Monroe Morning-World*, Feb. 14, 15, 26, 1957; *Times-Picayune*, Feb. 26, 1957; Michal Belknap, *Federal Law and Southern Order* (Athens: University of Georgia Press, 1995), 40–41.

39. *U.S. v. McEleveen*, 180 F. Supp. 10 (1960).

40. Frank T. Read and Lucy S. McGough, *Let Them Be Judged: The Judicial Integration of the Deep South* (Metuchen, N.J.: Scarecrow Press, 1978), 135, 153.

41. Neil R. McMillen, *The Citizens' Council: Organized Resistance to the Second Reconstruction, 1954–64* (Urbana: University of Illinois Press, 1971), 71–72; Jeansonne, *Leander Perez*, 240; Rainach, Humphreys interview, 25; Michael Beschloss, *Reaching for Glory: Lyndon Johnson's Secret White House Tapes, 1964–1965* (New York: Simon and Schuster, 2001), 155.

42. Howard, *Political Tendencies in Louisiana*, 360–89; Fred Dent, "Continuation of Report on Rapides Parish," typescript, Jun. 21, 1963; Morrison to personal friends, Jul. 9, 1963, both in box 15, Scott Wilson Papers, Special Collections, Tulane University. For McKeithen's racist campaign materials, see "Morrison Works to Destroy Segregation" and "All Smiles," election leaflets, both in campaign files, DeLesseps S. Morrison Papers, Tulane University.

43. Rainach to Thomas C. Williams, Jan. 13, 1955, box 2, Rainach Papers. For examples of the anti-Semitism of the Citizens' Councils in New Orleans and Shreveport see "Copy of telephone message by Citizens Council of Greater New Orleans," typescript, Jan. 25, 1964, box 2, Perez Papers; *Councillor*, May 8, 1970, reel 33/C56, Right-Wing Collection.

44. For evidence of black admiration for Huey Long, see Matthew Polk, interview by Kate Ellis, Jul. 22, 1994, New Iberia, Louisiana, Behind the Veil Oral History Project, Special Collections, Perkins Library, Duke University; J. H. Scott, interviewed by Joseph L. Logsdon, 1966, 44, J. H. Scott Papers, Earl K. Long Library, University of New Orleans; Joseph L. Logsdon, "Oral History of A. P. Tureaud, Sr.," transcript of tape 10, private collection of Joseph L. Logsdon.

45. Glen S. Jeansonne, "Longism: Mainstream Politics or Aberration? Louisiana Before and After Huey Long," *Mid-America* 71 (Apr.–Jul. 1989): 90; Harvey R. H. Britton, interview by Adam Fairclough, Nov. 4, 1987, tape recording, Fairclough Oral History Collection, Amistad Research Center.

FOUR

Massive Resistance and Minimum Compliance: The Origins of the 1957 Little Rock School Crisis and the Failure of School Desegregation in the South

John A. Kirk

Two assertions are central to this avowedly revisionist essay, which uses the case study of white reaction to the 1954 *Brown v. Board of Education* school desegregation decision in Little Rock, Arkansas, to suggest a new framework for understanding the emergence of white resistance to *Brown* in the South. The first assertion is that gradualism and tokenism employed under the banner of "minimum compliance" played a far greater role in the development of southern resistance to the *Brown* decision than has previously been acknowledged. With its defiant rhetoric and radical stance, massive resistance grabbed more headlines than minimum compliance, but it was precisely the latter's low-key and surreptitious approach to school desegregation that made it far more effective in undermining the *Brown* decision in the long run. The dangers of gradualism and tokenism were not lost on civil rights movement participants, including Martin Luther King, Jr., who in his 1963 "Letter from Birmingham City Jail," written almost nine years after *Brown*, noted that he had "almost reached the regrettable conclusion that the Negro's great stumbling block in his stride toward freedom is not the White Citizen's Counciler or the Ku Klux Klanner, but the white moderate . . . who paternalistically believes he can set the timetable for another man's freedom. . . . Lukewarm acceptance is much more bewildering than outright rejection."[1] King also anticipates my second assertion in his 1967 book *Where Do We Go From Here: Chaos or Community?* when he notes that the Supreme Court's 1955 implementation order for *Brown*, which became known as *Brown II*, was "a keystone in the structure that slowed school desegregation down to a crawl."[2] Although the *Brown* decision has received a great deal of attention from commentators and historians, far less has been written about the significance of *Brown II*. Yet it is my assertion that *Brown II* had a much greater impact on the development of white resistance to school desegregation than the first *Brown* ruling.

In shifting the focus from massive resistance to minimum compliance, and from *Brown* to *Brown II*, this essay encourages a rethinking of the emergence of southern resistance to school desegregation and the long-term impact of that resistance. One important point to note at the outset is that this study focuses on an Upper South city, which had a black population (about a quarter of Little Rock's one hundred thousand residents were black) that was smaller than many Lower South cities, and smaller than that of many southern rural areas as well. Different parts of the South offered different levels of resistance to school desegregation, and that resistance often developed more quickly and determinedly in places that had larger black populations, where whites felt more threatened by racial change.

Nevertheless, Upper South cities such as Little Rock played a pivotal role in the white southern reaction to *Brown*. When the Supreme Court handed down the two *Brown* decisions, it very probably did not expect Lower South states such as Mississippi and Alabama to rush to desegregate their school systems. It did, however, very probably expect Upper South states such as Arkansas and North Carolina to set the pace for school desegregation, and thereby to place pressure on surrounding rural areas, and for those rural areas in turn to place pressure on neighboring Lower South states, for compliance with *Brown*. In practice, the Court probably envisioned what might be described as a southern school desegregation domino effect. The fact that the process of school desegregation stalled at such an early point and so dramatically in a prime, progressive Upper South city like Little Rock was catastrophic for the strategy of school desegregation that the Supreme Court embarked upon, and its reverberations reached far beyond Little Rock.

The existing historical record of the 1957 Little Rock school crisis paints a picture of a moderate Upper South city hijacked by massive resistance. Little Rock appeared to be at the forefront of compliance with the *Brown* decision when the school board declared that it would work toward the peaceful desegregation of the city's schools. However, the night before the all-white Central High School was due to accept nine black students in September 1957, Governor Orval E. Faubus called out the National Guard to prevent the implementation of the desegregation plan, ostensibly on the grounds of preserving the peace. When President Dwight D. Eisenhower eventually persuaded Faubus to withdraw the state soldiers, a white mob frustrated attempts by the nine black students to attend Central High. This finally prompted Eisenhower to send in federal soldiers to ensure the safety of the black students. Central High spent one school year desegregated under armed guard. When the federal troops were withdrawn, Faubus closed all of the city's schools to prevent desegregation. Only when the white business community mobilized to gain control of the city school board did Little Rock return to a path of moderation, when it desegregated schools on a token basis.[3]

In tracing the origins of the Little Rock crisis to the early formation of local school policy in response to the two *Brown* decisions, and in particular to the development of a policy of minimum compliance, this essay offers a significant corrective to existing accounts of the school crisis and a suggestive framework for understanding the development of resistance to school desegregation throughout the South. In line with similar tactics used in other Upper South cities, minimum compliance was a policy that sought to employ gradualism and tokenism to delay and to limit the implementation of school desegregation for as long as legally possible. The driving force behind minimum compliance was that it theoretically placated those who did not want school desegregation by limiting integration to the bare minimum. At the same time, it allowed school districts to maintain that they were in fact implementing the law. Advocates of minimum compliance viewed such a stance as "moderate" in relation to the "extremes" of meaningful integration and the outright opposition to school desegregation offered by those who advocated massive resistance. Yet in fact, minimum compliance turned out to be simply a more diluted form of massive resistance that on the face of things offered a less harmful way of frustrating the process of school desegregation but that actually wreaked chaos. Therefore, although massive resistance and minimum compliance at first appeared to be quite different, their differences quickly narrowed in the years following the *Brown* decision, as they combined to undermine the process of school desegregation in Little Rock, in other Upper South cities, and ultimately throughout the South.[4]

Many of the observations and findings about the Little Rock crisis in this essay echo those of Numan V. Bartley's summary of events in his book *The Rise of Massive Resistance.* The most important difference is that Bartley attributes the failure of school desegregation in Little Rock to "an accumulation of failures by well-meaning leaders," whereas I identify the policy of minimum compliance as a much more calculating and premeditated attempt to circumvent the *Brown* decision.[5] In contrast to the civility that William H. Chafe identifies in the Upper South city of Greensboro, North Carolina, Little Rock instead exhibited cynicism in race relations. Certainly, the architect of minimum compliance in Little Rock, Superintendent of Schools Virgil T. Blossom, demonstrated little of the "personal grace that smooths contact with strangers and obscures conflict with foes," which Chafe cites as a hallmark of civility. Neither did he seem to possess "a way of dealing with people and problems that made good manners more important than substantial action" or evidence much "abhorrence of personal conflict, courtesy to new ideas, and generosity toward those less fortunate than oneself" in his dealings with Little Rock's black community. Blossom single-mindedly pursued a policy of minimum compliance and rode roughshod over any dissenting voices. His express aim all along was to frustrate the process of school desegregation by drawing up an implementation plan that purposefully pushed the law to its furthest limits. Meanwhile, those most likely to practice civility in Little Rock, the city's white business elite, stood by silently and did nothing.[6]

Blossom's intention to pursue a policy of minimum compliance with the *Brown* decision in Little Rock became apparent just four days after the Supreme Court ruling. As he started to outline the school board's plans to an expectant delegation from the black community, Blossom noticed that the "high spirits" with which the meeting began transformed into a "rapid [loss of] enthusiasm." Blossom told the black delegation that the school board did not intend to move ahead with desegregation immediately. Instead, it would wait for the expected announcement of the Supreme Court's implementation order the following year. In the meantime, Blossom indicated that he would take on the job of drawing up plans for what might happen if the Court forced Little Rock schools to desegregate. After Blossom finished his speech, Lucious Christopher (L. C.) Bates, owner and editor of the Little Rock–based *Arkansas State Press*, the state's leading black newspaper, stormed out of the meeting in outright disgust at the school board's perceived lack of commitment to implement a desegregation program. Others stayed, but the widespread disappointment in the black delegation was clear. Blossom tried to reassure them that he was not proposing to "delay for delay's sake, but to do the job right."[7] Privately, Blossom told whites of his intention to design a school desegregation plan that would provide "the least amount of integration over the longest period."[8]

Unhappy with the school board's response to the *Brown* decision, the black community, spearheaded by the Little Rock branch of the NAACP, pressed Blossom for a definite declaration of plans for desegregation. At a subsequent meeting, Blossom told Little Rock NAACP representatives that before any desegregation took place, the school board intended to build two new schools. Horace Mann High School would be built in the predominantly black eastern part of the city, and Hall High School would be built in the affluent white suburbs of the west. Blossom insisted that the two new schools, in black and white residential areas, respectively, would not have a set racial designation. Rather, Blossom assured local NAACP members, the school board planned to desegregate all three of the city's high schools, Horace Mann High, Hall High, and Central High, along colorblind attendance zones in 1957. Elementary schools would follow some time around 1960.[9]

The so-called Blossom Plan divided members of the Little Rock NAACP's executive board. L. C. Bates opposed the Blossom Plan, as he believed that it was "vague, indefinite, slow-moving and indicative of an intent to stall further on public school integration." Nevertheless, a clear majority supported the Blossom Plan and cautioned against pushing the school board too hard. Most felt that Blossom and the school board should be given a chance to prove their good intentions, that the plan they had drawn up was reasonable, and that, importantly, it would be acceptable to the white community. The local branch therefore decided against immediate action and instead awaited further developments.[10]

In April 1955, the Little Rock NAACP held a meeting in anticipation of the Supreme Court's implementation order. The main speaker was a field worker for the NAACP's Legal Defense Fund, Vernon McDaniels, who had spent six months in Arkansas assessing the school desegregation situation. McDaniels admitted that different communities would offer different degrees of resistance to school desegregation. Yet, he insisted, with increased efforts by blacks across the state to urge local school boards into compliance with the *Brown* decision, Arkansas represented the "brightest prospect among the southern states for integration."[11]

This upbeat assessment followed encouraging developments in the state after the *Brown* decision. A few school districts in the predominantly white northwest Arkansas had already moved to desegregate, whereas in many other southern states there was no progress at all. No widespread, organized campaign of resistance to school desegregation had developed, as had happened in other southern states. Moreover, the state legislature had delayed the one direct attempt to circumvent the *Brown* decision. State representatives from the heavily black-populated eastern Arkansas introduced a Pupil Assignment Bill to the 1955 Arkansas General Assembly that was designed to evade school desegregation by assigning black students to black schools and white students to white schools on grounds other than race.[12] A divided assembly agreed to delay the implementation of the measure until after the Supreme Court had announced its school desegregation implementation order.[13] The opposition to legislation designed to circumvent *Brown* indicated the presence of law-abiding influences in Arkansas that could hold at bay attempts by militant segregationists to align the state with massive resistance elsewhere in the South. Although the situation over school desegregation remained somewhat ambiguous, there were grounds for cautious optimism that a more definite timetable for desegregation would consolidate the state's position of moderation.

Yet to those who held faith in the ability of the Supreme Court's implementation order to clear a path for compliance with *Brown*, the words of the justices on May 31, 1955, came as a major blow. Instead of following up on its initial conviction, the court equivocated. The court's implementation order, which became known as *Brown II*, ambiguously told school boards that they must make a "prompt and reasonable start" to desegregate "with all deliberate speed." No definite deadline was set for when integration had to begin, and there was no indication of what exactly constituted compliance with the *Brown* decision, in terms of how many students were to be integrated and at what grades. Indeed, the Court even listed the "local problems" that might be given as reasonable excuses for delay. The Court decentralized the task of administrating school desegregation by handing this responsibility to federal district judges and to local school boards. The overall message to the South seemed to be that it could take as long as it wanted to desegregate schools. To many, this meant never.[14]

The reasons behind the Supreme Court's indecisiveness were complex. Rumors abounded that in exchange for unanimity over *Brown* some southern justices had managed to win the South the benefit of the doubt in awarding a lenient implementation order. The lack of political backing also seems to have played a major role. President Eisenhower continually refused to support the *Brown* decision strongly in public. In private, he admitted that he feared catastrophic massive resistance in the South if its racial mores were put so quickly and directly under threat. Southern leaders, emboldened by the delay between the school desegregation decision and its implementation order, warned of impending violence. Playing upon the fears of massive resistance voiced by the president, they warned of the need not to alienate the white population through forcing racial change too fast. White southerners increasingly sought to demonstrate the fears articulated by their leaders. Reluctance to implement the *Brown* decision quickly began to crystallize into direct opposition to it. Due to a perceived lack of support from other branches of the federal government and the public at large, together with divisions within its own ranks, the Court climbed down from its original lofty stance for racial change. Instead, it offered an ambiguous and confusing compromise.[15]

Brown II proved an important turning point for school desegregation in Arkansas. Whites such as Blossom who advocated a policy of minimum compliance saw the court implementation order as a mandate for further measures to limit the impact of *Brown*. In turn, this paved the way for the beginning of a movement toward outright defiance of the law and total opposition to school desegregation. Before the Supreme Court implementation order, the most outspoken opponents of school desegregation in Arkansas had looked to find a way to circumvent school desegregation through legal means. Encouraged by the reluctance to enforce the *Brown* decision, the first calls for resistance by any means came from an organized band of segregationists. This hardening of sentiment against desegregation among whites helped, in turn, to strengthen the resolve of blacks, as their earlier optimism that whites would implement the *Brown* decision vanished.

The feeling that *Brown II* meant that school boards could take as long as they liked to desegregate was evident when Virgil Blossom announced plans to modify his original school desegregation proposals. The most important development was the introduction of a transfer system that would allow students to move out of their assigned school attendance zone. Under the original Blossom Plan it was clear that new schools were being strategically placed to provide attendance areas that would ensure a majority black Horace Mann High and a majority white Hall High. The assignment of black students to Horace Mann High, although they lived closer to Central High, had confirmed the intentions of the school board to pursue a policy of minimum compliance and to limit the impact of desegregation as much as possible.[16]

Even so, the minimum compliance of the original plan still allowed for integration that involved several hundred pupils. The new plan, however, reflected the belief that *Brown II* allowed minimum compliance to be taken even further. Thus, the modified Blossom Plan allowed whites to opt out of attendance at Horace Mann High without giving blacks the right to choose to attend Hall High. Furthermore, it allowed only token integration at Central High. To encourage the shift of white pupils from Horace Mann High, the school board clearly designated it as a black institution by assigning an all-black teaching staff there. The school board then declared that it intended to open Horace Mann High as a segregated black school in February 1956, a move that would establish a clear precedent for black attendance the year before the school was supposed to desegregate.[17]

The revised Blossom Plan incensed members of the Little Rock NAACP's executive board, even those who had been willing to accept the superintendent's original proposal for school desegregation.[18] To add insult to injury, Blossom did not even bother to consult the NAACP about the changes. When local NAACP representatives met with the school board to request the immediate integration of the city's schools, the school board rejected the proposal outright.[19] Little Rock's stance set the pattern for the three other largest municipal school districts in the state. Fort Smith, North Little Rock, and Hot Springs all drew up plans that purposefully delayed any desegregation of schools until the state capital made the first move.[20]

The fact that *Brown II* encouraged not only backpedaling but also helped to create an active movement of opposition and resistance to school desegregation was first in evidence at Hoxie, a small settlement in northeast Arkansas. With a population of just over a thousand, Hoxie was close enough to the eastern Arkansas Delta to have a split school term to allow for the cotton-picking harvest. Yet it was atypical in that, with only fourteen black families living there, it did not reflect the density of the black population in other Delta areas.[21] On June 25, 1955, the school board at Hoxie voted, largely for financial reasons, to desegregate.[22] On July 11, the first day of integrated classes, a small group of disgruntled local men gathered outside the school to witness proceedings. Some parents voiced their misgivings, with one, a Mrs. John Cole, worriedly telling newspapermen that her eight-year-old daughter Peggy "feared Negroes." However, despite the apprehension surrounding integration, the consensus was that "we have to obey the law." Although there was some tension in classes at first, teachers soon made black students feel welcome, and normal school life quickly resumed. At noon recess, black and white boys tried out for the school baseball team together, and photographers even caught the fearful Peggy playing and walking arm in arm with black female students.[23]

Ironically, the very success of school desegregation at Hoxie made it the rallying point for massive resistance forces in the state. *Life* magazine reporters were present to document the event, producing an article that included a collection of pictures showing the mixing of black and white students.[24] Whereas other school boards were generally at pains to avoid the glare of publicity, desegregation at Hoxie became a national story. With the help and encouragement of segregationists in other states, particularly the closely neighboring Mississippi, local whites held a meeting in Hoxie. There, they elected Herbert Brewer, a local soybean farmer and part-time auctioneer, as chair of a new pro-segregation group.[25] Brewer and the Hoxie Citizens' Committee (HCC) picketed and petitioned the Hoxie school board in an effort to persuade its members to reverse their decision to desegregate. The school board held firm in its conviction and rebuffed the demands of segregationists. However, to provide a cooling-off period, the board closed the school two weeks before the scheduled end of term.[26]

The concession to close the schools early proved unfortunate, since it encouraged further disruption from segregationists. The gathering storm also helped to draw support from other segregationists across the state. White America, Inc., a Pine Bluff–based organization, sent the attorney Amis Guthridge from Little Rock to stir up the populace. James D. Johnson, head of the newly formed segregationist faction the White Citizens' Councils of Arkansas, followed soon after. The meeting of segregationist factions at Hoxie led to a pooling of resources and the formation of the Associated Citizens' Councils of Arkansas (ACCA). The ACCA became the main vehicle for white resistance to school desegregation in the state after the Hoxie campaign.[27]

Yet, for all the bluff and bluster of segregationists at Hoxie, they only met with a protracted defeat. The school remained desegregated the following term, and the courts issued an injunction to prevent any interference.[28] Unlike other such white activists in the South, Arkansas's White Citizens' Councils remained distinctly lacking in kudos. In some other southern states, the Citizens' Councils could count merchants, bankers, landowners, and politicians among their brethren. They could exert economic, political, and social influence alongside the angry rhetoric at mass rallies. In Arkansas, the militant segregationist voice came from those who had little community standing.[29] Membership figures underscored white Arkansans' lack of interest in the Citizens' Councils. Whereas Mississippi boasted three hundred thousand members, Arkansas recruited, at the highest and most likely overstated estimate, only twenty thousand members.[30]

Despite the ACCA's overall lack of credibility, the NAACP was keenly aware of the potential dangers of growing organized white resistance in Arkansas. The standoff at Hoxie prompted an increased urgency within the Arkansas State Conference of NAACP branches (ASC) to step up the pressure for school desegregation before similar tactics spread to other parts of the state. In December 1955, Little Rock's NAACP executive board members voted to file a lawsuit against the Little Rock school board. They contacted the NAACP's Legal Defense Fund southwest regional attorney, Ulysses Simpson Tate, who had worked with them previously, for advice on how to proceed. The Little Rock NAACP was especially concerned about plans to open Horace Mann High as a segregated school in February 1956. However, Tate cautioned against seeking an injunction to prevent the opening of Horace Mann High. Instead, he urged the branch to take the positive step of petitioning for the admission of black students to white schools when Horace Mann High opened.[31]

On January 23, 1956, thirty-three black students applied for admission to four different white schools in Little Rock. All principals of the schools refused entry to the students and referred them to Blossom. Daisy Bates, president of the ASC and wife of L. C. Bates, accompanied nine of the black students to Blossom's office. There, Blossom explained that he had to "deny their request . . . in line with the policy outlined [by the school board]." Blossom was adamant that school desegregation would take place, as planned, in 1957. Daisy Bates told reporters after the meeting: "I think the next step is obvious. We've tried everything short of a court suit."[32] On February 8, 1956, the ASC's attorney, Wiley A. Branton, filed suit in the U.S. District Court against the Little Rock school board for desegregation on behalf of thirty-three students under the title *Aaron v. Cooper*.[33]

At the trial in August 1956, the U.S. District Court backed the modified Blossom Plan. To a large degree, however, this reflected confusion within NAACP ranks about the nature of the trial rather than the persuasive arguments of school board attorneys or the soundness of Blossom's proposal. The Little Rock NAACP built its case on very specific terms that asked only for the enforcement of the original Blossom Plan. In order to reinforce the strength of its argument, branch members went to great pains to select individual examples of black students who faced particular hardship under the modified plan. Ulysses Simpson Tate had different ideas about the case. As previous dealings between the national, regional, state, and local NAACP had revealed in Arkansas, each often had its own agenda of concerns that could cause conflicts of interest and misunderstandings. Tate did not confer with local branch officials before the trial. When he flew into Little Rock the day before the scheduled hearings in the case, he claimed that he was too tired to take instructions and immediately retired to his room to rest. The next morning, Tate ignored the case built by the Little Rock NAACP and proceeded to argue the national NAACP line for the immediate and complete integration of all schools. This was the same line taken by the national NAACP in all of its other sixty-five integration suits against school boards in the Upper South at that time.[34] Since Tate was senior to Branton in the NAACP legal hierarchy, the local attorney deferred to him.[35]

Tate's line of argument lost the lawsuit by playing straight into the hands of the school board. Tate did not demand that the school board should live up to the promises it had already made. Rather, by demanding wholesale immediate integration, he allowed school board attorneys to contend that their clients were acting in accordance with the "with all deliberate speed" guidelines laid down by *Brown II*. Judge John E. Miller upheld their argument. Offering a shred of consolation for the local NAACP, Miller retained federal jurisdiction in the case to make sure that the school board now carried out the Blossom Plan along the lines that it had indicated in court.[36]

The Little Rock NAACP branch was naturally disappointed at the outcome of the lawsuit. In consultation with Wiley A. Branton, their attorney, Thurgood Marshall, the director-counsel of the NAACP Legal Defense Fund, and Robert L. Carter, special counsel to the NAACP, they decided to appeal.[37] The Appeals Court at St. Louis heard arguments in *Aaron v. Cooper* on March 11, 1957. Again, the court upheld the modified Blossom Plan, saying that the school board were indeed operating within a timetable that was reasonable, given the local problems of desegregation in the South. However, the Appeals Court reaffirmed Judge Miller's ruling that the school board was now obliged to carry out its modified plan, beginning with the desegregation of high schools in September 1957.[38]

Wiley A. Branton reported that in spite of the court defeat he was pleased by some aspects of the decision, particularly the affirmation by the Appeals Court that desegregation must take place the following school term. Branton felt that the ruling offered an important "cloak of protection against some die-hard, anti-integration groups who might still try to delay integration."[39] In a letter to the head of the school board attorney team, Archibald F. House, Branton insisted that "the plaintiffs feel just as strongly about the issues." Yet, he added, "time has made many of the problems moot and the opinion of the appellate court clarified some of the issues more favorably for us." Branton believed that the court decision left room for "give and take" that could "make for a spirit of goodwill and harmony among the students and patrons in the initial phase of school desegregation at Little Rock."[40]

Branton's optimistic outlook, despite the court defeat, came within the context of continuing positive developments in Arkansas. In the schools, with Little Rock under federal court order to desegregate, four other major municipal school districts—Pine Bluff, Hot Springs, North Little Rock, and Fort Smith—all drew up integration plans for September 1957.[41] By then, all of the publicly state-supported colleges and universities had begun to admit black students. In politics, six blacks were appointed to the Democratic State Committee by Governor Orval Faubus, two blacks were elected to the city councils of Hot Springs and Alexander, and two blacks were elected to school boards at Wabbaseka and Dollarway. Local groups and associations across the state made goodwill gestures promoting interracial harmony. Several religious groups integrated; an interracial Ministerial Alliance formed in Little Rock in 1956. Some county medical societies also integrated their memberships, along with the American Association of University Women in Conway and Fayetteville and the Little Rock League of Women Voters.[42]

The most striking development came in April 1956 when four municipalities—Little Rock, Hot Springs, Pine Bluff, and Fort Smith—successfully desegregated their public transportation systems. This occurred after a misunderstood Supreme Court ruling in *South Carolina Electric & Gas Co. v. Flemming* (1956), which many national newspapers reported as heralding the end of segregation in public transport. Amid the confusion, several bus companies in Upper South cities took the initiative to desegregate.[43] Even after discovering the mistake, the policy continued in Arkansas. All interstate waiting rooms for bus and rail transportation desegregated without incident.[44] This was in direct contrast to Montgomery, Alabama, where it took a much-publicized bus boycott led by Martin Luther King, Jr., and yet another U.S. Supreme Court ruling, *Browder v. Gayle* (1956), to compel the city to desegregate its buses.[45]

Despite these promising signs, the issue of school desegregation swiftly reached its denouement at Little Rock in the latter half of 1957. During the summer of that year, Blossom drew up attendance zones for admission to Central High that included two hundred black students. He then asked LeRoy Matthew Christophe and Edwin L. Hawkins, the principals of the black Horace Mann High and Dunbar Junior High, to determine how many of their students wanted to apply for transfer. Thirty-two pupils from Horace Mann High and thirty-eight from Dunbar Junior High indicated an interest in attending Central High. Blossom asked the principals to screen each student individually and to make a judgment as to their suitability for selection. This was based upon a range of factors, including intelligence (Blossom insisted that all those selected must possess an IQ of over one hundred), personality traits, and social skills. When this process was completed, the principals forwarded the names of suitable candidates to Blossom for further screening.[46]

Blossom forged ahead with the plans for attendance zones and screening without bothering to consult the Little Rock NAACP. The organization only learned of the new plans through the black community grapevine. Upon hearing the news, Daisy Bates contacted the principals of the two black high schools, who confirmed that the selection process was already underway. The principals suggested that Daisy Bates contact Blossom for an explanation of his actions. When she contacted Blossom, he agreed to meet with local NAACP officials.[47]

At the meeting, Blossom explained his actions by comparing the situation in the schools to the desegregation of baseball, where Jackie Robinson had been selected as the first black player because of his high personal standing, conduct, and morals. Similarly, Blossom said,

I feel that for this transition from segregation to integration in the Little Rock school system, we should select and encourage only the best Negro students to attend Central High School—so that no criticism of the integration process could be attributed to inefficiency, poor scholarship, low morals, or poor citizenship. [48]

Questioned by local NAACP officials, Blossom admitted that he could not legally turn down an application from a student simply because he or she did not meet his own personal criteria. However, Blossom made it clear that he would do everything to discourage such a candidate. With regard to the new attendance zone, which further limited the pool of potential black applicants to Central High, Blossom told the Little Rock NAACP that he was prepared to invoke the state's Pupil Assignment Law if any complaints were raised. Furthermore, Blossom asserted that he would make any final decision on transfers to Central High. "I know it is undemocratic, and I know it is wrong," Blossom told them, "but I am doing it."[49]

Blossom's continuing manipulation of the school desegregation process angered Little Rock NAACP members, particularly as the court suit seemed to rule out any further adjustments to the already modified Blossom Plan. Efforts to screen candidates, they complained, "seem[ed] to carry pursuasion [sic] and possibly pressure" and served only to instil "a feeling of inferiority, fear and intimidation" in black students. Moreover, they pointed out, the threat to use the Pupil Assignment Law clearly contradicted the "good faith" compliance demanded by ongoing court jurisdiction. Blossom responded that he had already discussed these matters with the judge and insisted that all the changes would stand.[50]

Since it was now too late to challenge the new measures in court, the Little Rock NAACP reluctantly accepted the further changes to the Blossom Plan. When the two black principals recommended thirty-two of their students to Blossom, he rigorously interviewed each of them again. As predicted by the Little Rock NAACP, Blossom used the selection process to further dissuade students from attending Central High. In one case, he reduced a prospective female student to tears by declaring that she lacked the right "scholastic background and emotional responsibility." When two talented black high school football players turned up at his office, Blossom warned them that their careers would come to a premature end if they attended Central High. Blossom ruled, adding yet another new proviso to school desegregation, that no black students would be allowed to participate in any of the social or sports activities at Central High. Upon hearing this, both students withdrew their application.[51] Finally, after a grueling ordeal, the number of students permitted to integrate Central High School stood at seventeen. After further black students withdrew, the number went down to just nine students. They were Minnijean Brown, Elizabeth Eckford, Ernest Green, Thelma Mothershed, Melba Pattillo, Gloria Ray, Terrance Roberts, Jefferson Thomas, and Carlotta Walls.[52]

In August 1957, as the prospect of desegregation at Central High drew closer, the Capital Citizens' Council (CCC) in Little Rock launched a last gasp attempt to halt the process of school desegregation. It filed a number of lawsuits that attempted to force the state to uphold its segregation statutes to prevent integration and invited two high-profile segregationists, the Georgia governor Marvin Griffin and the former speaker of the Georgia House of Representatives, Roy V. Harris, to speak in Little Rock. At the meeting, Griffin lauded the 350 present as "a courageous bunch of patriots." Harris told them that Griffin would use the highway patrol to resist school desegregation if necessary, and if that failed, he would enlist "every white man in Georgia."[53]

Although clearly unhelpful, neither the litigation nor the speeches by Griffin and Harris were serious enough to derail the desegregation process. The real bombshell came on August 27, when a newly formed segregationist group, the Mothers' League of Central High, filed suit in the Pulaski County Chancery Court.[54] Acting as spokesperson for the group, Mrs. Clyde Thomason claimed that recent events caused "uncertainty of the law, conflicting court decisions and a general state of confusion and unrest." This would lead to "civil commotion" if the school board implemented its desegregation plan. At face value, the Mothers' League suit appeared to be yet another futile bid to prevent desegregation. However, the League dramatically called Governor Faubus as its star witness. On the stand, Faubus testified that he believed violence would occur if plans for school desegregation went ahead, citing unsubstantiated reports of increased weapons sales in the city and the recent confiscation of revolvers from both white and black students.[55]

Chancellor Murray O. Reed, a Faubus appointee, ruled in favor of the Mothers' League and issued a restraining order against the school board, preventing its desegregation plan from going ahead. Attorneys for the school board promptly petitioned the U.S. District Court, asking it to forbid the implementation of Reed's order. On Friday, August 30, Judge Ronald Davies upheld the school board's petition and ordered school desegregation to proceed as planned the following Tuesday. Davies, from Fargo, North Dakota, was a temporary assignment to the bench because of an unfilled vacancy and was therefore a newcomer to events. Since Arkansas was the only southern state that belonged to the Eighth Circuit Federal Court District, temporary replacements often came from northern and midwestern states. Hailing from North Dakota, Davies was detached from the southern mores and local politics that governed issues of school desegregation and simply followed the letter of the law in his ruling.[56]

Upon hearing of Davies's decision, Faubus met with William J. Smith, his legislative counsel, and mooted the idea of calling out the National Guard to prevent school desegregation from taking place. Smith counseled against doing that until serious violence and disorder actually developed.[57] However, at 9 p.m., on Monday, September 2, the evening before Central High was due to desegregate, armed National Guardsmen began to cordon off the school buildings. At 10:15 p.m., Faubus broadcast a speech, carried by all local television and radio stations, claiming that he had evidence of impending violence in the city. Therefore, he had called out the National Guard "to maintain or restore order and to protect the lives and property of citizens."[58] Shortly after Faubus finished his speech, the school board issued a statement that "in view of the situation . . . no negro students [should] attempt to attend Central High or any white high school until this dilemma is legally resolved."[59] From that point on, events unfolded inexorably. When black students attempted to enter Central High, National Guard soldiers turned them away. The courts then ordered the troops removed from Central High and for school desegregation to proceed as planned. When Faubus removed the state soldiers, attempts by black students to study at Central High were frustrated by scenes of mob lawlessness. Finally, President Eisenhower acted decisively by sending in federal troops to preserve law and order and to ensure the safety of the nine black students.[60]

The eventual unraveling of school desegregation in Little Rock was rooted in a flawed policy of minimum compliance. In 1954, Blossom and the Little Rock school board drew up plans to desegregate three city high schools that would have involved a substantial number of students attending formerly segregated schools. During the three years after *Brown*, Blossom continuously modified his plan to limit the impact of desegregation as much as possible, at each step undermining efforts to ease a path for peaceful integration. Thus, by September 1957, the difference between minimum compliance with and massive resistance to *Brown* had narrowed to the barely distinguishable question of whether nine black students or whether no black students at all should attend just one city high school. As Blossom and the school board backtracked, the confidence and influence of massive resistance forces in the state grew. When the final push to halt school desegregation came from a small but dedicated band of segregationists in September 1957, the inherent flaws of the Blossom Plan became apparent. In concentrating school desegregation at only one city school, Blossom allowed Little Rock segregationists to marshal their slim resources to maximum effect. The fact that Central High was located in a working-class neighborhood injected class antagonisms into the already fraught question of school desegregation. Blossom sold his plan to a great number of social and civic groups, but almost all of these were exclusively white and middle class. Little attempt was made to engage wide-ranging community support or consensus, even for minimum compliance with the law. Indeed, Blossom was extraordinarily autocratic in taking control of school desegregation, to the extent that Little Rock's desegregation plan even bore his own name. Blossom earned his much-desired recognition from the city's elite for this—he was named Little Rock's "Man of the Year" in 1955—but it did nothing to prepare the wider community for school desegregation.[61]

Blossom's targeting of Little Rock's white business elite, evidenced in the groups to which he sold his plan for minimum compliance and the award they gave him for it, made them complicit in that policy. Elizabeth Jacoway characterizes the white business elite in Little Rock as "taken by surprise" by the events of September 1957. Jacoway contends that these men ultimately came to the rescue of the community, prodded by their wives' formation of the Women's Emergency Committee to Open Our Schools (WEC), mobilizing to defeat segregationist school board members and to reopen closed schools in August 1959. Such an account does not convincingly answer the crucial question of why the white business elite allowed the school crisis to occur in the first place. Viewed over the longer term from 1954 to 1957, the description of the white business community might more accurately be summed up as "struck dumb." After all, as Jacoway points out, the white business elite was a tightly knit and impressively organized group that had successfully waged campaigns in the postwar period to profoundly shape the economic and political future of the city.[62] Moreover, in stark contrast to the events of September 1957, in the first six months of 1963, the white business community, pressured by protest and demonstrations in the black community, moved swiftly and decisively to end segregation in virtually all public and in many private downtown facilities.[63]

There seems little doubt that the white business elite held the ability to facilitate the peaceful desegregation of schools in 1957. That they chose not to intervene can in part be attributed to their own ambivalence toward desegregation and in part to the fact that the Blossom Plan allowed them to ignore the integration controversy altogether. Under the Blossom Plan, the white elite received their own, segregated Hall High School, built in the affluent suburbs of the western part of the city. The decision of the white business elite to wash its hands of school integration was a grave error of judgment that cost the community dearly both in economic and in educational terms. Other business communities in other southern cities were left to learn from the mistakes of Little Rock. Some responded positively, while others still blindly followed a similar pattern of recalcitrance, and many subsequently paid a similar price.[64]

Ironically, it was Governor Faubus who proved one of the most effective combatants of massive resistance up until September 1957. Faubus held his own particular take on minimum compliance. In contrast to Blossom's brand of minimum compliance, which involved doing the legal minimum to enforce school desegregation, Faubus's minimum compliance involved doing the political minimum to keep segregationists happy while pursuing a policy of noninterference over school desegregation. Faubus's stance on school desegregation prior to September 1957 was wholly consistent with his personal and political background. Faubus was born in the Ozark Mountains of northwest Arkansas in 1910 and raised in a poor white farming family. His early political development was strongly influenced by his father, Sam, an ardent socialist. In 1935, Sam actually persuaded his son to enroll at the leftist Commonwealth College in Mena, Arkansas, where Orval spent several months. As a youth, Faubus worked variously as an itinerant farm laborer, lumberjack, rural schoolteacher, postmaster, and editor and publisher of the weekly *Madison County Record*. In 1942, he entered the U.S. army and served as a commissioned officer in Europe during World War II. Upon his return to Arkansas, Faubus began to pursue his political ambitions in earnest. In 1949, he joined the liberal reformist administration of Governor Sid McMath, sitting on the state highway commission and later becoming director of highways. Hailing from northwest Arkansas, Faubus had limited experience of interaction with blacks, yet he solicited the help of influential black political figures and actively sought black votes during his campaigns for governor.[65]

On the campaign trail in 1954, Faubus largely eschewed the politics of race and played down the impact of *Brown*, insisting that the matter should rest at a "local level with state authorities standing ready to assist in every way possible."[66] Throughout his first term in office, Faubus stuck by his decision not to interfere with school desegregation and steered clear of racial controversies. Although this stance did nothing to actively implement school desegregation, Faubus's refusal to become embroiled with segregationists prevented the efforts of Arkansas's White Citizens' Council to give the race question mainstream political exposure.[67] When directly challenged for the office of governor in 1956 by the head of Arkansas's White Citizens' Councils, James D. Johnson, Faubus did take on the segregationist mantle to win votes. However, he simply adopted and then diluted all of the measures proposed by his opponent to prevent segregation, and then painted Johnson as a "purveyor of hate."[68] Faubus thereby successfully gained reelection at a time when taking the most extreme segregationist stance appeared mandatory for electoral success in the South. The Citizens' Councils remained critical of him, lampooning him in their publications as "Awful Faubus" and demanding that he declare himself "either for the white folks or for the NAACP."[69] Neither was the population at large sure of Faubus's segregationist credentials. As one bemused *Arkansas Democrat* reader declared in 1957, "I consider the governor without peer in the art of carrying the water of segregation on one shoulder and the water of integration on the other without spilling a drop of either."[70]

This questioning of Faubus's intentions seemed quite justified when, shortly after the 1956 election, he sought to drop the segregationist mantle as quickly as he had donned it. Faubus failed to implement any of the prosegregation legislation that he had sponsored in the 1957 Arkansas General Assembly in order to win segregationist support for his own reformist agenda. He refused to make appointments to the State Sovereignty Commission, which formed the cornerstone of the state's prosegregation program. Without a quorum, the commission was unable to act upon any of the prosegregation measures passed by the General Assembly. Eventually, segregationist politicians had to file a lawsuit to force Faubus to fill the places on the commission.[71] Faubus's delay effectively undermined the prosegregation measures, since the commission was not able to hold its first meeting until August 30, just a week before school desegregation was due to occur.[72] Faubus's relapse to a more moderate stance on school desegregation once the immediate political necessity to adopt segregationist rhetoric had passed was also evident in his dealings with the Citizens' Councils. They repeatedly petitioned Faubus to use his authority as head of a sovereign state to prevent school desegregation from taking place. Faubus scoffed at any notion that he might intervene, telling the press "Everyone knows no state law supersedes a federal law" and "If anyone expects me to use them to supersede federal laws they are wrong."[73]

Faubus's final decision to throw in his lot with the segregationists in September 1957 came within the context of the failure of minimum compliance. In the lead-up to school desegregation, segregationist litigation and the speeches by Griffin and Harris exerted pressure on the process of integration. It became increasingly clear that Blossom and the Little Rock school board, whose stance all along had been that school desegregation was a necessary evil and that they would do all they could to minimize its impact, had fostered little actual support for desegregation to combat this pressure. Faubus made no attempt to solicit concrete support for desegregation, since he quite rightly perceived this as political suicide. What he did do was to follow a policy of noninterference, believing that he was offering protection from militant segregationists for local communities to get on with the process of desegregation. When the local community in Little Rock, in the shape of Blossom and members of the white business elite, came to Faubus at the eleventh hour to ask him to take a stand to help enforce a weak and insubstantial plan for school desegregation, the governor felt that they were asking him to take risks that they were not prepared to take themselves and asking him to sacrifice his political career in the process. Refusing to do this, and in the absence of any convincing groundswell of support to make school desegregation work in the city, Faubus chose to side with the segregationists, which he saw as the only viable choice for political survival.[74] Indeed, as it turned out, Faubus was right. He was reelected to an unprecedented third term of office in 1958 and for a further three terms after that. As Faubus tasted the fruits of success through his opposition to desegregation, his actions became more reckless and cavalier. Moreover, his electoral victories meant that Arkansas inherited a prosegregationist governor whose political career long outlasted the momentary influence of the Citizens' Councils and who proved a future obstacle in efforts to return a moderate image to Little Rock and to Arkansas after the school crisis.[75] Thus, the policy of minimum compliance turned a potential moderate ally into a potent enemy.

When Little Rock's schools eventually reopened in August 1959 after the white business community mobilized to wrest control of the school board out of the hands of segregationists, the policy of minimum compliance was resumed. Only four black students attended formerly segregated schools, with two assigned to Central High and two assigned to Hall High. Token integration prevailed until further federal intervention in the mid-1960s, this time by the Office of Education, which drew up more stringent desegregation guidelines. As with many other cities, Little Rock used a variety of further methods to limit integration, including so-called freedom of choice and so-called zoning plans. An equally familiar pattern of busing and resegregation followed in the 1970s and 1980s. The impact of the policy of minimum compliance therefore continued to have a much greater long-term impact on school desegregation in Little Rock than massive resistance.[76]

Events in Little Rock demonstrate that the impact of the two *Brown* decisions in southern communities needs careful scrutiny. Many of the assumptions, expectations, and foundations for what was to follow solidified during that period. One reading of those years might well insist that white resistance was an inevitable outcome of the Supreme Court directly threatening long-established southern racial mores. Another might, as I do here, insist that white southern massive resistance to school desegregation was not inevitable, particularly in Upper South states such as Arkansas. Rather, massive resistance emerged within a context of missed opportunities, a failure to mold community consensus, and a failure to cultivate respect and support for the law. When massive resistance failed, self-styled moderates used the furore it created to justify their already established policy of minimum compliance with the law. Yet it was the policy of minimum compliance that helped to bolster massive resistance in the first place. It was also the ongoing policy of minimum compliance after massive resistance had subsided that far more effectively undermined the process of school desegregation in Little Rock, in other Upper South cities and states, and eventually throughout the South.

Notes

1. Martin Luther King, Jr., "Letter from Birmingham City Jail," in *A Testament of Hope: The Essential Writings and Speeches of Martin Luther King, Jr.*, ed. James M. Washington (San Francisco: HarperCollins, 1986), 295.

2. Martin Luther King, Jr., *Where Do We Go From Here: Chaos or Community?* (New York: Harper and Row, 1967), 11.

3. See, for example, Dwight D. Eisenhower, *Waging Peace* (Garden City, N.Y.: Doubleday, 1965); Brooks L. Hays, *A Southern Moderate Speaks* (Chapel Hill: University of North Carolina Press, 1959), and *Politics Is My Parish: An Autobiography* (Baton Rouge: Louisiana State University Press, 1981); Orval E. Faubus, *Down from the Hills* (Little Rock: Pioneer Press, 1980), and *Down from the Hills Two* (Little Rock: Democrat, 1986); Virgil T. Blossom, *It Has Happened Here* (New York: Harper, 1959); Roy Reed, *Faubus: The Life and Times of an American Prodigal* (Fayetteville: University of Arkansas Press, 1997); Numan V. Bartley, *The Rise of Massive Resistance: Race and Politics in the South During the 1950s* (Baton Rouge: Louisiana State University Press, 1969), chapter 14; Elizabeth Jacoway, "Taken by Surprise: Little Rock Business Leaders and Desegregation," in *Southern Businessmen and Desegregation*, ed. Elizabeth Jacoway and David Colburn (Baton Rouge: Louisiana State University Press, 1982); Tony Freyer, *The Little Rock Crisis: A Constitutional Interpretation* (Westport, Conn: Greenwood Press, 1984); Corrine Silverman, *The Little Rock Story* (Tuscaloosa: University of Alabama Press, 1958).

4. On massive resistance, see Bartley, *Rise of Massive Resistance*. On Blossom's attitude to school desegregation, see Blossom, *It Has Happened Here*, 13–15.

5. Bartley, *Rise of Massive Resistance*, 252.

6. William H. Chafe, *Civilities and Civil Rights: Greensboro, North Carolina and the Black Struggle for Freedom* (New York: Oxford University Press, 1980), 8.

7. Blossom, *It Has Happened Here*, 11–13.

8. A. F. House to Arthur B. Caldwell, Jul. 21, 1958, box 5, folder 7, Arthur Brann Caldwell Papers, Special Collections Division, University of Arkansas Libraries, Fayetteville.

9. Georg C. Iggers, "An Arkansas Professor: The NAACP and the Grass Roots," in *Little Rock, U.S.A.*, ed. Wilson Record and Jane Cassels Record (San Francisco: Chandler, 1960), 286; Little Rock Board of Education to Legal Redress Committee NAACP, Arkansas, Sept. 9, 1954, Virgil T. Blossom Papers, Special Collections Division, University of Arkansas Libraries, Fayetteville.

10. Iggers, "Arkansas Professor," 286–87.

11. "The Status of Desegregation in Arkansas—Some Measures of Progress," group 2, series B, container 136, folder entitled "Schools, Arkansas, 1946–55," National Association for the Advancement of Colored People Papers, Manuscript Division, Library of Congress, Washington, D.C.; *Southern School News*, May 1955, 2.

12. *Southern School News*, Mar. 1955, 2

13. *Southern School News*, Apr. 1955, 7.

14. On *Brown II* and its aftermath, see J. Harvie Wilkinson III, *From Brown to Bakke: The Supreme Court and School Integration: 1954–1978* (New York: Oxford University Press, 1979), 61–95.

15. Wilkinson, *From Brown to Bakke*, 61–95; David R. Goldfield, *Black, White and Southern: Race Relations and Southern Culture, 1940 to the Present* (Baton Rouge: Louisiana State University Press, 1990) 81; Michael S. Mayer, "With Much Deliberation and Some Speed: Eisenhower and the *Brown* Decision," *Journal of Southern History* 52 (Feb. 1986): 43–76.

16. *Southern School News*, Jul. 1955, 3; Iggers, "Arkansas Professor," 287.

17. Iggers, "Arkansas Professor," 287.

18. Iggers, "Arkansas Professor," 287–88.

19. *Southern School News*, Sept. 1955, 10; Wiley A. Branton to William G. Cooper, Aug. 21, 1954, box 4, folder 10, Daisy Bates Papers, State Historical Society of Wisconsin, Madison.

20. *Southern School News*, Jul. 1955, 3; Aug. 1955, 15; Sept. 1955, 10.

21. Mildred L. Bond to Roy Wilkins, Aug. 6, 1955, box 4, folder 10, Bates Papers.

22. *Southern School News*, Aug. 1955, 15.

23. "A 'Morally Right' Decision," *Life*, Jul. 25, 1955, 29–31.

24. Ibid.

25. Cabell Phillips, "Integration: Battle of Hoxie, Arkansas," *New York Times Magazine*, Sept. 25, 1955, 12, 68–76.

26. *Southern School News*, Sept. 1955, 10.

27. Neil R. McMillen, "The White Citizens' Council and Resistance to School Desegregation in Arkansas," *Arkansas Historical Quarterly* 30 (summer 1971): 97–100; Jerry J. Vervack, "The Hoxie Imbroglio," *Arkansas Historical Quarterly* 48 (spring 1989): 22.

28. Arthur Brann Caldwell, "The Hoxie Case—The Story of the First School in the Old South to Integrate in the Wake of the *Brown* Decisions," 6–20, supplied courtesy of William Penix (attorney for the Hoxie school board).

29. The best guide to the White Citizens' Councils is Neil R. McMillen, *The Citizens' Council: Organized Resistance to the Second Reconstruction, 1955–1964* (Urbana: University of Illinois Press, 1971). On the composition of the ACCA, see "Race Relations in Little Rock Before 1957," series 1, box 20, folder 197, Arkansas Council on Human Relations (ACHR) Papers 1954–1968, typescript, Special Collections Division, University of Arkansas Libraries, Fayetteville.

30. Dianne D. Blair, *Arkansas Politics and Government: Do The People Rule?* (Lincoln: University of Nebraska Press, 1988), 65.

31. Iggers, "Arkansas Professor," 288–89.

32. *Southern School News,* Feb. 1956, 11.

33. *Southern School News,* Mar. 1956, 4; Wiley A. Branton, "Little Rock Revisited: Desegregation to Resegregation," *Journal of Negro Education* 52 (summer 1983): 253.

34. Iggers, "Arkansas Professor," 290. On earlier conflicts of interest and misunderstandings between the national, regional, state and local NAACP in Arkansas, see John A. Kirk, *Redefining the Color Line: Black Activism in Little Rock, Arkansas, 1940–1970* (Gainesville: University Press of Florida, 2002).

35. Freyer, *Little Rock Crisis,* 52.

36. Branton, "Little Rock Revisited," 254; Freyer, *Little Rock Crisis,* 56–58.

37. Rev. J. C. Crenchaw, "Our Reason for Appeal," typescript, n.d., box 4, folder 10, Bates Papers; Branton, "Little Rock Revisited," 255–56.

38. *Southern School News,* May 1957, 2; Branton, "Little Rock Revisited," 255–56.

39. "Statement by Rev. J. C. Crenchaw," typescript, n.d., box 4, folder 10, Bates Papers; *Southern School News,* May 1957, 2.

40. Wiley A. Branton to A. F. House, Jul. 10, 1957, Blossom Papers.

41. *Southern School News,* Jul. 1957, 10.

42. "What Is Happening in Desegregation in Arkansas" typescript, Jan. 1957, series 1, box 29, folder 302, ACHR Papers.

43. Catherine Barnes, *Journey from Jim Crow: The Desegregation of Southern Transit* (New York: Columbia University Press, 1983), 118–19; Ozell Sutton and Rev. Rufus King Young interviews. All interviews cited in this essay were conducted by me between 1992 and 1993 and are deposited in the University of Newcastle-upon-Tyne Oral History Collection.

44. "What Is Happening in Desegregation in Arkansas."

45. On the Montgomery bus boycott, see Adam Fairclough, *To Redeem the Soul of America: The Southern Christian Leadership Conference and Martin Luther King, Jr.* (Athens: University of Georgia Press, 1987), 11–35.

46. "Report of Conference Between Little Rock School Superintendent and NAACP Representatives, May 29, 1957," typescript, group 2, series A, container 98, folder entitled "Desegregation of Schools, Arkansas, Little Rock, Central High, 1956–1957," NAACP Papers.

47. Ibid.

48. Ibid.

49. Ibid.

50. Ibid.

51. Mrs. L. C. Bates to Mr. Robert L. Carter, Aug. 2, 1957, group 2, series A, container 98, folder entitled "Desegregation of Schools, Arkansas, Little Rock, Central High, 1956–1957," NAACP Papers; Blossom, *It Has Happened Here*, 19–21.

52. Daisy Bates, *The Long Shadow of Little Rock: A Memoir* (New York: David McKay, 1962), 59.

53. *Southern School News*, Sept. 1957, 6; Roy Reed, *Faubus*, 196–97; Robert Sherrill, *Gothic Politics in the Deep South* (New York: Balentine Books, 1969), 105–6.

54. On the Mothers' League, see Graeme Cope, "'A Thorn in the Side'? The Mothers' League of Central High School and the Little Rock Desegregation Crisis of 1957," *Arkansas Historical Quarterly* 57 (summer 1998): 160–90.

55. Warren Olney III, assistant U.S. attorney general, to Arthur B. Caldwell, U.S. attorney general, Sept. 13, 1957, box 5, folder 2, Caldwell Papers; Reed, *Faubus*, 199; Silverman, *Little Rock Story*, 6–7.

56. Branton, "Little Rock Revisited," 259–60; Reed, *Faubus*, 199–200; Silverman, *Little Rock Story*, 7.

57. Irving J. Spitzberg, *Racial Politics in Little Rock 1954–1964* (New York: Garland, 1987), 65.

58. "Telephone Report from Assistant U.S. Attorney James E. Gallman, Little Rock, Arkansas, on the integration situation, September 3, 1957," typescript, box 5, folder 2, Caldwell Papers; Reed, *Faubus*, 208.

59. "Telephone Report from Assistant U.S. Attorney James E. Gallman, Little Rock, Arkansas, on the integration situation, September 3, 1957"; Branton, "Little Rock Revisited," 260.

60. Kirk, *Redefining the Color Line*, chapter 5.

61. Bartley, *Rise of Massive Resistance*, chapter 14.

62. Jacoway, "Taken by Surprise."

63. Kirk, *Redefining the Color Line*, chapter 6.

64. Jacoway and Colburn, *Southern Businessmen and Desegregation*; Tony Badger, "Segregation and the Southern Business Elite," *Journal of American Studies* 18 (Apr. 1984): 105–9.

65. Faubus interview. For a more detailed account of Faubus's upbringing and political career see Reed, *Faubus*.

66. *Southern School News*, Mar. 1955, 2. On the reactions of liberal southern politicians to *Brown*, see Tony Badger, "Fatalism, Not Gradualism: Race and the Crisis of Southern Liberalism, 1945–1965," in *The Making of Martin Luther King and the Civil Rights Movement*, ed. Brian Ward and Tony Badger (London: Macmillan, 1996), 67–95.

67. Faubus interview.

68. *Southern School News*, Aug. 1956, 3; Reed, *Faubus*, 178–79; Faubus interview.

69. *Southern School News*, Sept. 1955, 10; McMillen, "White Citizens' Council," 108.

70. *Arkansas Democrat*, Aug. 3, 1957.

71. *Southern School News*, Aug. 1957, 7.

72. *Southern School News*, Jul. 1957, 10; Aug. 1957, 7.

73. McMillen, "White Citizens' Council," 104; Reed, *Faubus*, 188.

74. Warren Olney III, assistant U.S. attorney general, to Arthur B. Caldwell, U.S. attorney general, Sept. 13, 1957; Faubus interview.

75. Kirk, *Redefining the Color Line*, chapters 5 and 6.

76. *Arkansas Gazette*, May 23, 1965; Aug. 30, 1966; Dec. 17, 30, 1967; University Task Force on the Little Rock School District, *Plain Talk: The Future of Little Rock's Public Schools* (Little Rock: University of Arkansas, 1997), 19; "School Desegregation in Little Rock, Arkansas," staff report of the U.S. Commission on Civil Rights, Jun. 1977, Special Collections Division, University of Arkansas Libraries, Fayetteville, 4–5; Wilkinson, *From Brown to Bakke*, 104.

FIVE

The Fight for "Freedom of Association": Segregationist Rights and Resistance in Atlanta

Kevin M. Kruse

Ａt first glance, Atlanta may seem an unlikely place to explore the mind-set of massive resistance. Unlike more famous battlegrounds in the struggle over segregated education, Atlanta has often been singled out as a unique source of racial moderation and enlightenment in the Deep South. This reputation, of course, was founded on a long record of compliance with court-ordered desegregation. During the 1950s, Atlanta desegregated a wide variety of public places and, in so doing, christened itself "the city too busy to hate." Most famously, in August 1961, Atlanta yielded to court orders and deseg-regated four of its public high schools with a great deal of publicity and a total lack of violence. Reporters who had covered the course of massive resistance from Little Rock to New Orleans were stunned to see a southern metropolis desegregate its schools with so much pride and so little disruption. *Newsweek* toasted "a proud city," while the *New York Times* praised Atlanta for providing a "new and shining example of what can be accomplished" by "people of good will and intelligence." *U.S. News and World Report* heralded a "New Mood in the South," and *Look* magazine likewise anointed Atlanta "the leader of the New South." The ultimate praise, however, came from President John F. Kennedy, who opened his evening news conference with congratulations "for the respon-sible law-abiding manner" with which Atlanta had desegregated its schools. "I strongly urge all communities which face this difficult transition to look closely at what Atlanta has done."[1]

But those with an interest in segregationists should look closely at Atlanta as well. Just as the city's moderates proved prescient in accepting desegrega-tion, so too did its segregationists lead the way in crafting new rationales for resistance. Unlike their counterparts in the Deep South, who stuck with mas-sive resistance to the bitter end, segregationists in moderate urban centers like

Atlanta found themselves forced to articulate a new defense of white supremacy, a rationale that rested less on a denial of the civil rights of blacks and more
on a defense of the supposed rights of whites. In retrospect, such an invocation
of "segregationist rights" may seem insincere. Indeed, in the vast majority of
historical work, segregationists have largely been portrayed simply as an opposition group suppressing the rights of others, either "civil rights" writ large or
any number of individual entitlements, such as the rights of African Americans
to vote, assemble, speak, or protest. Segregationists, of course, *did* stand against
those things, and often with bloody and brutal consequences. But segregationists, like all people, did not think of themselves in terms of what they opposed
but rather in terms of what they supported. Anyone seeking to understand segregationists—not to excuse or absolve them, but understand them—must first
understand how they understood themselves. Even though the conventional
wisdom, then and now, held that segregationists were only fighting *against*
the rights of others, in their own minds, these whites were instead fighting *for*
rights of their own—such as the supposed "right" to select their neighbors, their
employees, and their children's classmates, the "right" to do as they pleased with
their private property and personal businesses, and, of course, the "right" to
remain free from what they perceived to be dangerous encroachments by the
federal government.

To be sure, all these positively defined "rights" were rooted in a negative
system of discrimination and racism. But in the minds of segregationists, these
rights existed all the same. Indeed, from their own perspective, segregationists were the ones fighting for individual freedom, not the "'so-called' civil
rights activists." As they liked to point out, it was the civil rights movement that
aligned itself with a powerful central state, demanded increased governmental
intervention in local affairs, and waged a sustained assault on the individual
economic, social, and political prerogatives of others. By contrast, segregationists claimed they stood for the rights of the individual to do as he pleased
and, as a result, to discriminate as he saw fit. Ultimately, these white southerners understood their defense of segregation as a defense of their *own* liberties
rather than a denial of others'.[2]

Although segregationists invoked a broad range of supposed rights, at heart
their claims were encompassed by a single concept, which they commonly characterized as their "freedom of association." Throughout the campaign for massive resistance to school desegregation and, more noticeably, during its wake,
southern segregationists increasingly invoked their right to "freedom of association" as justification for their cause. Importantly, they did not define "freedom of association" *positively*, in terms of what outside groups they could join,
but *negatively*, in terms of which groups of outsiders they could shun. In their

struggle to preserve segregated education, for example, white parents insisted that they had a right to choose what kind of schools their children attended and, more to the point, what kind of children attended school alongside their own. Throughout their struggle to preserve segregated education, these whites remained committed to the concept of "freedom of association" and resolved to preserve it at any cost.

During the era of massive resistance, the "freedom of association" rationale became a common theme used by white parents to defend segregated schooling. "Is it not every father's and mother's inalienable right and duty to choose, for their children, associates and companions for life?" worried one father in 1956.

> If so, how can they when the right of segregation is taken away from them, *and tell me who has that right*? If you do away with segregation in schools, churches, and public places, for our children and young people, you tie the hands of our fathers and mothers to make the kind of homes they would like to have for their off-spring, and which is the very foundation of our schools and churches and the very spirit of the Constitution.

Other Atlantans agreed. "We can't choose who we send our Children to School with, and it won't be long before we will have to ask who we can visit and who can visit us," complained another father in 1957. "How far are we from a Russian form of Government?" Blacks were entitled to their rights, these white parents reasoned, but not at the expense of whites' rights to choose their own associates. "I want the negro to enjoy his freedom but I dont want any part of them," said one man. "I dont want any one to tell me Ive got to sit with them have my children go to school with them invite them into my home . . . which shall it be? give us liberty or give us death?"[3]

As these grassroots cries of "freedom of association" grew louder, segregationist politicians picked up on the theme as well. In the late 1950s, for instance, Georgia's governor, Ernest Vandiver, frequently spoke of "freedom of association" and "freedom of choice" in his many speeches in support of school segregation. In a sign of the issue's popularity and power, the governor even attempted to pass an amendment to the state constitution, one that declared that "freedom from compulsory association at all levels of public education shall be preserved inviolate." While the amendment never passed, the central concept behind it remained a strong theme in segregationist resistance. This was particularly true for those who disdained the crude racism of groups like the Klan and instead embraced a resistance shrouded in middle-class values of rights and respectability. In Atlanta, for instance, such an organization, called the Metropolitan Association for Segregated Education, repeatedly echoed the theme. "My views on the 'school crisis,' the 'sit-ins,' 'kneel-ins,' etc., remain summarized in the phrase 'freedom of association,'" the group's president noted in a typical statement from 1960. "It is perfectly alright if people who want integration have all the integration they want, provided those who feel otherwise (including me, of course) are granted the same 'freedom of choice'" to do otherwise. In this formulation, whites insisted that segregation represented not a social system in which whites denied the rights of blacks but rather one in which whites and blacks respected the rights of each other.[4]

As the date of Atlanta's public school desegregation grew closer, white segregationists invoked their "freedom of association" more and more frequently. In May 1961, just three months before the city's schools were set to desegregate, the clash came to a head. As school officials read through requests from black students seeking transfers to white schools, they found one application quite unlike the others. A seventeen-year-old white girl, Sandra Melkild, sought a transfer from Northside High, which would desegregate that fall, to Dykes High, which would remain all-white. The sole reason for Sandra's request, her application stated succinctly, was her desire "to maintain freedom of association." In the words of her father, William Melkild, "the rights to equal education are inseparably connected with rights to freedom of association. This freedom is the right to associate with whom one pleases and the right not to associate with whom one pleases." Sandra Melkild had a right, her family insisted, not to be "forced" to attend school with blacks against her will.[5]

William Melkild and similar segregationists portrayed their children as the victims of the civil rights movement, which they characterized as a campaign seeking the "forced association" of the races. "Disallowing the transfer of Sandra Melkild, who is seeking freedom of association, while ... permit[ting] the transfer of 10 Negroes seeking forcible association," the father charged, would "set the most disturbing precedent in this city and state since Reconstruction days." School officials, however, worried about setting other precedents. First, they feared that giving a white student the freedom to change schools would allow black students to change schools as well. That precedent would destroy their intricate plans for keeping desegregation to a merely nominal level and would thus, as Georgia's attorney general warned, "lead to massive wholesale integration of the worst sort." Second, the school board worried that other white parents would make transfer requests, too. Only the Melkilds had thought to make the request during the two-week window for applications, but many more had expressed interest since. For these reasons, the school board rejected the request.[6]

Refusing to accept defeat, William Melkild secured a hearing before the State Board of Education in August 1961. As in earlier appeals, he claimed his daughter had been denied a fundamental freedom, "the right to associate with whom one pleases and the right not to associate with whom one pleases." Governor Vandiver had appointed much of the state board. Loyally, the board members followed his lead in defending whites' "freedom of association." Paul Stone, for instance, claimed the Atlanta school board had "grossly abused its discretion" in the matter by "forcing a child to go into a situation that is very distasteful" to her. When an attorney for the Atlanta school board argued that "freedom of association" had no legal foundation at all, Stone retorted that it had the backing of "human law." By a vote of seven to two, he and his associates swiftly reversed the Atlanta board's decision.[7]

Suddenly, just weeks before the scheduled desegregation of Atlanta's schools, the city's plan for controlled, token integration threatened to fall apart. Judge Frank Hooper, who presided over Atlanta's desegregation suit, interrupted his vacation to settle the controversy. As many predicted, Hooper claimed the Melkild request was motivated by racial factors and therefore invalid. "She didn't show any reason for a transfer except for the fact that some Negroes had been admitted to a school that she was attending," he later recalled. Ultimately, the judge ruled against the Melkilds not because of any enlightened racial sensibility but rather because he, like the Atlanta school board, feared wide-scale white flight. "If the Atlanta Board of Education was compelled . . . to allow a transfer from Northside High School of all the white students," he ruled, "the practical effect would be to vacate the school as to all white students desiring to transfer." The remainder of the "desegregated" school system would invariably follow suit, he predicted, since "whenever any Negro students transferred into an all-white school," that institution would "be abandoned by all who desired to do so." Hooper refused to sanction such an exodus.[8]

Although the courts refused to accept the "freedom of association" rationale, segregationists still clung to it. Long after the apparent demise of massive resistance, whites in Atlanta continued to invoke their supposed rights to a segregated education. Initially, segregationists had reason to believe they could get what they wanted within the public school system. When the Atlanta school board unveiled its plans for controlled desegregation of the public schools, for instance, whites noted with pleasure that the board had apparently appropriated both the logic and the language of "freedom of association." Like many other school boards across the South, the Atlanta board adopted a program of pupil placement known as a "freedom of choice" plan. On paper, such programs seemed an equitable approach to desegregation, since they theoretically allowed all parents, black or white, to send their children to the schools of their choice. But closer examination showed that, in practice, such plans parceled out the "freedom of choice" on decidedly uneven terms. White parents were able to keep their children enrolled in overwhelmingly white schools and thereby maintain segregated education. Black parents, however, had to petition individually for their children's transfer and then overcome a complex and extended series of bureaucratic obstacles. "We've got a saying around here," noted an officer of the NAACP, "that it's easier to go to Yale than to transfer from one public school to another in Atlanta."[9]

In time, however, pressure from the courts and civil rights activists alike weakened the school board's ability to use the "freedom of choice" ruse as a means for maintaining segregated schools. In early 1964, the Atlanta Board of Education responded to pressure from the federal courts and greatly accelerated its plans for integration in the upcoming school year. For the first years of the "freedom of choice" system, black students had been confined to dangerously overcrowded schools, even as significant space in white schools remained unused. Now that would change. "We're going to fill every empty seat in high school classrooms this fall," the board member Sara Mitchell announced. Transfers for black students, which had been tightly limited under the original "freedom of choice" approach, were now granted in great numbers. While only eighty-five requests had been approved in 1963, for instance, the school board granted over seven hundred in 1964. Segregationists were horrified. "It will mean only one thing," warned a white weekly paper, the *Metropolitan Herald*. "White residents of these areas will sell their homes and leave the city limits just as quickly as they can." "Call it prejudice, ignorance, or whatever you like," the editors said, but "white families are not going to live long in a school area where massive integration of the schools is in effect. They are not going to expose their children to such an explosive condition for long."[10]

The impact of mass transfers was perhaps clearest at West Fulton High School. As early as 1957, city officials warned that residential racial changes would soon affect the school. "There seems to be an impending change— already in progress—partly brought about due to the Negro population moving closer," a report noted. "This socio-economic situation is a grave problem." As long as Atlanta limited the number of black students transferred, changes in the surrounding neighborhood had little impact. In 1962, for instance, just two black students attended West Fulton; in 1963, the number was still only nine. In a school whose total enrollment approached 1,200, such token numbers meant that the degree of actual integration was negligible. The acceleration of Atlanta's desegregation plan, however, ended that. Over half of the transfer requests granted by the city in 1964 were to West Fulton. When the school opened that fall, blacks outnumbered whites by a slight margin. Stunned by the sudden changes, whites withdrew their children with astonishing speed. Over the first week of classes, white enrollment plummeted from 607 to 143. School officials tried to stop the white flight from West Fulton but had little success. The superintendent, John Letson, for instance, met with hundreds of students to convince them that, in the wake of the Melkild decision, there would be no "mass transfers" to other, "less heavily integrated" schools. The students, however, swore they would never return and devoted their time to eulogies to the "old West Fulton." One girl became so choked with emotion she was unable to finish her prepared remarks; another fainted and had to be revived by a school nurse. Their parents proved to be just as stubborn, as over two hundred angry mothers and fathers stormed the school board meeting the following week. The school board caved, granting transfers for 150 white students who wanted to leave. As the school went, so went the surrounding neighborhood. Just a month later, the changes were astonishing. "It's virtually a Negro community now," observed a white cook who worked across from the school. "I sure hoped I wouldn't be around to see it."[11]

A similar pattern developed that year at Kirkwood Elementary. Though Atlanta's elementary schools had yet to be desegregated, black parents showed up at the still-white school in August 1964, hoping to register their children there. All the nearby black schools, they noted, were horribly overcrowded. Whitefoord Avenue Elementary, for instance, had been transferred to black use only a few years before, but it was already dangerously full. Students there, like some 5,400 other black elementary students in the city, were taught in half-day "double sessions." Classes convened in hallways, the teachers' lounge, a clinic room, and even the janitor's washroom. As enrollment at the black school surged to nearly 650 students over capacity, still-white Kirkwood remained 750 under capacity. When the black parents were turned away, they staged pickets at the white school and launched a boycott of the black ones. Under pressure, the school board announced in December 1964 that black children would be allowed to attend Kirkwood Elementary after the holidays. White children there, however, would be allowed to maintain their "freedom of association" through transfers to other, still-white elementary schools within the system. As an added insult, white teachers were allowed to flee as well. The results were dramatic. On the Friday before the black children were to arrive, there were still 470 white boys and girls enrolled at Kirkwood Elementary, plus a full slate of white teachers and staff. When the black students showed up the following Monday, they found only seven white children in the building, with just the white principal.[12]

As it became clear to all sides of the segregation struggle that the "freedom of choice" approach would not keep real racial changes from coming to the public schools, white parents searched for new ways to maintain "freedom of association" for their children. For many parents, private schools stood as the most attractive alternative. In truth, private schools had been serving as a segregationist refuge for nearly a decade. Even before the desegregation of Atlanta's public school system, during the late 1950s, whites flocked to the city's private schools. One prestigious academy, for instance, saw its enroll- ment increase tenfold—from one hundred students to one thousand—over the course of just four years. The headmaster appreciated the reasons why. "In all candor," he confided to a reporter, "the segregation-desegregation strug- gle gives impetus to the development of private schools." When the NAACP lawsuit for desegregation of the public schools was delayed a year, he noted, "we had forty cancellations in one week." But as desegregation of the public schools became ever more likely in the eyes of white parents, they moved their children to private schools in record numbers. In 1959, for instance, one acad- emy tripled its enrollment, while a second registered one thousand students and turned away 1,600 more.[13]

In an effort to help all whites send their children to such segregated private schools, Georgia's leaders had created a system of tuition grants as part of the state's machinery of massive resistance. Although the legislation made no refer- ence to race, it noted that, if the public schools were "forced" to integrate, stu- dents seeking to escape the "intolerable conditions" of the public schools would be eligible to receive funds from the state for a private education instead. And, as planned, once Atlanta's public schools desegregated in 1961, the tuition grant system went into effect the following fall. More than one thousand grants were approved that year, for a total of over $186,000. Although the grants had been meant to help whites flee from the few schools that were then being desegre- gated, evidence soon showed otherwise. The *Atlanta Constitution* reported that 83 percent of the recipients had been enrolled in private schools well before desegregation began. (One recipient was a local black educator who had been sending his children to a northern prep school and was now happy to let seg- regationists help pay their way.) Furthermore, hundreds of the recipients lived in areas outside Atlanta, where no desegregation existed and, thus, where there was no "need" to flee the public schools. As such stories came to light, most leg- islators soured on the plan. Even State Senator Garland Byrd, who had cham- pioned tuition grants while lieutenant governor, came to denounce them as a "subterfuge" that only helped "a privileged few." The legislature tightened the administration of the law and, by the time the 1963 school year began, not a single tuition grant had been issued throughout the state. As a practical result, only wealthy whites would be able to use segregated private schools as a means of maintaining "freedom of association" for their children.[14]

For private schools, their new status as the last bastion of segregated edu- cation in Atlanta was an uncomfortable one. Nowhere was this unease more keenly felt than in the prestigious private academies with religious affiliations. During the late 1950s, religious leaders and educators had stood at the forefront of Atlanta's moderate coalition in counseling the calm acceptance of court-ordered desegregation. Through a pair of forthright "Ministers' Manifestoes," a series of Sunday columns in the *Atlanta Constitution*, and countless sermons to their own congregations, these churchmen had taken a principled public stand for the acceptance of desegregated schools. Suddenly, in the early 1960s, these religious leaders found themselves confronted with the same situation in their own still-segregated institutions. Wrestling with this problem publicly and painfully, many found it hard to practice what they had quite literally been preaching.[15]

Some quickly moved to correct the problem. Roman Catholic schools, for instance, made it clear they wanted no part in segregation. Soon after his appointment to the Atlanta archdiocese in 1962, Archbishop Paul Hallinan aggressively pressed for the desegregation of all eighteen elementary and high schools under his jurisdiction. Shortly thereafter, the Greater Atlanta Council on Human Relations (GACHR) took stock of the remaining religious schools. The largest and most popular ones generally hedged the issue. For instance, the main Presbyterian schools, Westminster and Trinity, noted that they had received application forms from African Americans yet had never admitted a black student. Trinity corrected that oversight in April 1963, enrolling the daughters of Andrew Young, the civil rights activist and future mayor of Atlanta. Westminster, meanwhile, continued to bar blacks. In 1963, for instance, a black professor of anthropology at Atlanta University tried to enroll his daughter there. Despite her academic qualifications, the headmaster was not optimistic about her chances. "He said it was very disturbing," noted a GACHR activist, but "that unfortunately a lot of people who have money are opposed to it." As expected, her application was denied.[16]

A similar but more sensational situation unfolded the same year at Westminster's Episcopal counterpart, the Lovett School. The "Lovett Crisis," as it would forever be known, began simply enough in August 1962. On a flight to Atlanta, Reverend John Morris, a liberal Episcopal priest, found himself chatting about segregated schools in that city with an African American woman. "She asked about Lovett, whether it was segregated, etc.," Reverend Morris recalled. "I knew of no policy, but promised to advise her about it later." In the end, he could find no official policy at the school. But Reverend Morris understood that, throughout the past decade, the Episcopal Diocese of Atlanta had repeatedly come out against segregated education and the forces of massive resistance. Now that massive resistance had been defeated in Georgia and the public schools of Atlanta had been desegregated, it only seemed logical that the private schools associated with the Diocese would do likewise. There-fore, Reverend Morris told his traveling companion that Lovett would appar-ently welcome children of all races. And so, she and her husband submitted an application to the school for their son, a young boy named Martin Luther King III.[17]

Despite the Diocese's past stance against massive resistance, the Kings' application sparked considerable controversy in the church and its school. After a great deal of public embarrassment and private deliberation, Lovett's trustees sent Coretta Scott King and Martin Luther King, Jr., a curt letter in February 1963 informing them that "under present circumstances" the acad-emy could not accept their son. In response, local activists launched an inten-sive protest campaign, urging church leaders to heed their own advice and accept school desegregation in the institutions they controlled. Rather than submit to pressure, the Diocese dug in its heels. Over the next months and years, the Lovett crisis only worsened. A significant rift grew within the church, matched only by the considerable controversy outside it. Local priests stood on picket lines around Lovett and even went on hunger strikes at the diocesan cathedral. Meanwhile, leading figures of the civil rights movement and the media singled out the school as a sign of the lingering segregationist resistance in the South.[18]

Notably, throughout the turmoil, the leaders of the Diocese and the Lovett School repeatedly invoked the "freedom of association" rationale in their defense. "Personally, I have been in complete sympathy with the negro in his quest for decent treatment," noted the Reverend Alfred Hardman, who served as both the dean of the Cathedral of St. Philip and the chairman of the Lovett board. "I am still willing to stand up and be counted as being in accord with his seeking the right to vote; to public transportation; to hotel accommodations; to worship in any church, etc." But the Lovett School was another matter. "I feel strongly," Dean Hardman confided, "that both the negro and the white man has some individual rights. Among these I would include the right to pay for and operate a school accepting only those he chooses and to reject any applicant he doesn't want for any reason he deems good."[19]

In the end, private academies like Lovett successfully used the "freedom of association" argument to maintain segregated education for years. In the realm of public education, the same rationale had been twice dismissed by the courts—first, when the Melkilds offered it as an overt argument for segrega-tion, and then, when the school board used it as a covert means of minimizing desegregation. Private schools, however, remained free to discriminate. And thus, for those select whites who were willing and able to pay for the privilege of "freedom of association," segregated education remained a legally accept-able and socially attractive option. Those who could not, however, resolved that there was only one remaining way for them to secure their supposed rights—abandoning the public school system altogether.

Indeed, as the degree of actual desegregation increased throughout the 1960s, whites steadily fled from Atlanta's public schools. By 1970, white enrollment in the school system was already half what it had been at its peak in 1963. While whites and blacks had been equally represented in the 1964–65 school year, black students outnumbered whites by margins of two to one in 1969 and then three to one in 1971. In individual schools, the racial imbalance was even more acute than those overall ratios suggested, since most of the city's students were educated in schools predominantly of one race. As late as the 1969–70 academic year, only 20,000 students in a system of over 100,000 pupils attended schools that were classified as "desegregated." The bar for considering schools "desegregated" had been set extremely low—a school merely needed a minimum of 10 percent of both blacks and whites in its student body—and yet only 34 out of 117 public schools met the standard. Frustrated by white flight, school officials threw up their hands. "I don't know what you can do," shrugged Benjamin Mays, the black head of the school board, "to keep white folks from being scared if you move into their neighborhood."[20]

The continued segregation of Atlanta's public schools made it clear that the "freedom of choice" concept had been little different from the old segregationist trope of "freedom of association." To be sure, southern whites defended the new phrase with as much passion as they had defended the old. As an official with the Department of Health, Education and Welfare (HEW) later marveled, in the 1960s, "freedom to choose one's own school was being talked about in the South in the same breath as the freedoms of speech and assembly under the First Amendment." Southern moderates certainly understood the significance and sought to educate the nation about it. In 1969, Ralph McGill turned his column in the *Constitution* into an open letter to Robert Finch, who, as the incoming HEW secretary for the Nixon administration, would lead the federal government's oversight and enforcement of school desegregation. "There is all too often no freedom in the freedom of choice plan," McGill noted frankly. "It too frequently is freedom in reverse. It offers a segregationist, racist-dominated community or board an opportunity to proclaim a free choice, while they covertly employ 'persuasions' to maintain segregation or meager tokenism." The "freedom of choice" approach, McGill warned, was simply segregation in a subtler form. "It will be the greatest tragedy with the most foreboding consequences if public school officials are allowed to perpetuate dual school systems," he warned Secretary Finch. "You may be assured, sir, that the freedom of choice plan is, in fact, neither freedom nor a choice. It is discrimination."[21]

The federal courts agreed. In 1968, the U.S. Supreme Court indicated in *Green v. New Kent County, Virginia,* that "freedom of choice" plans were no longer sufficient to fulfill the court's desegregation mandate and needed to be replaced with more aggressive approaches. Like many other cities, Atlanta shifted to a program of majority-to-minority student transfers as a way to create a greater racial balance in city schools. In 1971, the court signaled in *Swann v. Charlotte-Mecklenburg Board of Education* that metropolitan-wide busing programs could be used to aid and enlarge such an approach. While other cities adopted such plans, black leaders balked at the idea in Atlanta. "Massive busing would be counterproductive at this point," Benjamin Mays sighed. "We'd end up with no whites to bus." Lonnie King, a former student activist who then led the local chapter of the NAACP, agreed with the school board president. "There were no white kids to bus," he mused later. "You'd be busing children from an 87 percent black school to another 87 percent black school."[22]

Instead of seeking a solution through busing, the school board and the local NAACP forged a negotiated settlement in 1973 that critics christened the "Atlanta Compromise." For their part, the board promised to increase student transfers, create a program of biracial magnet schools, further integrate school staffs, and make aggressive moves towards increasing the number of blacks in administrative positions. In exchange, the NAACP agreed to drop its ongoing lawsuit against the school board and ease its demands for massive, metropolitan-wide busing. While the Atlanta Compromise ended the legal struggles over school segregation, it did nothing to stem the tide of white flight from the city's public schools. In fact, whites continued to abandon the city's public schools at a staggering rate. In 1973, whites still made up 23 percent of the total enrollment. By 1985, however, that figure had fallen to just 6 percent. By 2002, the overwhelmingly black character of Atlanta's public school system was unmistakable. Of the city's ninety-three schools, fifty-four had only one or two white students enrolled, while another twenty-one had no white students at all.[23]

One of the primary causes of lowered white enrollment in the city's public schools, of course, was the larger pattern of flight of whites to the suburbs. To be sure, white families still remained inside the city of Atlanta during the 1970s and 1980s, but their children attended private schools by a margin of nearly two to one. (In 1985, the city's school system had only 7,000 white students out of a total enrollment of 110,000. Private academies, meanwhile, enrolled about 12,000 students, the vast majority of whom were white.) White flight to the suburbs, as a means of maintaining "freedom of association" not only in schools but in countless other public and private spaces, had been strong and steady since the demise of massive resistance. In 1960, the total white population of Atlanta stood at barely more than 300,000. Over the course of that decade, roughly sixty thousand whites left Atlanta. During the 1970s, another 100,000 whites—nearly half of all white Atlantans—would flee the city as well.[24]

Not surprisingly, the suburbs to which these whites fled were overwhelmingly white. In 1970, for instance, the booming suburbs of Cobb County were 96 percent white. The same year, Gwinnett County's population was 95 percent white, while the suburban section of north Fulton County stood at an astonishing 99 percent white. Because these suburban areas had so few black residents with whom these whites would be "forced" to associate in the schools and other public spaces, whites found them to be an ideal location for maintaining the goals of racial separatism they had sought for so long. Once there, these suburbanites proved as determined to preserve their "freedom of association" in their new environments as they had inside the city, if not more so. As a state legislator from the Atlanta area put it in 1971, "the suburbanite says to himself, 'The reason I worked for so many years was to get away from pollution, bad schools and crime, and I'll be damned if I'll see it all follow me.'" Likewise, in 1975, Joe Mack Wilson, later mayor of the Cobb County seat of Marietta, summed up the suburban attitude with an appropriate image. Pointing to the Chattahoochee River, which runs between the county and the city, he tried to explain to an outsider the worldview of his constituents. "They love that river down there," he said. "They want to keep it as a moat. They wish they could build forts across there to keep people from coming up here."[25]

For many whites, settlement in the suburbs represented the culmination of a decades-long pursuit of "freedom of association." Notably, in their migration from the city to the suburbs, segregationists had not merely changed addresses but changed the ways in which they thought and spoke about what they understood to be their fundamental rights. During the days of massive resistance, "freedom of association" had been offered as little more than a thinly disguised justification for racism. But over time, as the theme appeared again and again in the rhetoric and rationales of disaffected whites, their cause came to be seen—by them and by society at large—as ultimately less about race and more about rights. Although massive resistance may seem to be a relic of the past, the legacies of discrimination and white flight are ones that still must be reckoned with today.

Notes

1. Virginia H. Hein, "The Image of 'A City Too Busy to Hate': Atlanta in the 1960s," *Phylon* 33 (fall 1972): 207; *New York Times*, Aug. 31, 1961; *Newsweek*, Sept. 11, 1961; *U.S. News and World Report*, Sept. 11, 1961; *Reporter*, Sept. 15, 1961.

2. In stressing the individualistic aspect of segregation, this study borrows from Alan Brinkley's astute analysis of "individualistic conservatism" writ large. See Alan Brinkley, "The Problem of American Conservatism," *American Historical Review* 99 (Apr. 1994):

415–19, as well as Michael Kazin, "The Grass-Roots Right: New Histories of U.S. Conservatism in the Twentieth Century," *American Historical Review* 97 (Feb. 1992): 136–55.

3. James W. Tarpley to James C. Davis, Mar. 1956, box 31, James C. Davis Papers, General Correspondence Series, Special Collections, Robert W. Woodruff Library, Emory University, Atlanta; E. A. Veale to Ralph McGill, Sept. 1957, box 24, Ralph E. McGill Papers, Special Collections, Robert W. Woodruff Library, Emory University, Atlanta; Anonymous to James C. Davis, Sept. 30, 1957, box 32, Davis Papers.

4. *Atlanta Journal*, Nov. 19, 1960, Aug. 8, 1961; *Southern School News*, Mar. 1961; Benjamin Muse, *Ten Years of Prelude: The Story of Integration Since the Supreme Court's 1954 Decision* (New York: Viking Press, 1964), 224.

5. *Atlanta Journal*, May 16, Aug. 7, 11, 1961, *Atlanta Constitution*, May 17, 19, 1961; *Southern School News*, Jun. 1961; *Atlanta City Directory, 1962*.

6. *Atlanta Journal-Constitution*, Jul. 2, 1961; *Atlanta Journal*, May 16, Jun. 9, 23, Jul. 7–11, 1961, *Atlanta Constitution*, May 17–19, Jun. 29, 1961; *Southern School News*, Jun., Aug. 1961; minutes, Atlanta Board of Education, Aug. 14, 1961, Atlanta Public School Archives, Atlanta (hereafter APSA).

7. *Atlanta Journal*, Aug. 7–9, 15, 1961; *Atlanta Constitution*, Aug. 8, 1961; Eliza Paschall, notes, Aug. 8, 1961, box 1, Eliza Paschall Papers, Special Collections, Robert W. Woodruff Library, Emory University, Atlanta.

8. *Atlanta Constitution*, Aug. 16, 17, 1961; *Atlanta Journal*, Aug. 16, 17, Dec. 13, 20, 1961; *Atlanta Journal-Constitution*, Aug. 29, 1961; transcript, Hearing in Motion for Further Relief, *Calhoun v. Latimer*, copy in box 27, Austin T. Walden Papers, Archives, Atlanta Historical Society, Atlanta; *Southern School News*, Jan. 1962.

9. James T. Patterson, *Brown v. Board of Education: A Civil Rights Milestone and Its Troubled Legacy* (New York: Oxford University Press, 2001): 100–101; *Atlanta Journal*, Apr. 21, 1961.

10. *Atlanta Journal*, Aug. 21, Nov. 20, 22, 1963; Mar. 7, 12, 27, 30, 1964; May 25, 1964; Jun. 24, 1964; July 14, 29, 1964; Aug. 11, 1964; *Atlanta Constitution*, Apr. 7, Jul. 14, 29–30, 1964; *Atlanta Times*, Jul. 29, 1964; Ronald H. Bayor, *Race and the Shaping of Twentieth-Century Atlanta* (Chapel Hill: University of North Carolina Press, 1996), 230–31; *Metropolitan Herald*, Jun. 10, 1964, copy in reel 110, part 11, Southern Regional Council Papers, Microfilm Collection, Special Collections, Robert W. Woodruff Library, Atlanta University, Atlanta; minutes, Atlanta Board of Education, Jul. 13, 1964, APSA.

11. "Summary of Evaluation at West Fulton," typescript, Mar. 20, 1957, APSA; "Transfer Students–1962," list, box 18, Herbert T. Jenkins Papers, Archives, Atlanta Historical Society, Atlanta; list, "Transfer Students, 1963–1964," box 18, Jenkins Papers; "Statistical Report, 1964–1965," typescript, APSA; *Atlanta Journal*, Jun. 4, Sept. 8, 1964; Officer R. B. Moore to Supt. C. Chafin and Capt. W. L. Duncan, Sept. 8, 1964, box 18, Jenkins Papers; *Atlanta Constitution*, Sept. 9, 1964; minutes, Atlanta Board of Education, Sept. 14, 1964, APSA; Sara Mitchell Parsons, *From Southern Wrongs to Civil Rights: The Memoir of a White Civil Rights Activist* (Tuscaloosa: University of Alabama Press, 2000), 109–10; Bayor, *Race and Atlanta*, 234; *Atlanta Times*, Sept. 15, 27, 1964.

12. *Atlanta Journal*, Aug. 28, 31, Sept. 1, 22, Dec. 16, 1964, Jan. 26, 1965; Parsons, *Southern Wrongs*, 83; Bayor, *Race and Atlanta*, 230–34; *Southern School News*, Sept., Oct. 1964; flyer [Sept. 22, 1964], box 18, Jenkins Papers; Susan M. McGrath, "From Tokenism to

Community Control: Political Symbolism in the Desegregation of Atlanta's Public Schools, 1961–1973," *Georgia Historical Quarterly* 79 (Winter 1995): 856–57; *Atlanta Constitution*, Jan. 26, 1965.

13. Telex report, [n.d., 1961], box 12, *Newsweek*, Atlanta Bureau Files, Special Collections, Robert W. Woodruff Library, Emory University, Atlanta (hereafter NAB); James M. Sibley to Joseph Cumming, Oct. 14, 1963, box 8, NAB; *Southern School News*, Oct., Nov. 1959.

14. Minutes, Atlanta Board of Education, Aug. 13, 1962, APSA; *Southern School News*, Mar., Apr., Nov. 1962, Mar. 1963; *Atlanta Journal*, Dec. 6, 19, 1961, Oct. 16, 19, 1962; Feb. 6, 13, 15, 18, 20, Apr. 25, 29, 1963; May 2, 7, 1963; Aug. 23, 1963; Calvin Trillin, *An Education in Georgia: Charlayne Hunter, Hamilton Holmes, and the Integration of the University of Georgia* (Athens: University of Georgia Press, 1991), 47–48.

15. *Atlanta Constitution*, Nov. 23, 1955; *Atlanta Journal-Constitution*, Oct. 20, 27, Nov. 10, 17, Dec. 8, 15, 22, 1957.

16. *Southern School News*, Jul., Aug. 1962; Eliza Paschall, *It Must Have Rained* (Atlanta: Center for Research in Social Change, Emory University, 1975), 87, 150; Andrew Young, *An Easy Burden: The Civil Rights Movement and the Transformation of America* (New York: HarperCollins, 1996), 197; Paschall to Dr. William Pressly, May 30, 1962, box 2, Paschall Papers; typewritten draft report, [n.d., 1961], box 12, NAB; Eliza Paschall to Kay Hocking et al., Feb. 20, 1963, Paschall Papers.

17. John B. Morris, *Episcopal Society for Cultural and Racial Unity Newsletter*, Aug. 6, 1963, box 1, Episcopal Society for Cultural and Racial Unity (ESCRU) Collection, Special Collections, Robert W. Woodruff Library, Emory University, Atlanta.

18. John B. Morris, *ESCRU Newsletter*, Aug. 6, 1963, box 1, ESCRU Collection; Joseph A. Pelham, "Memorandum on Lovett School," Apr. 8, 1963, box 61, McGill Papers.

19. Alfred Hardman to Ralph McGill, Jun. 29, 1963, box 50, McGill Papers.

20. Patterson, *Brown*, 100–101; Clarence N. Stone, *Regime Politics: Governing Atlanta* (Lawrence: University of Kansas Press, 1989), 103; Frederick Allen, *Atlanta Rising: The Invention of an International City, 1946–1996* (Atlanta: Longstreet Press, 1996), 176.

21. J. Harvie Wilkinson, *From Brown to Bakke: The Supreme Court and School Integration* (New York: Oxford University Press, 1979), 109; *Atlanta Constitution*, Feb. 4, 1969; Leon E. Panetta and Peter Gall, *Bring Us Together: The Nixon Team and the Civil Rights Retreat* (New York: Lippincott, 1971), 79.

22. Peter H. Irons, *Jim Crow's Children: The Broken Promise of the Brown Decision* (New York: Viking Press, 2002), 199–233; Wilkinson, *From Brown to Bakke*, 116–18, 136–39; Stone, *Regime Politics*, 103; Bayor, *Race and Atlanta*, 247.

23. John Egerton, *The Americanization of Dixie: The Southernization of America* (New York: Harpers, 1974): 89–93; Stone, *Regime Politics*, 104–6; Bayor, *Race and Atlanta*, 247–51; *New York Times*, May 6, 1985; *Atlanta Journal-Constitution*, Aug. 10, 2002.

24. *New York Times*, May 6, 1985; U.S. Bureau of the Census, *U.S. Censuses of Population and Housing: 1960*, vol. 1, part 8, *Census Tracts: Atlanta, Ga., Standard Metropolitan Statistical Area* (Washington, D.C.: U.S. Government Printing Office, 1962), table P-1; U.S. Bureau of the Census, *1970 Census of Population and Housing*, vol. 1, part 14, *Census Tracts: Atlanta, Ga., Standard Metropolitan Area (and Adjacent Area)* (Washington, D.C.: U.S. Government Printing Office, 1972), table P-1; U.S. Bureau of the Census, *1980*

Census of Population and Housing, vol. 2, part 80, *Census Tracts: Atlanta, Ga. Standard Metropolitan Statistical Area* (Washington, D.C.: U.S. Government Printing Office, 1983), table P-2.

25. *Atlanta Journal-Constitution,* May 3, 1987; *New York Times,* Jun. 2, 1971; Peter Applebome, *Dixie Rising: How the South Is Shaping American Values, Politics and Culture* (San Diego: Harcourt, Brace, 1996), 35.

PART TWO

Segregationist Ideology

SIX

White South, Red Nation: Massive Resistance and the Cold War

George Lewis

In late June 1961, James Jackson Kilpatrick, editor of the *Richmond News Leader*, returned from a fact-finding trip to the Soviet Union. "Good to have you back," wrote Kilpatrick's fellow newspaperman Leon Dure, before adding, "unarrested and unbrain-washed, yet."[1] References to the Soviet Union as a Machiavellian power that often resorted to underhand tactics were common in the Cold War period. Dure's lighthearted approach to such matters was perhaps not so common but does serve to suggest some diversity in the response of American citizens to the pressures of the global conflict. The correspondence between the two men is also an appropriate reminder that the Cold War was of immediate concern to southern white supremacists, for both Kilpatrick and Dure emerged as important strategists in the South's massive resistance campaign. Kilpatrick, the better known of the two, became a leading propagandist for the southern cause in a series of *News Leader* editorials. Dure played an altogether quieter—though no less pivotal—role, for he contributed the phrase "freedom of choice" to the vocabulary of resistance, a phrase that soon became common currency as southern legislatures drew up plans to circumvent *Brown*.[2]

Given that both the Cold War and southern resistance began to precipitate concurrently in the late 1940s, it is not surprising that the global concerns of the Cold War made a telling contribution to the atmosphere and context in which massive resistance was played out. By the late 1950s, there was no mistaking the two issues that most troubled white southerners. As Kilpatrick's fellow Virginian and former state governor, John Battle, wrote at the end of 1958, "my first wish in 1959 for Virginia is a program of racially segregated public school education which will not be held invalid by the federal courts, and for the nation the end of the cold war and with it lasting peace."[3] Nor was the acknowledgment of the centrality of these twin threats the sole preserve of politicians. The region's businessmen, who played a significant role, if a less conspicuous one than their political counterparts, in the outcome of massive resistance—especially in the Upper South—echoed those concerns. As the owner of a southern air conditioning company explained to a fellow executive, "two of the biggest, if not the biggest problems which will face our generation, are communism on the international front and the race issue on the domestic front. Both," he concluded, "can easily become fraught with emotionalism and cause both sides to make serious mistakes."[4]

Historians who have concentrated on the white South's response to racial change, however, have been guilty of viewing massive resistance in domestic isolation. A wave of recent historical works has begun to explore the impact that the United States' domestic race relations had on the wider Cold War, and vice versa. The work of historians such as Mary Dudziak and Azza Salama Layton has, however, focused squarely upon matters of federal policy—whether foreign or domestic—and on presidential attempts to control the impact that continued racial inequality in the South had on the nation's wider global image.[5] In adding to that growing body of work, Thomas Borstelmann has carefully examined the ways in which a catalogue of racial assumptions, held by a succession of policy-makers and political leaders in Washington, has affected notions of postwar white supremacy throughout the world, most notably in relation to southern Africa. In positioning himself within a "growing movement to reunite the internal and external sides of the American past," however, Borstelmann is also drawn inexorably to the power brokers and playmakers of the nation's capital.[6] As a result, there is still precious little that is known about the effect that Cold War hostilities had within the white South at a state, or even a regional, level. Attempting to redress that imbalance, Jeff Woods has argued that the Cold War was not only of concern to federal politicians in Washington but also was of such concern to segregationist politicians that many imported the tactics of federal anticommunist committees south of the Mason-Dixon line in an attempt to shore up "southern nationalism." Even Woods's reevaluation, however, has failed to note that, alongside the leaders of massive resistance, the new Cold War context for race relations also had a telling effect on those supporting segregation at the grassroots: this was in no way a solely elitist phenomenon.[7]

For segregationist politician and constituent alike, the Cold War affected the tenor of their intellectual arguments, and altered the vocabulary of resistance. In short, as the personal papers, correspondence with constituents, printed polemic, and speeches of resistance leaders and politicians across the South clearly demonstrate, the language of the new global conflict infused the rhetoric of resisters at all levels of society. The extent to which Cold War–influenced language was common to the region as a whole, from the cosmopolitan suburbs of Washington, D.C., to the furthest reaches of the Mississippi Delta, must serve as a reminder that the phenomenon of massive resistance was not simply a product of the Deep South's demagogues but was also to be found in the Upper South. It is, moreover, when the varied and variable reaction of resistance forces to Cold War concerns are examined across the entire region that splits and divisions within the white South can be most easily seen. It is those fissures that have too long been glossed over by historians content to focus solely on the intricacies of the African American side of the freedom struggle. A close analysis of segregationists' reaction to the Cold War climate also serves to emphasize that they were as willing, and at times as able, to adapt to their new surroundings as their federal counterparts. Indeed, as different threats appeared, starting with *Brown* in 1954, and later including the deployment of federal troops in Little Rock in 1957 and, for example, the direct action of the sit-in demonstrations of 1960, many resisters proved themselves adept at reacting to the Cold War climate to provide novel defenses of their position.

There are compelling arguments to suggest that, at least in part, federal support for *Brown* was motivated by its use as an instrument of Cold War foreign policy.[8] In the South, *Brown* was, for obvious reasons, often central to the rhetoric employed by both sides of the battle for racial equality. Indeed, both segregationists and desegregationists sought to use the decision as an exemplar of the ills of American society. For desegregationists, the very fact that such a decision was needed in the first place highlighted inequalities that for too long had been deep-seated in American life. For segregationists, it served to highlight the interventionist policies of a succession of overbearing federal administrations. If it is hardly surprising that both sides of the segregation struggle were united in recognizing the impact that *Brown* would have on their way of life, it is, perhaps, less expected that both freely used the language of the Cold War to articulate their concerns. It was in the two sides' immediate reaction to *Brown* that the new Cold War language of southern resistance first came to prevalence. Many supporters of desegregation echoed the view of federal policy shapers that *Brown* had to be obeyed because it fulfilled an important foreign policy objective. In what was commonly perceived to be a bipolar global conflict between communist East and democratic West, *Brown* offered the United States a useful tool to prove to a worldwide audience that its constitution was, at heart, an egalitarian document. In an era in which white colonialism was in retreat across the globe, the United States could simply not afford to repel the nonwhite governments of newly independent, postcolonial nations with continued examples of racism.[9] It was a point that was not lost on Harry Emerson Fosdick, a prominent member of the NAACP, who wrote to a Florida businessman in the wake of the decision, to argue that it would be "ironic if discriminations were to persist long after the Voice of America proudly announced a bright new emancipation to the peoples of Asia, Africa and Latin America."[10]

Although it is tempting to assume that all segregationists were united in their dismissal of *Brown* as a necessary foreign policy instrument, that was not necessarily the case. There was, in fact, little uniformity on the subject. Herman Talmadge, the rabidly racist governor of Georgia, publicly proclaimed his refusal to cave in to federal decisions emanating from Moscow; for every Herman Talmadge, there was a Harry Byrd, quietly noting that there would be "difficult days to come." The "eyes of the world," Byrd realized, would be watching the racial situation in the South very closely.[11] Given a rare opportunity to elucidate the white South's position in a national magazine, the *Saturday Review*, Clifford Dowdey noted in October 1954 that the "educated Southerner is well aware of the considerations of world politics which were involved in this decision; he strongly suspects that these considerations much influenced the unanimity of the Court, and he declines the role of obstacle to the 'march of human freedom.'"[12] Similarly, a number of grassroots segregationists, if only grudgingly, began to acknowledge the role that foreign policy considerations must have played in the Supreme Court's schools decision. Indeed, a growing number tried to explain to their political leaders that the new exigencies of the Cold War were fast catching up with established southern racial practices, and now had to be taken into account. For those southerners who had been brought up in the belief that white supremacy was axiomatic, those new pressures provided one of the few rational explanations for the unanimous nature of the Supreme Court's desegregation ruling. "Unless the Supreme Court did it to offset Communistic propagander [*sic*]," wrote one Virginian constituent to his governor in June 1954, "I cannot see how they could have come to a unanimous decision."[13] Similarly, one North Carolinian explained to Thomas Pearsall, then in charge of formulating the Tarheel State's response to the Supreme Court's schools edict: "The world situation made the [*Brown*] decision inevitable."[14]

The number of white southerners who forcefully opposed the *Brown* decision is not, in itself, remarkable, but the number who chose to do so by immersing their worries in the language of the Cold War is significant. South Carolina's Jane Revill, for example, besought her political leaders to realize that the decision "falls in line with communism," because it encroached on individuals' rights to choose his or her own associates, and those of his or her children. While acknowledging that pressure did exist for a visible change in U.S. racial policy, she dismissed such pressures out of hand. "The segregation decision is being considered as a compromise with communism," she said, "whereas in reality it is a measure of surrender to communism."[15] Others shared her sentiments. *Brown*, for example, was "no answer to 'world opinion' but is the road to communism."[16] Although such rhetoric was most prevalent in the period between the first and second *Brown* decisions, there were some segregation-ists who were so convinced by its efficacy that they continued the argument throughout the resistance period. In January 1958, for example, the Arkansas Representative Ezekiel C. Gathings proclaimed to Congress: "Comintern agents realized that . . . nothing could be better designed for their purpose than a deci-sion by the Supreme Court . . . striking at the most sensitive of all questions . . . that of integration of the White and Negro races"; "that they eventually found this," he concluded, "cannot be denied."[17]

In the years following *Brown,* many massive resistance leaders were pain-fully aware of the consequences of the Supreme Court's ruling on the long-term segregation of southern society and, as a result, were fully cognizant of the need to present a united segregationist front in the battle against federally mandated desegregation. With that in mind, a separate strand of Cold War–influenced, post-*Brown* resistance rhetoric was developed to fulfill a specific purpose: it was designed to win over those white southerners whose commitment to segrega-tion had begun to waver in the face of the federal judiciary's assault, and those whose morale had begun to flag. For example, the *Dixie-American,* a newspaper based in Birmingham, Alabama, printed a story in early March 1956 that clearly sought to implicate the Soviets in the racial disturbances that surrounded Autherine Lucy's attempts to enroll at the University of Alabama. The tone of the article was deliberately provocative and was designed to enrage segrega-tionists into ever more defiant postures by further demonizing the forces sup-porting desegregation. Citing reports made by the German Youth Organization on East German radio, the *Dixie-American* published an article entitled "East German Reds Hop Bandwagon of Agitators Riding Lucy Coattails." It said that "the Communists have offered Autherine Lucy a scholarship to attend an East German University," an offer that left the *Dixie-American* somewhat upbeat. If she decided to take up the offer, the article continued, "and has the cour-age of her convictions that miscegenation is the wave of the future, it is to be hoped that similar scholarships can be provided by the East German reds" for all those at the university who supported her.[18] Indeed, East Germany proved to be something of a favored target for southern segregationists. In June 1961, Senator Olin Johnston announced that his sources had uncovered "a new line" in East German "perversion." Drawing upon an article published in South Car-olina's *Columbia Record,* he announced that "Communist East Germany has opened an American Negro agitation training center in the Saxony industrial city of Bautzen. The center was grandly titled 'the Institute for the Advance-ment of the Negro Race' and was concerned with 'training squads of African Negro agitators who, after completing training in East Germany, will return to their home countries to await infiltration into US Negro population centers." All the indications are that it was a fabrication, but a fabrication based—at least in part—on real events. As part of the ongoing Cold War propaganda battle, there were reports that the East Germans had offered the Little Rock children a place in their "unsegregated" and "egalitarian" schools, so as to draw further attention to the inequities of the U.S. position. On the other hand, whatever was claimed by Senator Johnson, no contemporary southerner was likely to be in a position to refute his claims with authority, so it was really a carte blanche to undermine civil rights protesters. So intent were East Germans in carrying out their plans, the report claimed, that they had brought students to the center on scholarships from Guinea, Ghana, Congo, Liberia, and Togo.[19]

This prevalence of Cold War themes in resistance rhetoric needs to be explained beyond the simple truth that both the Cold War and massive resistance developed concurrently in the late 1940s. From a segregationist point of view, such language at least offered the white South the opportunity of recasting what was, in essence, a regional struggle to uphold racial separation as a national battle against a foreign, totalitarian enemy. If used intelligently and effectively, rebranding civil rights agitation not as the work of the South's racial enemies but as the work of the nation's Cold War foes could even remove race from the intellectual debates surrounding massive resistance altogether. By depicting racial clashes as but a localized theater of a global war, the parameters of the desegregation struggle could, effectively, be shifted. No longer would massive resistance be seen as the struggle of the renegade South against the rest of the nation. Instead, it was possible to remove blame for racial disturbances from the South altogether, as well as to depict the region as the last bastion of true Americanism fighting against a single, un-American enemy.

S. J. Thompson, a prolific resistance propagandist from Greenwood, South Carolina, produced a widely distributed one-page broadsheet in the summer of 1954, giving perhaps the earliest example of the attempts of certain segregationists to carry out this repositioning. Agents of communist powers were the same all over the world, according to Thompson. "They have been trying to find a way to destroy the Southern States for more than twenty years for no other reason except that nearly all the white people in the Southern States are one hundred percent American."[20] As resistance began to gather pace, the argument gained in currency. In 1955, the outspoken newspaper columnist Nell Battle Lewis, an "unqualified opponent of integration," said unequivocally that any effort to bring about desegregation was "an integral part of the Communist conspiracy to 'divide and conquer,' to disrupt our existing society and make us ripe for revolutionary changes."[21] By the time the sit-ins had provided a concrete example of the lengths to which black activists were willing to go to achieve desegregation in February 1960, such rhetoric had found its way into the vocabulary of electioneering. Robert Dupree, campaigning as an independent in the Florida gubernatorial race of 1960, claimed that an end to desegregation would mean that "the standard of living in this country would be lowered, while the crime rate would rise. The communists would gain," he concluded, "while our country would be undergoing an internal turmoil plus the [resultant] lowered standard of living."[22] It was not the South that would suffer but the nation as a whole.

As nonviolent direct action campaigns aimed at ending segregation increased in both number and intensity across the South, so segregationists turned their attentions away from the *Brown* decision to focus on the new threat that such activism posed. Faced by civil rights campaigns that had been specifically designed to draw attention to continued de facto segregation in the South long after *Brown* had ended its de jure equivalent, resisters in turn altered their focus. They stepped up their attempts to prove that racial disturbances were not simply southern problems but were, in fact, national problems provoked by communist forces. Some segregationists showed that they, too, understood the subtleties that the international situation now demanded, and buttressed their earlier arguments against *Brown* with arguments designed to prove that Russian race relations were no better than those in the South. If that could be done successfully, then much of the Soviet Union's propaganda on racial inequality within the United States would surely be rendered meaningless. An article published in the *New York Times* on June 5, 1963, by the journalist Cyrus L. Sulzberger, was read into the *Congressional Record* later that month with some glee, as it highlighted the inequitable racial position within the Soviet sphere. According to Sulzberger, the Sino-Soviet split that had begun to emerge at the Bandung Conference in 1955 led the Chinese government into a series of pronouncements designed to embarrass the Soviet government on *its* racial record. This was music to southern ears. To the Soviet Union's "acute embarrassment," wrote Sulzberger, "the Chinese cleverly report US Negro discontent and unsavory incidents of violence—to Soviet disadvantage. Pieping [the Chinese capital] takes pains to remind its propaganda clientele that the USSR is predominately 'white' and, by inference, in no position to preach theory to 'colored' lands." The Soviets, concluded Sulzberger, were every bit as guilty of racism toward the non-Europeans within their borders as southern segregationists were against African Americans. Although racism in the USSR was "officially taboo," it had "never been erased."[23] Drew L. Smith, a member of the Louisiana Bar, seized on the opportunity of portraying Soviet race relations as being as flawed as those of the South. In an article entitled "Russia, Communism, and Race," Smith drew his readers' attention to the presence of some 168 million Slavs within the Soviet Union, as well as 18 million "native people of Turco-Tatar stock who are dark or yellow-skinned with a distinct oriental appearance," and a handful of Africans living in the Abkahazian Republic. The treatment of all such groups, concluded Smith, served as a vivid reminder that "the

Russians do not in practice grant racial equality to non-Russian peoples in the Soviet Union." In order to back up his position, Smith picked his source material for maximum effect, quoting a report made by none other than Supreme Court Justice William O. Douglas—one of those political figures, in the mind of the white South, who was personally responsible for desegregation. Smith quoted remarks that were attributed to Douglas in one of the Library of Congress's publications, a brochure entitled "The Soviet Empire: The Prison House of Nations and Races."[24] During a visit by Douglas to the Soviet Union, the brochure reported, Douglas "found the public school system segregated and that they were being operated to favor the Russians and to the disadvantage of the natives."[25] Segregation, Smith was at pains to suggest, was not a singularly southern problem.

Homogeneity among massive resisters must not be taken for granted, however. Even within the segregationist South, there were voices that urged caution, with the growing awareness that massive resistance itself could be perceived as poor Cold War propaganda. That, in turn, would effectively hand another weapon over to the desegregationist cause. In September 1957, for example, the *Durham Morning Herald* published an editorial that was scathing in its assessment of the ongoing racial crisis at Little Rock. "A small group of people," it maintained, "and they the worst, are responsible for the disorders that have attended desegregation of some Southern schools recently. . . . What has the violence and the uproars of recent days accomplished to offset the damage done to the good name of the US abroad?" it asked, before concluding that "rabid segregationists ought to ponder that question."[26] Less sympathetic was an editorial in the *Richmond News Leader* dealing with the new wave of sit-in demonstrations that began in early 1960. This was trespass, thought the *News Leader*, and was in brazen defiance of property rights. Nevertheless, it urged a certain amount of caution. "Last week's Communist *Worker* devoted two full pages to a report from Richmond, in which correspondents exulted in heightened tensions and gleefully exhorted the Negroes to further provocations. The Communists live on friction and thrive on divisiveness," the paper concluded, for "this sort of thing is their meat."[27] Clearly, there was a balance to be struck between using the Cold War to bolster the segregationist cause and falling victim to the conflict's wider concerns.

If much of the Cold War rhetoric in massive resistance was based upon somewhat capricious claims of Soviet involvement in racial disturbances, and equally ephemeral attempts to pin down a clear-cut subversive enemy, the deployment of troops in Clinton, Tennessee, in September 1956, in Sturgis and Clay in Kentucky in the same year, in Little Rock in 1957, and in the Deep South on a number of separate occasions in the 1960s gave resisters a less nebulous target. The use of troops proved to be pivotal to massive resistance, for, although Eisenhower vacillated and procrastinated over the deployment of federal forces in Little Rock, when they were eventually sent in, it signaled that the administration was willing to back up federal desegregation decisions with military might. The irony of deploying U.S. forces internally, however, while Soviet forces remained at large externally, was not lost on the supporters of massive resistance. One irate Texan, for example, noted in a telegram dispatched to all southern governors that "Kennedy calls out troops for Mississippi, [and] builds political prestige in Harlem while Russia builds naval bases in Cuba." Another complained that he could not explain to his son "why no troops have been sent to Cuba (not even token air support at the Bay of Pigs) and yet an army invaded Mississippi."[28] As a satirical segregationist advertisement for the "National Association for Agitation of Colored People" put it, "Join the NAACP and 'Boss' the Country—Join the Army and See the South!"[29]

Segregationists were further aggravated by the knowledge that, in the midst of Cold War tensions in the late 1950s, U.S. troops were secretly and specifically being trained not for confronting the Russians but for confronting racial protesters in the South. A prosegregation resident of Bessemer City, North Carolina, wanted to avoid having to struggle with his own sons face to face in any ensuing conflict over desegregation. "Please don't force me to fight our three sons in army, marine and air corps," he wrote beseechingly in February 1956, upon hearing of Estes Kefauver's threat to use troops to enforce *Brown*. News of the deployment of Russian troops in Hungary, in November 1956, to put down student- and worker-led anti-Soviet demonstrations provided too awkward a similarity with the potential deployment of troops to quell racial disturbances in southern states. E. P. Shuford, from Martinsville, Virginia, wrote to Eisenhower, saying: "[you] condemn Russia for going into Hungary. Now you go into Little Rock. Don't ever criticize Russia any more."[30]

Sensing an opportunity for reclaiming at least some of the moral high ground in the desegregation struggle, southern politicians strove to make as much political capital as possible out of the troops issue, especially after Eisenhower's deployment of the 101st Airborne at Little Rock. In a speech given in October 1957, Senator Harry Flood Byrd of Virginia sought to use the troops issue to resisters' advantage. He reported that he had heard from a constituent who had just received a letter from her husband, a member of the armed forces. Her husband had reported: "This afternoon I was on a raiding party (aggressor). We had to harass them and see if they could repel us. Our only weapons were rocks, yes, *rocks*." Byrd was outraged. "When the international crisis is what it is," he thundered, "and Russia has shown superiority in missile development, to train troops to stop rioting appears so ridiculous that I can hardly believe what I see and hear. We can be certain," he concluded, "that troops so trained can accomplish little against the brutality of those who may threaten us." When Byrd demanded more information on the subject from the secretary of the army, he was told that such information "would be incompatible with the public interest."[31] The Mississippi judge Tom P. Brady, whose "Black Monday" address has been dubbed "the inspiration and first handbook of the [Citizens'] Council movement," was also scathing about the deployment of troops in Little Rock. In a speech entitled "The Red Death," which he gave at a number of different venues throughout 1957, Brady berated Eisenhower. "The advice which he took and the deed which he committed in sending armed troops in to Little Rock to bludgeon and bayonet helpless citizens was in fact a lethal dagger which has been plunged into the heart of the Republican party," he said. "No longer can it maintain that it is the conservative, constitutional party of America. There is no such party. Its titular head in Little Rock," he concluded, "committed the very acts which it so loudly denounced that had taken place in Hungary. The grim Communist specter of a totalitarian government has at last placed its iron heel on the throat of a sovereign state."[32] It proved to be so popular a line of argument among segregationists that South Carolina's Strom Thurmond was still alluding to it in the summer of 1963, when he made great play of reading an account of the deployment of troops at Little Rock into the *Congressional Record*. Thurmond theatrically withheld the identity of the account's author from his audience, quoting: "The Federal Government has the power and the duty to use troops and whatever other constitutional means are available to enforce the law of the land." The use of the word "constitutional" in such a context, Thurmond believed, "might lead some to think a good American has said these words." With a final flourish, he revealed that the words "were uttered eighteen months before Little Rock's Federal troop intervention by Benjamin J. Davis, chairman of the Negro Commission of the US Communist Party."[33]

Southerners continued to accuse the federal government of Soviet-style totalitarianism during the 1960s. "Certainly," wrote one southerner in response to the planned armed escort of Freedom Riders in 1961, "it would take great gall and hypocracy [*sic*] for anyone to criticize the despicable actions of Castro, Hitler and Khrushchev in subduing their people and not give equal attention to our own at the present time."[34]

Again, though, there is less symmetry in the ways in which segregationists responded to the troops issue than might be expected, as opposition to the use of troops did not unite the white South. Certainly, many wanted to know why precious military resources were being squandered. True to the isolationist traditions of the region, however, other white southerners felt that it was the Cold War that was squandering those resources and not internal disturbances, and that more troops should be used to quell internal subversion at the expense of foreign entanglements. How could the United States justify spending "over 40 billion dollars on defense to oppose communism abroad, when we are, step by step, imposing the declared program of the communists at home?" asked one Virginian. President Kennedy, said one Savannah resident, "uses our money to fight Communism abroad. Why doesn't he take that money and fight it here in the US?" Likewise, the use of troops at Ole Miss to ensure James Meredith's enrollment in 1962 "cost the government 4¼ million dollars," according to one Texan. "Why doesn't Bobby use soldiers to put Communists in jail?" he wondered.[35]

The Cold War, then, offered massive resisters a number of new strategies, as well as adding a number of new concerns. More than anything, perhaps, it was adaptable, providing as much ammunition against the *Brown* decision in 1954 as it did against the use of troops in Little Rock in 1957, or the armed escort of the Freedom Riders four years later. Equally important was the central role it played in rejuvenating some of the more established weapons in the South's existing resistance arsenal. In seeking to stave off desegregation, resisters put forward a complex web of arguments and counterarguments for perpetuating racial inequality, the vast majority of which had been used by the South for well over a century. While wider attitudes toward explicit racism had changed over time, however, the vast majority of the defenses of the southern segregationist position had not altered since the Civil War, and as a consequence some of the most trusted weapons in the southern armory were beginning to look decidedly weary by the 1950s. The new vocabulary of the Cold War, coupled with a shared willingness by segregationists to adapt to their surroundings, proved to be a revitalizing force for many of the more traditional forms of southern defiance.

The ideology of anticommunism that drove the United States' foreign policy in the Cold War era had also long been used by some southern segregationists in the domestic arena. Indeed, anticommunism and redbaiting had become established parts of the South's defensive canon, in a tradition of protecting white supremacy that stretched back almost a century. Writing in 1850, for example, the plantation owner George Fitzhugh attacked any form of government that advocated "free competition" over and above what he saw as the "feudal" systems of the Old South. The egalitarian philosophy put forward by communists in France, he wrote, was always bound to fail, for government was God's work, and any attempt "to establish government on purely theoretical abstract speculation, regardless of circumstance and experience, has always failed." Communists would also fail in their attempts to obtain egalitarian brotherhood, Fitzhugh believed, in a society built upon a hierarchical understanding of the races.[36] Efforts by the nascent Communist Party of the United States (CPUSA) to court African American members in the interwar years only served to solidify a link in many segregationists' minds between communist subversion and enforced racial equality.[37]

Even before the concerns of the Cold War had begun to saturate the South, a significant number of segregationists had built upon the former Confederacy's traditions of antiradicalism, its distrust of outsiders, and its suspicions of the CPUSA to taint as "subversive" or "communist" any individual or organization who threatened the region's conservative social structure and entrenched racial mores. The consensus of foreign policy anticommunism ushered in by the Cold War merely confirmed that, if resisters chose to redbait their foes in the domestic sphere, they would be doing so in a broadly supportive climate. With that in mind, many of the region's white supremacists did, indeed, decide to press their claims that civil rights activists were part of an orchestrated, communist plot. Such attacks were not simply the reflexive, blanket response to civil rights protests that many have assumed, however. Anticommunism may have been used in the first instance to attack proponents of racial change, but that was not its sole purpose. In the aftermath of racially motivated violence or civic unrest in the South, anticommunism also offered more astute segregationists the opportunity to deflect culpability away from their own actions and instead lay the blame for those disturbances on often ill-defined, "subversive" outside forces. In the years following the integration of Central High School in Little Rock, for example, many of Arkansas's politicians attempted to absolve themselves from any responsibility for the violent, mob-led upheavals that greeted the first batch of black students to enroll at Central High. "It was back in the 1920's that Communists began telling Negroes about plans to take over the southern part of the United States," noted the Arkansas congressman Dale Alford in February 1959, as well as the plan to "secede from the rest of our country, and establish a 'black Soviet.' Fantastic?" he asked rhetorically. "Yes, but not fantasy. This is a well-established fact, documented by the official Communist press."[38] It was not native Arkansans' actions that had necessitated the deployment of federal forces, Alford was insinuating, but communist-backed insurgents.

For the majority of resisters, the Cold War climate added legitimacy to anticommunism, especially when it was harnessed in concert with broader attempts to portray civil rights protestors as subversives. Indeed, Alford, Thurmond, and others, such as Senator James O. Eastland of Mississippi, redbaited civil rights advocates almost at will. Virginia's William Munford Tuck, for instance, a former governor and a massive resistance–era congressman, remained committed to the tactic more than a decade after *Brown*. In the autumn of 1965, sensing the impending failure of his cause, Tuck was desperate to rally support for one last stand, and was still seeking to do so by drawing attention to the un-American—and therefore tacitly "pro-Soviet"—nature of civil rights activity. "Any and all of these menacing so-called Civil Rights groups," he told one correspondent, are "lawless and un-American," and it was those groups who were responsible for the recent "national turmoil and strife, and for much of the bloodshed which has gone on in America in the last months and years."[39] It should be stressed, though, that, while anticommunism continued to be deployed by a majority of the region's white supremacists, it was never adopted wholesale. A consensus of anticommunism in international affairs did continue unabated throughout the massive resistance years, but, for a number of reasons, its appeal began to diminish in the domestic arena. Southerners had always remained somewhat distrustful of its most high-profile proponent, the Wisconsin senator Joseph "Tail Gunner Joe" McCarthy, not least because of his Republicanism and Catholicism. McCarthy relaunched his floundering political career on Lincoln Day in 1950 in Wheeling, West Virginia, with claims of subversion in the federal government. In the next four years, however, his reckless approach to anticommunism, his choice of increasingly high-profile targets, his bullying of defendants, and the paucity of hard evidence with which he attempted to back up his claims proved unsustainable. When he decided to take on "subversives" in the U.S. army in 1954, his anticommunist crusade finally unraveled; he was censured by Congress, and he descended into political oblivion as quickly as he had risen. His decline created more uncertainty about his methods in the minds of the South's more discerning resisters. Eastland was still able to bring his anticommunist Senate Internal Security Subcommittee road show to the South in the years following McCarthy's fall, but by that time, the luster of domestic anticommunism had begun to dim, and the size of the audience that was willing to take segregationists' anticommunist charges at face value was diminishing. A sizeable minority of resisters, while remaining committed to white supremacy, proved increasingly reluctant to use domestic anticommunism as a means of maintaining that supremacy in the South. By the late 1950s, regardless of the Cold War climate, the decision of whether or not to redbait was often a very personal one, and was by no means automatic.[40]

Whilst Woods's analysis of anticommunism in the South has carefully mapped out the role of state investigative and redbaiting committees in the region, such as that commanded by Eastland, his concentration on Cold War–inspired anticommunism is so disciplined that it neglects to take into account the other aspects of massive resistance that were affected by the concerns of the global conflict.[41] Although it was the most obvious beneficiary of Cold War concerns, anticommunism was not the only southern resistance measure to be transformed. Perhaps the best example of the adaptability of resistance rhetoric in this context is provided by a weapon that had given the southern cause longer service than even anticommunism: states' rights. Judge William "Wild Billy" Old, a staunch segregationist who reportedly owned a Zippo lighter with a Confederate flag on the front that played "Dixie" when opened, had in 1956 urged the South to embark upon the ultimate course of states' rights action: interposition.[42] Although several former Confederate states formally passed interposition resolutions, Old's attempts to save the South from federal interference by championing their sovereign rights proved makeshift, lightweight, and, in the final reckoning, legally untenable. Instead, it was left to the new language of the Cold War to provide the means of reinvigorating states' rights, as what had been a pivotal argument in the southern case against northern invasion became an argument to resist—or at least to retard—Soviet infiltration. "Our whole constitutional republican form of government is based on the principle that the States reserve unto themselves all rights not specifically delegated to the Federal Government," proclaimed the Defenders of States Rights and Individual Liberty, a quasi–Citizens' Council organization, in a radio broadcast of 1957. Outlining the traditional rationale behind the South's adherence to such arguments, the broadcast continued: "Our founding fathers realized . . . that this was the only protection the people could have . . . from all-powerful centralized bureaucracy." Adding the new Cold War ingredients, it concluded: "It is much easier for those who would overthrow our form of government to subvert and infiltrate centralized government than it is to go into forty-eight separate states and do the same thing." States' rights, more than simply saving the South from desegregation, would save the nation from Soviet invasion.[43] As the Virginia senator A. Willis Robertson made clear to the Richmond Bar Association, "the present plan of the Communists is to break down the rights of states because they know that no dictatorship can be created in this country as long as we have 48 independent states."[44]

The renovation of states' rights, and its emergence as a weapon fueled by Cold War anxieties, was paralleled by other traditional arguments of the white South. Those who promoted miscegenation—dubbed "Mixiecrats" by one Alabama resister in 1957—were also recast in the light of the Cold War climate as agents of the Soviet Union.[45] In many ways, rebranding miscegenation as a Cold War issue was more obvious a move than doing so for states' rights, given the CPUSA's long and often vocal advocacy of racial and social equality. The perceived perils of miscegenation were clearly enunciated in a sermon by the segregationist preacher W. D. Moody in November 1957. Speaking only weeks after the Soviet Union had launched Sputnik, Moody laid the blame for America's apparent sluggishness in the space race on two separate, yet related, issues: interracial breeding, which he claimed lowered the intelligence of American citizens; and the country's preoccupation with internal racial matters. The "brain power of America was gone," claimed Moody, before wondering rhetorically when "the Russians shot thire [sic] First Sputnik, what was the brain power of America doing?" Waging war on "God's Little Children" by imposing the decision of nine men in Washington.[46] In a similar vein, the Defenders of

State Sovereignty followed up their states' rights radio bulletin with one on the perils of miscegenation—the obvious result, in Defenders' minds, of school desegregation. Moreover, it was a result that, in one hazily defined way or other, was linked to Soviet plans for world domination. The broadcast argued that the racial makeup of the United States was inherently different from that of other slave societies in South and Central America because, unlike former Spanish and Portuguese colonies, the "founders of the future United States maintained their practice of non-amalgamation rigorously, with only slight racial blendings along the fringes of each group." The promotion of racial separation was, therefore, an integral part of the makeup of U.S. society. As a result, it was "nonsense to say that racial discrimination . . . is 'Un-American.'" The continued separation of the races, it was argued, was, in the broader picture, an assertion of pure Americanism, not to be diluted by Soviet-style policies of race-mixing.[47]

In many ways, then, the Cold War impacted on massive resistance as forcefully as massive resistance impacted on the Cold War. Segregationists were well aware of its presence, even if some refused to bow to its strictures. Perhaps surprisingly, many more demonstrated a pragmatic flexibility by adapting themselves to the opportunities that the global conflict offered them. In the main, the Cold War both rejuvenated long-used defenses of the southern position, and offered the region a range of rhetorical and intellectual weapons that had been unavailable before hostilities between East and West had begun to crystallize. The Soviet Union's use of troops to brutally repress an uprising in Hungary, barely a year before U.S. troops were dispatched to Little Rock, proved too good an opportunity for many segregationists to resist. Likewise, widespread claims that Soviet schooling denied equal rights to Russia's own ethnic groups were seized upon as offering extenuating circumstances for the South's ongoing racism. Even more significantly, the Cold War at the very least offered southerners the opportunity to discuss the increasingly thorny issue of segregation in new, masked ways. If the ills of southern race relations could be blamed upon Cold War Soviet agitators, the entire struggle to uphold segregation could be revised as a battle to defeat the nation's Cold War foe. That, too, was important: the South's foe was then a determinedly national one, and the region's problems, subsequently, were no longer peculiarly regional. The fact that not all southern segregationists chose to use these new, Cold War–inspired defenses, however, is an ongoing testament to the lack of homogeneity among resistance forces, and to the often very individual ways in which the majority of white southerners collectively sought to maintain their segregated way of life. If, as one recent history has suggested, the evolving civil rights movement, and the changes that it wrought, "cannot be understood apart from the international context of the Cold War," then neither, most emphatically, can the concerted white supremacist opposition to that change, which coalesced as massive resistance.[48]

Notes

1. Leon Dure to James Jackson Kilpatrick, Jun. 20, 1961, box 1, James J. Kilpatrick Papers, Manuscripts Division, Special Collections Department, University of Virginia Library, Charlottesville.

2. For more on Dure's role, see James H. Hershman, Jr., "Massive Resistance Meets Its Match: The Emergence of a Pro–Public School Majority," in *The Moderates' Dilemma: Massive Resistance to School Desegregation in Virginia*, ed. Matthew D. Lassiter and Andrew B. Lewis (Charlottesville: University Press of Virginia, 1998), 104–33. See esp. 127–30.

3. "What Is Your First Wish in 1959 for 1. Virginia 2. The Nation?" John Battle's reply to telegram from Associated Press to Battle and five former Virginia governors, Dec. 30, 1958, box 1, John S. Battle Gubernatorial Papers, Archives and Research Services, Library of Virginia, Richmond.

4. Agnew H. Bahnsen, Jr., Bahnsen Company (Air Con) Winston-Salem, to Grady Allred, K&W Cafeterias, Winston-Salem, Sept. 19, 1963, box 346, Terry Sanford Gubernatorial Papers, State of North Carolina Department of Cultural Resources, Division of Archives and History, Raleigh.

5. Mary Dudziak has analyzed the ways in which the constraints of the Cold War, and the need of the United States to appeal to nonwhite citizens in nascent postcolonial states, led a succession of presidential administrations to try to curb the worst excesses of racism within the United States in general, and below the Mason-Dixon Line in particular. Azza Salama Layton has sought to link American civil rights activity not to the domestic policies of federal governments but to their foreign policies. Mary Dudziak, *Cold War Civil Rights: Race and the Image of American Democracy* (Princeton: Princeton University Press, 2000); Azza Salama Layton, *International Politics and Civil Rights Policies in the United States, 1941–1960* (Cambridge: Cambridge University Press, 2000).

6. Thomas Borstelmann, *The Cold War and the Color Line: American Race Relations in the Global Arena* (Cambridge, Mass.: Harvard University Press, 2001); quotation, ix.

7. Jeff Woods, *Black Struggle Red Scare: Segregation and Anti-Communism in the South, 1948–1968* (Baton Rouge: Louisiana State University Press, 2004). On Woods's definition of southern nationalism, see especially 1–5. On the subject of political elitism, Woods sees the southern Red Scare as being driven by an "interlocking network of local, state, and federal institutions."

8. See especially Mary L. Dudziak, "Desegregation as a Cold War Imperative," *Stanford Law Review* 41 (Nov. 1988): 61–120.

9. Such was the pace of the independence movement that, in 1960 alone, independence was granted to Zaire, Somali, Dahomey, Upper Volta, Ivory Coast, Chad, Congo Brazzaville, Gabon, Senegal, Mali, and Nigeria. In 1961, Sierra Leone and Tanzania became independent, in 1962 Jamaica, Trinidad and Tobago, and Uganda, in 1963 Kenya, and in 1964, Malawi and Zambia.

10. Harry Emerson Fosdick to Charles J. Williams, May 21, 1954, box 110, Thomas B. Stanley Gubernatorial Papers, Archives and Research Services, Library of Virginia, Richmond.

11. Harry F. Byrd, "Bits and Pieces," typescript, box 1, Harry Byrd, Sr., Papers, Manuscripts Division, Special Collections Department, University of Virginia Library, Charlottesville. For Talmadge's outraged reaction, see Herman E. Talmadge, *You and Segregation* (Birmingham, Ala.: Vulcan Press, 1955), esp. vi–viii.

12. Clifford Dowdey, "A Southerner Looks at the Supreme Court . . . But the Klan Will Not Ride Again," *Saturday Review*, Oct. 9, 1954, 9–11, 35–38; quotation, 9.

13. Harry H. Roberts to Battle, Jun. 2, 1954, box 100, Stanley Papers.

14. J. W. Seabrook to Thomas Pearsall, Dec. 21, 1954, box 1, Thomas Jenkins Pearsall Papers, Southern Historical Collection, Wilson Library, University of North Carolina at Chapel Hill.

15. Jane Revill to William B. Umstead, Jun. 24, 1954, box 58.2, William B. Umstead Gubernatorial Papers, State of North Carolina Department of Cultural Resources, Division of Archives and History, Raleigh.

16. Thomas F. Walker to Stanley, Jun. 11, 1954, box 100, Stanley Papers.

17. *Congressional Record*, Jan. 14, 1958, A220.

18. "East German Reds Hop Bandwagon of Agitators Riding Lucy Coattails," *Dixie-American*, Mar. 4, 1956, 7.

19. *Congressional Record*, Jun. 8, 1961, 9918–19.

20. S. J. Thompson, "Segregation of the Races," Aug. 19, 1954, box 102, Stanley Papers.

21. Nell Battle Lewis to Luther Hodges, Apr. 2, 1955, box 41.1, Luther H. Hodges Gubernatorial Papers, State of North Carolina Department of Cultural Resources, Division of Archives and History, Raleigh.

22. Robert Dupree to Luther Hodges, Aug. 19, 1960, Hodges Papers, box 522.

23. *Congressional Record*, Jun. 24, 1963, 11435.

24. *The Soviet Empire: Prison House of Nations and Races; A Study in Genocide, Discrimination, and Abuse of Power. Prepared, at the Request of the Subcommittee to Investigate the Administration of the Internal Security Act and other Internal Security Laws of the Committee on the Judiciary, United States Senate, Eighty-fifth Congress, Second Session* (Washington, D.C.: U.S. Government Printing Office, 1958).

25. "*Russia, Communism, and Race*, by Drew L. Smith, Member of the Louisiana Bar, New Orleans, Distributed by Federation for Constitutional Government, LaSalle Street, New Orleans," box 4, Virginia Commission on Constitutional Government Papers, State of North Carolina Department of Cultural Resources, Division of Archives and History, Raleigh.

26. Editorial, *Durham Morning Herald*, Sept. 19, 1957.

27. Editorial, *Richmond News Leader*, Mar. 9, 1960.

28. Philip Braubach telegram, Sept. 29, 1962, and S. H. Conger to Sanford, Oct. 2, 1962, both in box 232, Sanford Papers.

29. "Membership Application for NAACP: Better Known as National Association for Agitation of Colored People or National Association for Advancement of Communist Party," flyer, box 16, Guy Benton Johnson Papers, Southern Historical Collection, Wilson Library, University of North Carolina at Chapel Hill.

30. H. V. Carver to Sam Ervin, Feb. 15, 1956, folder 1119, Sam Ervin Papers, Southern Historical Collection, Wilson Library, University of North Carolina at Chapel Hill;

E. P. Shuford to Eisenhower, copied to Thomas Stanley, Sept. 26, 1957, box 107, Stanley Papers.

31. "Speech by Senator Harry Flood Byrd (D.Va.) Henrico County Democratic Banquet, October 11, 1957, Richmond, Virginia," typescript; reply from Secretary of the Army, both in box 4, Byrd Papers.

32. Neil R. McMillen, *The Citizens' Council: Organized Resistance to the Second Reconstruction, 1954–64* (Urbana: University of Illinois Press, 1994), 17. "The Red Death, A Complete Address in Sacramento, California by Judge Tom P. Brady of Mississippi in 1957," typescript, folder 4028, William Munford Tuck Papers, Manuscript and Rare Books Department, Earl Gregg Swem Library, College of William and Mary, Williamsburg.

33. *Congressional Record*, Aug. 7, 1963, 13662.

34. Fran Harris to Sam Ervin, May 21, 1961, folder 2512, Ervin Papers.

35. Landon B. Lane to Bill Tuck, May 5, 1959, folder 4068, Tuck Papers; David Humphrey to Terry Sanford, Sept. 3, 1961, box 111, Sanford Papers; G. C. Inge to Terry Sanford, Jan. 21, 1963, box 374, Sanford Papers.

36. George Fitzhugh, "Sociology for the South," in *Slavery Defended: The Views of the Old South*, ed. Eric L. McKitrick (Englewood Cliffs, N.J.: Prentice-Hall, 1963), 34–50.

37. In 1924, for example, only five years after its inception, the CPUSA had proclaimed that "the Negro workers of this country are exploited and oppressed more ruthlessly than any other group." At its Sixth Congress in 1928, the Comintern publicly recognized the South's African Americans as an oppressed group and proclaimed that they had the right to secession within the United States. The CPUSA then formulated twelve demands for ending black oppression, including a demand for the "abolition of the whole system of race discrimination. Full racial, political and social equality for the Negro race." Harvey Klehr, *The Heyday of American Communism: The Depression Decade* (New York: Basic Books, 1984), 324.

38. *Congressional Record*, Feb. 17, 1959, 2545.

39. William Tuck to Albert Tatum, Sept. 28, 1965, folder 4343, Tuck Papers.

40. For more on those segregationists who refrained from redbaiting, including Virginia's David Mays, North Carolina's Wesley Critz George, and, to a certain extent, Arkansas's J. William Fulbright, see George Lewis, *The White South and the Red Menace: Segregationists, Anticommunism and Massive Resistance, 1945–1965* (Gainesville: University Press of Florida, 2004).

41. Woods, *Black Struggle Red Scare*.

42. Earle Dunford, *Richmond Times-Dispatch: The Story of a Newspaper* (Richmond, Va.: Cadmus, 1995), 365. First formulated in the Kentucky-Virginia resolutions of 1798, interposition held that the legislatures of individual sovereign states could intercede to protect their own citizens, if the federal government overstepped its authority.

43. "Defenders of State Sovereignty and Individual Liberties Broadcast no. 16: Could the Integration Decree be a Blessing in Disguise?" typescript, box 21, Sarah Patton Boyle Papers, Manuscripts Division, Special Collections Department, University of Virginia Library, Charlottesville.

44. Robertson quoted in *Times-Dispatch*, Nov. 26, 1957, 6.

45. R. M. Harper to Wesley Critz George, Dec. 6, 1957, box 6, Wesley Critz George Papers, Southern Historical Collection, Wilson Library, University of North Carolina at Chapel Hill.

46. W. D. Moody to Thomas Stanley, Nov. 22, 1957, box 107, Stanley Papers.

47. "Defenders of State Sovereignty and Individual Liberties Broadcast no. 17: Mixes Blood [*sic*] and Mixed Schools," typescript, box 21, Boyle Papers.

48. Borstelmann has written: "The far-reaching changes that swept through the American South in the second half of the twentieth century cannot be understood apart from the international context of the Cold War. The evolving civil rights movement fit into the larger story of decolonization and the Cold War struggle over world leadership and the meaning of 'freedom'"; *Cold War and the Color Line*, 270.

SEVEN

Disunity and Religious Institutions in the White South

David L. Chappell

Just how massive was "massive resistance"? Comparison of the civil rights struggle to well-known freedom movements elsewhere affords some perspective. According to the Southern Poverty Law Center's tally—embodied in Maya Lin's great marble monument in Montgomery—forty people were killed in civil rights–related violence in the South in the 1950s and 1960s. The apartheid regime in South Africa beat that figure in a single day, killing sixty-seven people at Sharpeville in 1960. More recently, Chinese authorities killed over 2,500 dissidents in the immediate aftermath of Tiananmen Square. Closer to home, it took over six hundred deaths on the battlefields of the American Civil War to abolish slavery.

It was a moral outrage that even one person was killed defending his constitutional rights in the 1950s–1960s. Still, it would seem that, by worldwide historical standards, violent resistance to freedom movements tends normally to be more comprehensive and peremptory than was the case with the movement for desegregation and reenfranchisement in the American South in those years. This is not to minify the terrorism in the white South—or the terrorism's psychological and political effects, which, as the historian Dan Carter and others have rightly noted, extended the direct damage. But it is important to see not simply how racist or opportunistic or destructive segregationism was—it was all those things—but also the ways in which it failed. It failed to inspire the sort of support that white southerners mustered one hundred years earlier, or that white South Africans mustered at the same moment across the ocean.

The most efficient way to get at the inability—or the unwillingness—of modern white southerners to fight on the scale or with the intensity of their ancestors or their contemporaries in South Africa, I think, is to compare the white South's political leaders to its religious leaders. The religious leaders of the white South did not live up to the expectations generated by their elected political leaders. This says something about the cultural depth and pervasiveness of the white South's commitment to the defense of segregation, and sharpens suspicions that a considerable amount of segregationist politics was opportunistic bluff and posturing.

The elected leaders were overwhelmingly segregationist—all but three of the South's U.S. senators signed the Southern Manifesto of 1956, which pledged them all to do their best to nullify the Supreme Court's *Brown* decision (the three who did not sign were from the periphery of the South, Tennessee and Texas). In every major Deep South election in which segregation was an issue over the next ten years, the segregationist candidate won.[1]

But religious leaders did not go that way. In 1954, the two Protestant denominations that still maintained a pure southern identity overwhelmingly passed resolutions supporting desegregation. In the Southern Baptist Convention (SBC), the vote was about nine thousand to fifty: this sounds like the proportion of the white southerners who supported segregation, but in the SBC that was the vote supporting desegregation. In the southern Presbyterian church (the Presbyterian Church in the U.S., or PCUS, as opposed to the North's PCUSA), the vote supporting desegregation was 239 to 169, or about three to two. At the start of the struggle, the white South's religious leaders appear to have been diametrically opposed to its political leaders.

Of course, there was strong opposition to these positions within the southern churches. There were celebrated cases of moderate or integrationist ministers being expelled from their pulpits.[2] That is part of a strong backlash that most scholars of southern religion have detected in the churches.[3] Nobody seems to have any idea how many such expulsions occurred, though it is doubtful that the numbers were high. Then again, the issue is not raw numbers but the symbolic, "chilling" effect of expulsions on other would-be moderates, religious and secular.

It is possible to get a reasonably reliable count of instances of another form of backlash. In the SBC papers, there are what at first appear to be a significant number of resolutions from churches that express dissent from the integrationist policies of their regional denominational policies. (In the PCUS papers, there are a much smaller number of such resolutions, only a handful.) The SBC numbers are, by my count, as follows. Eight SBC congregations sent resolutions withdrawing financial contributions to the SBC in reaction to its pro-*Brown* resolution. An additional nineteen SBC congregations either threatened to withdraw or requested that their contributions be earmarked for nonintegrationist activity. Finally, an additional forty-eight SBC congregations, without any threat or concrete action, protested the SBC's integrationist position. There were 31,297 churches in the SBC in 1957: all the segregationist resolutions sent by churches add up to about a quarter of 1 percent of the total.[4]

It is possible (though doubtful) that a significant number of similar resolutions were discarded or lost. But even if the number were doubled or quadrupled, it would appear that the resistance of southern churches to public school desegregation was far from massive.

There were efforts to change this situation. Segregationists were able to find a few ministers willing to take a public stance for segregation. Yet even those few ministers who tried to lend clerical authority and respectability to the cause were not very strong. The most widely published and often-cited segregationist preacher was the Rev. G. T. Gillespie of Jackson, Mississippi, who was known for a single speech in 1957. (He died in 1958.) Other segregationists, including Billy James Hargis, the famous right-wing crusader from Tulsa, borrowed almost all their biblical arguments about segregation from Gillespie.[5]

In his speech, Gillespie said:

> While the Bible contains no clear mandate for or against segregation as between the white and negro races, it does furnish considerable data from which valid inferences may be drawn in support of the general principle of segregation as an important feature of the Divine purpose and Providence throughout the ages.

As was the case with other segregationist ministers, Gillespie was particularly hesitant when speaking about the Bible, giving the whole speech a tentative tone. He was hedging segregationists' bets, not exhorting them with a vigorous call to arms.

The most decisive statement Gillespie made in his entire speech was: "Concerning matters of this kind, which in the inscrutable wisdom of God have been left for mankind to work out in the light of reason and experience without the full light of revelation, we dare not be dogmatic."[6] Similarly, Rev. Edward B. Guerry, an Episcopal priest of Charleston, South Carolina, wrote in a segregationist collection of essays, "we should endeavor to respect the sincere convictions of those who disagree with us. No one can assume for himself an attitude of infallibility on a matter so complex as this racial question."[7] Other than such careful, respectable, and unassailable statements, segregationist publications rarely gave space to clergymen or to religious arguments.

It is important that Gillespie and Guerry—and almost all the literate ministers who joined the segregationist cause—did not base their case extensively on the Bible.[8] There was occasional lip service to the biblical story of the Curse of Ham, the Tower of Babel story, and the passage from Acts 17 where God set "the bounds of habitation" for the nations of men. These references appear in angry letters in various archival collections but usually from laypeople, not clergy. Seg-regationists do not seem to have had much confidence in these biblical or theo-logical arguments and did not use them much. The most famous segregationist preacher, Rev. Wallie Amos Criswell of Dallas, Texas, in his much-reprinted segregationist speech to the South Carolina legislature, referred to the Bible only once, in making a warmup joke that had nothing to do with segregation. That speech, the only segregationist statement Criswell is known to have made, suggests that his commitment to the cause was hardly deep or impassioned. A true believer would surely have repeated and developed his argument.

Nobody knows what Criswell might have thought privately or off the record. He and other preachers may have indulged in the sort of hocus-pocus that occasional letter-writers used to try to show that the Bible sanctioned seg-regation.[9] The Baptist historian Paul Harvey is also working on these questions, and he finds some evidence of a "folk" theology of biblically justified segrega-tion in at least a few scattered letters from laypeople; such a theology was only rarely echoed by ministers.

In his published speech, Criswell did not stoop to any claim that the Bible sanctioned segregation. By 1968, Criswell had repudiated segregationism alto-gether. That year he became president of the SBC, at which point he said that segregation had never been justified on the basis of the Bible.[10]

Segregation's biblical sanction was a matter of deep concern that should not be underestimated. The South was "the Bible Belt": inerrantist and literalist views ran high. The question of the biblical provenance of their traditions and taboos was, for many white southerners, a subject of great soul-searching. It was not simply propaganda.

Letters from Sunday-school teachers to the SBC's Sunday School Board seek guidance on the biblical perspective on segregation. Clifton Allen, the head of the board, answered much of this mail, treating it as an expression of sincere anguish on the part of moderates and would-be segregationists. He patiently spelled out how the Bible could not support segregation. Allen, like nearly all prominent officials of the SBC and PCUS, gained a reputation as a social liberal and was roundly denounced by segregationists.

But one of the most important conservatives in the white southern church was quite frank about the Bible, too. "Christians should recognize that there is no biblical or legal justification for segregation," said L. Nelson Bell, in a public forum run by *Life* magazine in October 1956. Bell was editor of the *Southern Presbyterian Journal*, the organ of Presbyterians who were trying to pull the PCUS to the right, socially and theologically. Bell was a segregationist: his pri-vate correspondence makes it clear he believed in white supremacy. Still, in public he consistently said: "It can be safely affirmed that segregation of the races by law is both unchristian and un-American."[11]

"By law" was the key phrase. Bell believed segregation was part of the natural order, that black as well as white people preferred to be separate. They would both maintain segregation, spontaneously and voluntarily, like oil and water, if Jim Crow laws were abolished. Bell's racism, he often implied, was stronger—more confident—than that of those who insecurely resorted to legal compulsion.

Bell was always struggling to hold on to his more frankly bigoted and militant allies, but the strain wore him down and wrecked at least three important friendships. One of those was with Rev. Arnette Gamble of Hollandale, Mississippi, who kept insisting in letters to Bell: "To think that segregation could or would be maintained without segregation laws, is to be quite unrealistic." Removal of laws would "inevitably result in miscegenation, . . . a development I believe God disapproves," Gamble said. Gamble hit upon the inadjudicable difference that split segregationist ranks everywhere. Whereas Bell had faith in voluntary segregation, Gamble said: "The people of Mississippi know" that racial barriers "can only be maintained by force."

Bell soon broke off relations with Gamble, his longtime partner in promoting social and theological conservatism. Bell said the effort to keep talking was futile, as Gamble had become just like other political fanatics, who were bad for conservatism. Bell made a note to himself at the end of Gamble's last letter to him, in 1962: "I did not answer his letter as he is much like [the extreme Fundamentalist] Carl McIntire—nothing I might write would please him."[12]

Bell, as a social and theological conservative, defined himself as part of the Evangelical (with a capital *E*) movement, which in the 1940s broke away from what Bell and other conservatives saw as the narrow and vindictive tribalism of Fundamentalists like McIntyre and Bob Jones, Sr. (Evangelicals, who ultimately gained great popularity—and the resentment of Fundamentalists—through the crusades of Billy Graham, were more ecumenical and tolerant of doctrinal differences than Fundamentalists. They were often biblical inerrantists, like Fundamentalists, but unlike Fundamentalists, they did not insist that all their followers toe the inerrantist line.) It would be dangerously narrow and exclusive, Bell thought, to try to go down a segregationist road—even if one confined one's strategic targets to the white South, which few Evangelicals were content to do. The breakdown of Bell's relationships with Gamble and other key supporters illustrates how hard it was for a segregationist like Bell to maintain religious leadership, how risky it increasingly was to speak on the matter.

The course most southern clergymen pursued was simply not to speak on the matter. Rather than try to defend segregation or particular versions of it, most segregationist churchmen cleaved to a safer, more moderate position, one that had a long and legitimate historical pedigree in their churches—which legal segregation, as a new, modern institution, did not. The segregationists' pleadings develop a common theme: opposition to social preaching. Gillespie's coconspirator at Bellhaven College, Morton Smith, ended his segregationist argument by quoting the Westminster Confession's injunctions against mixing religion and politics: "'Synods and Councils are to handle and conclude nothing, but that which is ecclesiastical, and are not to intermeddle with civil affairs which concern the commonwealth.'" Smith explained; "Jesus, our King, did not seek social reform, but salvation of sinners."[13]

This line of the Westminster Confession became a mantra for segregationist Presbyterians.[14] They could not get their denomination to reverse its prointegration proclamations. Their falling back on blanket opposition to all social preaching was a tacit concession that they could not win on the merits. (It was unconvincing in any case, in light of all they preached about drinking, divorce, and communism.) Most of them dared not argue the point on principle. They believed that if churches, even their own southern white churches, were politicized further, things would go badly for segregationism.

Related to this antipolitical line of segregationist ministers is the big surprise in all the material the segregationists left behind: the most prominent and vigorously asserted religious theme in white supremacist propaganda of the 1950s and early 1960s is not Noah's curse on Ham or the statements in Acts 17 about God's ordaining the "bounds of habitation" of the separate nations or even traditional American Protestant opposition to social preaching. It is, rather, anticlericalism.

A segregationist in Chattanooga, Tennessee, for example, denounced the PCUS's prointegration statement, saying:

> The sad part of this is that just as the rulings of the Supreme Court and their violations of the Constitution have made so many people lose respect for and confidence in the Courts—so the leaders in our churches are forcing many members to lose respect for and confidence in our churches and its leaders.[15]

The Mississippi congressman John Bell Williams sought help from the head of the Association of Citizens' Councils, William J. Simmons, in financing a new segregationist publishing venture, to be called the *American Christian.* Williams urged Simmons to help distribute such a magazine among church people, where, he said, it "might do much to offset the integrationists' propaganda they are hearing from the pulpits."[16] A segregationist publication called the *Christian Layman* lumped "white church women" together with southern preachers. This in an article titled "Is the South Being Betrayed by Its Ministers and White Church Women?" The article claimed: "Priests, ministers and white church women are *unquestionably* leaders in the struggle for southern deseg-regation."[17]

Religion turned out to be utterly disappointing to the segregation move-ment as a whole. William D. Workman, the author of the most dispassionate and well-documented segregationist book, said that in the face of pervasive pressure to desegregate, which was coming "with almost nauseating frequency" from clergymen, including southern white clergymen, "the Southerner feels a strain on his religion as well as on his temper."[18] Roy Harris, the Georgia power broker and publisher, and president of the Citizens' Councils of America, was more blunt. When the Methodist hierarchy dared to send his church a new minister who had signed a statement against closing schools to prevent inte-gration, Harris boasted, "I ain't been to church since."[19] The best-selling seg-regationist author Carleton Putnam addressed the southern white clergy with even sterner language: "You watch the federal government take forcibly from the South while you sit with your hands folded in prayer," Putnam said.

> I'm tired of the sort of combined ignorance and stupidity you have shown. I'm tired of your timid conformity with the popular drift. And finally, I'm tired of your milk and water suggestions that we pass the buck to God while you support a policy which forces the white children of the South against the wishes of their parents into associations they understand better than you do. [20]

Perhaps the ultimate anticlerical statement came from a supporter of the South Carolina senator Strom Thurmond who wrote the senator in 1955:

> By now it should be evident to the pro-segregation forces that their real opponent in the fight to provide for the preservation of the white race in America is the so-called christian religion. . . . It should also be evident that segregation in the U.S. is a lost cause unless the pro-seg-regation forces organize across state lines, po[o]l their knowledge and resources, and launch a frontal assault on organized religion.[21]

The effort to get the churches out of politics was a gambit, played by the laymen who led the segregationist cause. One of the most important conser-vative lay leaders in the country was the Texas billionaire J. Howard Pew of Sun Oil, a key figure in the broad secular conservatism that was percolating along with religious conservatism in the 1950s. Pew spoke to the Foundation of the Presbyterian Church in March 1958, emphasizing the apolitical mission of the church. Pew translated the Westminster Confession into a "Ban on Secular Affairs" (a subtitle of Pew's printed speech).[22] Pew envisioned (and helped to create) the national right-wing movement that eventually took over the Republican Party of George W. Bush and the country. Pew's main ally in the southern Presbyterian Church was L. Nelson Bell, the intellectual leader of the antimodern, antiliberal movement in that church. Though Bell believed in segregation, he did not want to stake his journal or his movement on its defense. He tried to adopt what he considered a reasonable conservative stance—one very close, incidentally, to that articulated by James J. Kilpatrick of the *Richmond News Leader*, probably the most influential segregationist intellectual in the country.

Bell agonized over his defense of strictly voluntary segregation, which alienated many fire-eaters. But it was worth losing friends and allies, because of an important factor that has been strangely ignored in the scholarship on the civil rights struggle. That factor was Bell's son-in-law, Billy Graham, the most popular, most influential white minister in the South, if not the world.

After some waffling, Graham took a very firm line after 1954 that he would never allow segregated seating in his crusades. Like Bell, Graham frankly and publicly said that segregation could not be justified biblically. *Ebony* magazine published an article about Graham in September 1957, praising him for his stance. The title was "No Color Line in Heaven: Billy Graham." That same year, Graham hosted Martin Luther King, who gave the opening prayer one evening in Graham's "crusade" at Madison Square Garden in New York. Graham praised King there for the "social revolution" he was leading.[23]

Graham frequently had to deal with segregationist baiting.[24] One of his admirers, though she had been thrilled at all Graham was doing to revive conservative Christianity, was shocked when she learned of Graham's statements and practices on race. "I think it is most unfortunate that Billy Graham has joined the liberals in the idea of intergration[.] He is definitely hurting his cause and his standing in the South."[25] Bell was Graham's mentor and publicity agent, and his papers reveal a great deal about the construction of Graham's public image.[26] Bell's answer to an irate segregationist conveys the flavor of many letters he wrote defending his son-in-law.

> Billy is anxious to preach the gospel to all who will hear, and in Charlotte there have been a few Negroes sprinkled through the auditorium and a few in the choir, but no one has said anything about it and it seems that a real Christian spirit has prevailed. As a matter of fact, quite a number of Negroes have made professions of faith there. When all is said and done, that is the one and final solution to our race and all other problems.[27]

U.S. News and World Report estimated that 20 percent of Graham's audience in New York was black.[28] Comparable estimates of his southern audiences are apparently not available, but there are a few photos in Graham's scrapbooks that show black faces among the crowds at his southern crusades.[29]

Despite his open integrationism, southern politicians accommodated Graham. Governor George Bell Timmerman of South Carolina protested against Graham's plans to speak on the lawn of the state capitol in October 1958.[30] Graham was supported by the pastor of the largest SBC church in Columbia. Timmerman reached a compromise whereby Graham preached to a nonsegregated crowd on a military base nearby. Governor Wallace of Alabama also allowed Graham to desegregate a huge public stadium in Montgomery in 1965, after the horrible clashes at Selma. Going along with Graham was a chance that segregationist politicians took, for it was more dangerous to oppose such a massively popular figure.

The SBC and PCUS were eager to jump on Billy Graham's bandwagon, seeing it as a modern-day Great Awakening. So was every local ministerial association in the South with which Graham's organization had contact. Graham preached an ecumenical conservative Protestantism from which churches in the South were eager to benefit. Graham's people coordinated their visits with local ministers. They, in turn, promoted Graham. Their pews and collection plates filled up long after Graham left.

There was one more kind of pressure that militated against segregationism in southern white churches. This came from missionaries abroad, especially in Africa. Missionaries wrote back to their home churches that racial discrimination, dramatized by violence at Little Rock and elsewhere—as reported in newspapers all over the world—was crippling American and especially southern missions (as well as the so-called home missions to Negroes in the U.S.). The missions were a huge investment of southern white churches, and a point of pride and honor. In 1956, the SBC had 248 missionaries in Africa alone, on a budget of two million dollars, and growing. In 1958, SBC had sixty staff members of its Home Mission Board devoted to "Negro Work," with a budget of $200,000.

The missions put the southern white churches, one might say, in precisely the same position that decolonization put the U.S. government: competing for the allegiance of the newly independent populations of Africa and Asia. Recent books by Mary Dudziak, Azza Layton, and others finally document the point that historians had always assumed about a Cold War motive behind the U.S. government's sudden switch to integrationism after World War II.[31] We need a book on the equivalent pressure from missionaries on southern white churches. Southern missionaries were competing not only with the Communist International but also with rival churches, especially Catholics. The SBC and PCUS officials both indulged in a bit of anti-Catholic bigotry in urging their parishioners to ease up on the black folks. They almost seem to be offering anti-Catholic feeling as compensation for giving up racism, as though to conform to some cosmic law of conservation of bigotry.[32]

Segregationists could not live by politics alone. Especially in an age of political demagoguery—which was widely ridiculed and satirized, then as now, in the South as well as the North—they needed more than elected officials to fulminate about their alleged rights and traditions. They needed cultural legitimacy. They needed what black southerners, in very visible, headline-grabbing showdowns, suddenly appeared to have: deeply rooted institutions in their communities that were ready to inspire and to teach discipline to dedicated masses who mobilized in the community with a spirit of sacrifice and hard work.

The white churches of the South were torn by too many conflicting interests and motives to match that commitment. They did not care deeply enough about segregation to make its defense the most important thing in their lives. Roy Harris, the Georgia power broker and segregationist firebrand, once goaded a white audience, "You have to hand it to Martin Luther King and his group: they're willing to go to jail for their beliefs."[33] He ought to have added that they were also willing to go to church.

Martin Luther King challenged the southern white clergy, from his great pulpit in the Birmingham Jail, not for its militant opposition but for its neutrality. He criticized the southern white clergy for its failure, in effect, to stand up for what they knew was right. Segregationists criticized the southern white clergy for exactly the same sin, but with less confidence than King that they could win it over to their side.

King had seen it all from the start in Montgomery, when he had written to an incredulous Bayard Rustin that "the effect of White Citizens['] Council and Ku Klux Klan intimidation" was the opposite of what one might expect. In Alabama, King wrote, the segregationist organizations "have given our people more determination to press on for the goal of integration." And it wasn't just that black people felt provoked. "There is a general feeling that these organizations will destroy themselves through internal decay.... These organizations are putting as much pressure on white people as they are on Negroes."[34] A white southern minister, Glenn Smiley—one of the rare "inside agitators" who supported the civil rights movement—had reported from Montgomery on the eerie feeling of a city under siege by black Baptists. Smiley sensed then that moderate solutions were no longer possible. There was bitter talk among white folk—frustration that looked increasingly brittle, increasingly unable to congeal—while black folk walked around with knowing smiles. "Strange," Smiley said, "whites are scared stiff and Negroes are calm as cucumbers."[35]

Notes

1. The best treatment of the Southern Manifesto is Tony Badger, "The Southern Manifesto," paper delivered at the annual meeting of the Southern Historical Association, Orlando, Florida, November 1993. On the electoral payoffs of segregationism, see Earl Black, *Southern Governors and Civil Rights: Racial Segregation as a Campaign Issue in the Second Reconstruction* (Cambridge, Mass.: Harvard University Press, 1976).

2. I treat a few perhaps representative examples in *A Stone of Hope: Prophetic Religion and the Death of Jim Crow* (Chapel Hill: University of North Carolina Press, 2004), chapter 7.

3. See Wayne Flynt, *Alabama Baptists: Southern Baptists in the Heart of Dixie* (Tuscaloosa: University of Alabama Press, 1998); Randy Sparks, "'A Search for Life's Meanings': Mississippi's White Sunday Schools, White Churches, and the Race Question, 1900–1967," paper presented at the annual meeting of the Organization of American Historians, San Francisco, April 1997, and Randy Sparks, *Religion in Mississippi* (Jackson: Mississippi Historical Society, 2001), chapter 10; Mark Newman, "The Arkansas Baptist State Convention and Desegregation, 1954–1968," *Arkansas Historical Quarterly* 56 (autumn 1997): 294–313, "The Baptist State Convention of North Carolina and Desegregation, 1945–1980," *North Carolina Historical Review* 85 (Jan. 1998): 1–28, and *Getting Right with God: Southern Baptists and Desegregation, 1945–1995* (Tuscaloosa: University of Alabama Press, 2001); Lee Porter, "Southern Baptists and Race Relations, 1948–1963" (Th.D. diss., Southwestern Baptist Theological Seminary, Fort Worth, 1965). Also illuminating on the southern Baptists were Foy Valentine, "A Historical Study of Southern Baptists and Race Relations, 1917–1947" (Th.D. diss., Southwestern Baptist Theological Seminary, Fort Worth, 1949), John Lee Eighmy, *Churches in Cultural Captivity: A History of the Social Attitudes of Southern Baptists* (Knoxville: University of Tennessee, 1972), and Edward Queen, *In the South, the Baptists Are the Center of Gravity: Southern Baptists and Social Change, 1930–1980* (Brooklyn: Carlson, 1991). Paul Harvey's soon-to-be-published work on a Baptist "folk theology" of segregation may provide a breakthrough in understanding the lay side of the apparent divide between clergy and laity over segregation; see Harvey, "Religion, Race, and the Right in the Baptist South, 1945–1990," in *Religion and Politics in the South*, ed. Glenn Feldman (Tuscaloosa: University of Alabama Press, forthcoming). On Presbyterians, see Joel Alvis, *Religion and Race: Southern Presbyterians, 1946–1983* (Tuscaloosa: University of Alabama Press, 1994).

4. I treat these cases in greater detail in *Stone of Hope*, chapter 7. The resolutions are to be found in Christian Life Commission Files, box 11; Executive Committee Files, boxes 1, 54, 66, 73, 76, 82, 88, loo; Brooks Hays Papers, box 2; Clifton Allen Papers, no box number, all in Southern Baptist Convention (SBC) Archives, Nashville, Tennessee.

5. Hargis devoted a whole chapter to Gilespie's argument, excerpted from the famous speech here quoted, beginning with Gillespie's phrase "While the Bible contains no clear mandate for or against segregation." Hargis himself is a bit more confident: "It is my conviction that God ordained segregation," he is at pains to insist, by way of introducing Gillespie. "It is impossible for me to otherwise interpret Acts 17:26"—which he quotes, with the first clause on monogenesis in lower-case, and the quotation "AND HATH DETERMINED THE TIMES BEFORE APPOINTED, THE BOUNDS OF THEIR HAB-

ITATION" in capitals. Hargis, "The Truth About Segregation," pamphlet published by Evangelist Billy James Hargis, Tulsa, n.d., copy in George Wallace Papers, RC2 G 320, Alabama Department of Archives and History, Montgomery. For a similar but more extreme version of this, see Rev. Carey Daniel, "God the Original Segregationist," typescript, box 340, Sam J. Ervin Papers, University of North Carolina at Chapel Hill. The rather obscure Church of Christ preacher from Columbia, Tennessee, Rev. Leon Burns, rehearsed the same arguments as Gillespie and Daniel but did not mention them until the end, and devoted less than three pages of his sixteen-and-a-half-page pamphlet to them. Burns, *Why Desegregation Will Fail*, speech delivered at West Seventh St. Church, Columbia, Tennessee, Mar. 24, 1957, distributed by author. Copy in Clifton Allen Papers and reprinted in *Augusta Courier*, June 16, 1958.

6. Gillespie, *A Christian View on Segregation*, reprint of address, Nov. 4, 1954 (reproduced by the Citizens' Council, Jackson Mississippi), in series 5, box 146, Citizens' Council of America Literature Collection, Special Collections Division, University of Arkansas Libraries, Fayetteville, and in ser 3.A, box 282, National Association for the Advancement of Colored People Papers, Library of Congress (hereafter NAACP Papers). Another tract that follows Gillespie's pattern is Dr. Charles O. Benham (editor of *National Forecast* magazine of Topton, North Carolina), "X-Raying the Racial Issue: Is Integration Scriptural?" pamphlet, copy, RC2 G320, Wallace Papers. A briefer and somewhat less coherent argument, using the same Old Testament references, is in *Christian Battle Cry* 1 (Apr. 1956), copy, ser. 3.1, box 21, NAACP papers. This was reprinted in the *Natchez Times*, Nov. 22, 1954. I am indebted to Steven Niven for directing me to this reference.

7. *Essays on Segregation*, ed. T. Robert Ingram (Houston: St. Thomas Press, 1960), 18–19.

8. Among segregationists, and especially among southern ministers, Bible-quoting is the exception rather than the rule. Such attempts at segregationist prooftexting as crop up in letters and other sources from the period are far more likely to come from laypeople than from preachers. Paul Harvey confirms this in his independent research; see his "'God and Negroes and Jesus and Sin and Salvation,'" in *Rethinking Religion in the American South*, ed. Beth Schweiger and Don Mathews (Chapel Hill: University of North Carolina Press, forthcoming).

9. Here is a succinct example of folk belief on the biblical warrant of segregation, in a letter of protest to Billy Graham. Note how fleeting and undeveloped the references are, and how little the argument depends on them: "I note on your broadcast you have Integration, which I do not think is Scriptural—O.T., Deut., 3–8—and N.T., Acts 17–26; both you and your father [he means "father-in-law"] are such good Bible students, you have possibly already compared these two verses from the O., & N.T., of course, we all know about the Tower of Babel, and many other passages . . . it is my idea, if He had intended Integration, etc., he would have made all of us of one color or race. It is my idea the Old Book does not teach Integration, so I think it is wrong, as integrating, as it has in the North, will in some cases lead to amalgamation; take Mexico, Spain, etc., third or fourth 'raters.'" Edward Jones to Mr. Graham, Oct. 15, 1958, box 15, folder L, Nelson Bell Papers, Billy Graham Center, Wheaton, Illinois.

10. See Chappell, *Stone of Hope*, chapter 6, and Porter, "Southern Baptists and Race Relations," 28, 97. Criswell had ample opportunities to speak out on the record—he was

a popular speaker and published often. See, for example, "The So-Called Social Gospel," *Baptist Standard*, Sept. 22, 1949. In *The Bible for Today's World* (Grand Rapids, Mich.: Zondervan, 1965), Criswell lays out his commitment to a nearly literalist hermeneutic, probably the issue he cared most about and developed most in his published work. This and Criswell's other books barely mention racial issues in passing, and do not bother to provide any justification of segregation.

11. Bell, "A Round Table Has Debate on Christians' Moral Duty," *Life*, Oct. 1956, 160. Bell added:"It can be demonstrated with equal force that forced integration of the races is sociologically impracticable and at the same time such forced alignments violate the right of personal choice." The issue, for Bell, was force.

12. W. A. Gamble to Bell (associate editor) and H. B. Denby (editor) of the *Southern Presbyterian Journal*, Feb. 10, 1956; Bell to Gamble, Feb. 18, 1956; Gamble to Bell, Aug. 5, 1961; Bell to Gamble, Aug. 16, 1961; Gamble to L. Nelson Bell, Aug. 24, 1962; the last quotation is a typed note "to file," added to the carbon of the secretary's letter that was sent, in Bell's absence, to Gamble, Sept. 25, 1962; all in folder 26–15, Bell Papers.

13. The Westminster Confession continues, after "commonwealth": "'unless by way of humble petition in cases extraordinary; or by way of advice or satisfaction of conscience, if they are thereunto requested by civil magistrates'" (article 32, sec. 4). The *Southern Presbyterian Journal* also printed a statement adopted by the Session of First Presbyterian, Jackson, objecting to the PCUS's Report to the Ninety-seventh General Assembly, again quoting the Westminster Confession's strictures against involvement of Synods and Councils in "civil affairs."

14. In 1956, when a constituent wrote to Senator Sam Ervin from North Carolina, the most important segregationist leader after Byrnes's retirement, questioning his commitment to segregation as "opposed to the teachings of Christ," Ervin replied: "The Constitution of the United States is supposed to be interpreted acccording to the principles of constitutional law and not according to anyone's religious opinions." H. Larry Ingle to Ervin, Feb. 13, 1956, and Ervin to Ingle, Feb. 20, 1956, box 15, Ervin Papers.

15. She also said churches were cooperating with communist groups: "having been brainwashed themselves seek to brainwash their members." She was taken aback at the report of her denomination's Christian Relations Council: "I am surprised that so many—so many true loyal Southerners supported it.... The action of the Assembly of the Southern Presbyterian church in its last two meetings has done far more harm than good.... My negro cook says—'God made me black and He made you white—HE made us different—if he had wanted us the same HE would have made us the same." She called for cleaning the "liberal teachers" out of the seminaries. Mrs. Willard Steele of Chattanooga to Bell, Jun. 2, 1958, folder 47–8, Bell Papers.

16. "At least," Williams continued, "it would give the congregation the basis for demanding explanations from 'integrationist' pastors." J. B. Williams to W. J. Simmons, Jun. 14, 1957, box RO33-BO19-S2-10383, J. B. Williams Papers, Mississippi Department of Archives and History, Jackson, Mississippi.

17. The article claimed to quote an (undated) article from *McCall's*. It targeted Robert Graetz, erroneously calling him southern (he was a northerner who pastored an all-black Lutheran congregation in Montgomery). *Christian Layman*, Oct. 1958. I have been able to find only one issue of this publication, in box 10395, Williams Papers. The issue is devoted mostly to reprinting segregationist editorials and speeches.

18. William D. Workman, *The Case for the South* (New York: Devin-Adair, 1960), 109. See also the organ of the Louisiana Citizens' Councils, *Councilor*, Jul. 1957, 1, 4, copy, ser. 3.A, box 282, NAACP Papers.

19. Harris quoted in *Atlanta Constitution*, Feb. 3, 1960.

20. Putnam in the *Jackson Daily News*, Oct. 27, 1961, and *Jackson State Times*, Oct. 27, 1961. In an earlier statement, Putnam had denounced the Catholic Bishops' statement that "segregation cannot be reconciled with the Christian view of our fellow man" in November 1958. In a letter to Cardinal Spellman, Putnam said the bishops were accessories to a "crime against the South." *Citizens' Council* 4 (Dec. 1958).

21. This supporter suggested that Thurmond organize all leaders of the southern states to expose falsehood and "notify the heads of the various religious organizations sponsoring integration that they will be exposed as fakirs and their religion as a myth, just so much modern witchcraft." He noted that Christianity was "organized and operating under the banner of the one and only God, the Jewish God, the one and only race, the human race, with justice, equality, liberty, peace and plenty for all regardless of the laws of Malthus and Darwin." Thurmond responded, though briefly and noncommittally. Robert A. Wade of Hagerstown, Maryland, to Thurmond, Dec. 23, 1955, folder 1956–12, Segregation, Strom Thurmond Papers, Clemson University Archives, Clemson, South Carolina.

22. "Another basic tenet of Presbyterianism is that the corporate Church shall not become involved in matters that are properly the concern of the State. Well did our for[e]bears know that intervention in secular affairs would largely impair the ability of the Church to fulfill its mission." He quoted the Westminster Confession to support this. *Southern Presbyterian Journal*, Apr. 9, 1958, 7–9.

23. See Chappell, *Stone of Hope*, chapter 7.

24. See, for example, the angry mail in the George Wallace Papers. One telegram came in opposing Wallace's meeting with Graham: "I would hope that the white people of Alabama would give Billy Graham the cold shoulder on his current integration mission to Alabama. Some of his recent statements concerning Alabama and integration leaves us to believe up here that he's going down there to cram it down your neck he seems to have moved into the camp with Senator Javits and Adam Clayton Powell." Another told Wallace: "We hope you will not be in the integrated audience to hear Billy Graham." Paul Maston to Wallace, Apr. 24, 1965; Mrs. L. P. Munger to Wallace, Jun. 16, 1965, both in box RC2 G312, Wallace Papers.

25. Mrs. Willard Steele to L. Nelson Bell, Jun. 2, 1958, folder 47–8, Bell Papers.

26. Graham's own papers have so far been opened only to a select few, myself not among them. Most Graham scholars have to rely on the papers of Graham's various organizations, and the papers of his associates, especially Bell. A very thorough and apparently dispassionate treatment by one of the few who had access to Graham's papers—the best single book on Graham—is William Martin, *Prophet with Honor: Billy Graham* (New York: Morrow, 1991).

27. Bell also told this irate follower that he appreciated the "fine Christian spirit with which you disagree with [Billy] with reference to integration. Let me say that Billy does not believe in integration any more than you and I do. The point is that he feels, along with me, that *legal* or forced segregation is unchristian and that segregation should be on a voluntary basis." Bell to Edward Jones, Oct. 21, 1958, folder 15–15, Bell Papers. Bell

insisted to a different writer: "Billy has *not* stirred up racial strife. Apparently you have been reading some of the hate literature—some of it inspired by Communists—which revels in attacking those whom God is using." Bell to William McIntire, Jan. 14, 1959, folder 15–15, Bell Papers. Similar disavowals of Graham's intention to lead integration appear in Bell to Mrs. Peake of Norfolk, Aug. 7, 1956, folder 41–11, Bell Papers.

28. Martin, *Prophet with Honor.*

29. These scrapbooks are available at the Billy Graham Center, Wheaton, Illinois.

30. Graham had preached on the capitol grounds years before, to a segregated crowd, and nobody raised a fuss then. Timmerman said he was not protesting on racial grounds but claimed that church-state separation would be threatened by Graham's appearance on state property. Bell wrote to A. C. Miller, head of the SBC's Christian Life Commission, that the issue was beclouded by "extremists on both sides." As for Governor Timmerman, he said: "Someone has misinformed him about Billy's policies." The race issue never comes up when Graham preaches, Bell told Miller (one of the most notorious racial liberals in the white South): people of both races sit where they like without fanfare. Bell pointed out that the newspapers did not report on the frequent integration of Graham's audiences. Bell suspected that "Dr. Bob Jones, who has been fighting Billy so constantly, might not have given this idea to Governor Timmerman—giving him a very inaccurate picture of Billy's position. I know that Dr. Jones said that if [Graham] came to preach in Greenville, South Carolina, he would raise the issue there"; Bell to Miller, Oct. 13, 1958, folder 43-12, Bell Papers. And see exchange between Miller and Bell, Oct. 17 and 22, 1958, folder 43-12, Bell Papers.

31. Mary L. Dudziak, *Cold War Civil Rights: Race and the Image of American Democracy* (Princeton, N.J.: Princeton University Press, 2000); Azza Salama Layton, *International Politics and Civil Rights Policies in the United States, 1941–1960* (Cambridge: Cambridge University Press, 2000); Thomas Borstelmann, *The Cold War and the Color Line: American Race Relations in the Global Arena* (Cambridge, Mass.: Harvard University Press, 2001).

32. A 1958 SBC report noted, among the "current trends among Negro Baptists," not only a disconcerting movement toward the rival (northern) American Baptist Convention but also "the bid of the Catholic hierarchy for the Negro people and the Catholic gains in Negro membership"; Victor Glass and A. C. Miller, "Southern Baptists and the Negro," committee report to SBC, 1958, Race Relations Collection, SBC Archives, Box 1, p. 8.

33. Harris quoted in *Time,* Apr. 7, 1961.

34. Martin Luther King to Bayard Rustin, Sept. 20, 1956, reel 4, folders 246–47, Bayard Rustin Papers, Bethesda, Md.: University Publications of American, 1988, microfilm collection.

35. Smiley to FOR's J. Swomley, dated [by a different hand] Mar. [2?] 1956, reel 4, folder 242, Rustin Papers.

EIGHT

The Theology of Massive Resistance:
Sex, Segregation, and the Sacred after *Brown*

Jane Dailey

Asked to explain the victories of the civil rights movement, activists have often replied: "God was on our side." In his autobiography, the Southern Christian Leadership Conference (SCLC) staff worker (and future Atlanta mayor) Andrew Young reports his conviction that "God was showing us a way to change the world. Even when we could see no human way that we could realistically change the racist power of the South and the nation, we felt the spirit leading us on."[1] Civil rights leaders at the time also portrayed themselves and their cause as divinely sanctioned, positioning segregationists clearly across the fence. "We have the strange feeling down in Montgomery that in our struggle we have cosmic companionship," Martin Luther King revealed in 1956. "We feel that the universe is on the side of right and righteousness. That is what keeps us going." But he went further. Speaking of the boycott in another context, King portrayed segregationists as wayward Christians, who, like the prodigal son, "have strayed away to some far country of sin and evil."[2]

Religious supporters of black civil rights did not simply consider segregation unconstitutional: they considered it a sin, and its Christian champions heretics. The director of Religious Life at the University of Mississippi, the Baptist minister Will Campbell, believed that racism was a "heresy" infecting white southern Protestantism. Howard Kester, the executive secretary of the Fellowship of Southern Churchmen, considered the gospel preached in southern churches spiritually innutritious, resulting in "pellagra-souled Christians."[3] Integrationist Christians, referring time and again to the apostle Paul's notion of the church as the "body of Christ" (Ephesians 4), denounced their segregationist brethren for poisoning and polluting that body. "The Church is first of all the body of Christ, and in that Body we are one, not races or clans," declared one white Mississippi Methodist minister. Martin Luther King agreed. "[The]

[151]

church is the Body of Christ. So when the church is true to its nature it knows neither division nor disunity. I am disturbed about what you [segregationists] are doing to the Body of Christ." The beloved community, as King explained on another occasion, had to be integrated because "segregation is a blatant denial of the unity which we all have in Jesus Christ."[4] Segregation, in other words, was a theological as well as a social and political fallacy.

On the whole, historians have subscribed to King's version of the sacred history of the civil rights movement. Most books written about the struggle for racial equality emphasize the central role that religion played in articulating the challenge that the civil rights movement offered the existing order of segregation. There are good reasons for this. As Aldon D. Morris noted in *Origins of the Civil Rights Movement*, black churches were the "institutional center" of the African American freedom struggle. Although more recent scholarship has broadened both the organizational and ideological genealogy of the civil rights movement, even those historians who qualify the influence of the black church on the movement recognize the importance of the religiosity of black and white southerners in structuring their views on civil rights.[5]

The religiosity of antiintegrationists has not fared so well in the scholarly literature. Some of the historians most engaged with the religious beliefs of civil rights activists have, almost in the same breath, denigrated the religious faith of segregationists. While in recent years a number of scholars have written sensitively about the "theology of segregationism" and "a theology for racism," few have treated segregationist ideas about religion with the care that has been devoted to proslavery ideology and thinkers.[6]

In their response to the arguments of King and others, Christian segregationists entered an argument as old as the church itself: In what ways could and should the world of the flesh be made like the world of the spirit? Taking the tack that normative Christians have taken since the second century, antiintegrationists pitted the pastoral Paul, providing guidelines for the day-to-day administration of Christian communities, against the eschatological Paul, proclaiming the impending end of time and the irrelevance of life in the flesh. There are distinctions on earth (different languages, races, sexes), segregationists argued; these distinctions are created by God; and although humans can all become one in spirit through conversion to Jesus, and although once the Messiah comes all earthly distinctions will pass away, in this world and in this flesh, earthly distinctions are real—and Christians should not rebel against them. In his May 30, 1954, sermon "Integration or Segregation?"—reprinted widely in newspapers and circulated in pamphlet form—Rev. James F. Burks of Bayview Baptist Church in Norfolk, Virginia, rebutted the efforts of integrationists to cloak themselves in Christian righteousness. "The spiritual 'oneness' of believers in the Lord Jesus Christ actually and ethically has nothing to do" with the issue of segregation, Burks explained. Spiritual kinship differed from physical kinship, just as the spiritual and secular worlds differed. "If integration of races is based upon the contention that men are all 'one in Christ,' then the foundation is not secure. The idea of 'Universal Fatherhood of God and Brotherhood of Man' is MAN'S concoction and contradicts the Word of God," Burks charged. "Those who are 'one in Christ' are such through a spiritual union and certainly not physical." Citing Deuteronomy 32:8 and Paul in Acts 17:26 on the division of peoples, Burks insisted that, from a theological perspective,

> We are interested—finally and absolutely—in what the Word of God teaches about the races of men. . . . The Word of God is the surest and only infallible source of our facts of Ethnology, and when man sets aside the plain teachings of this Blessed Book and disregards the boundary lines God Himself has drawn, man assumes a prerogative that belongs to God alone.

Citing Paul's pastoral letters once again, Burks warned: "The Anti-Christ will consummate this [rebellious] attitude by opposing and exalting Himself above God."[7]

This chapter considers white southern reactions to the civil rights movement—in particular, reaction to the decision in *Brown v. Board of Education*—as a religious conflict over orthodoxy between two strongly held Christian traditions. For the historian (as opposed to the believer), orthodoxy is the product not of revelation but of conflict, in which the victory of one interpretation over another is historically produced rather than divinely ordained. Historians of the civil rights era tend to pass over this conflict and, ignoring or condemning the testimony of the many who believed that segregation was "the commandment and law of God," award the palm of orthodoxy to the colorblind, universalist theology of the "beloved community."[8]

When historians do this they participate in what was perhaps the most lasting triumph of the civil rights movement: its successful appropriation of Christian dogma. At the same time, they miss the titanic struggle waged by participants on both sides of the conflict to harness the immense power of the divine to their cause. Viewing the civil rights movement as in part an argument about competing claims to Christian orthodoxy will help scholars and students better understand the arguments made by either side of this struggle and the strategic actions they took.

White southerners had a rich arsenal of arguments against desegregation, and they deployed them against different targets. Segregationists did not make religious arguments against black suffrage, for example, or against integration of the armed forces. Southern white conservatives did not hurl scripture against the Federal Equal Protection Commission. Segregationists made religious arguments in very specific instances, under specific circumstances, at specific moments in time. One of those times was immediately following the announcement of the *Brown* decision, which sharpened dramatically the theological debate among southern Christians.[9]

The influence of religion, of course, may be seen in many aspects of southern life. This chapter explores how religion served as a vessel for one particular language crucial to racial segregation in the South: the language of miscegenation. It was through sex that racial segregation in the South moved from being a local social practice to a part of the divine plan for the world. It was thus through sex that segregation assumed, for the believing Christian, cosmological significance. Focusing on the theological arguments wielded by segregation's champions reveals how deeply interwoven Christian theology was in the segregationist ideology that supported the discriminatory world of Jim Crow. It also demonstrates that religion played a central role not only in articulating the challenge that the civil rights movement offered Jim Crow but also in *resistance* to that challenge.

• • •

I will begin where segregationist Christians began: with the Bible. When civil rights supporters quoted the apostle Paul's argument in Acts 17 that "[God] hath made of one blood all nations of men for to dwell on the face of the earth," segregationists responded by reciting the second half of this verse, in which the God who created all men "decreed the time and limits of their habitation." Reliance on this particular verse freed segregationists from the discredited "separate creations" theory (polygenesis) cited by proslavery advocates a century earlier. It also meant that the biblical defense of segregation could exist side by side with contemporary anthropology cited by Christian supporters of integration.[10]

But segregation did not rest on Paul alone. Turning to their Bibles, antiintegrationists found many narratives that supported a segregated world. White ministers and laypeople across the South offered a biblically based history of the world that accounted for all of the significant tragedies of human history, from the Fall and the Flood through the Holocaust, in terms of race relations. Binding the narrative together and linking the catastrophes of the past with the integrated apocalypse to come was the chief sin in the service of the Antichrist: miscegenation.[11] The notion that the sin committed in the Garden of Eden was sexual in nature stretches back centuries. By the Middle Ages, rabbinical readings of the Fall commonly considered the serpent a male, since it lusted after Eve.[12] Proslavery apologists in the nineteenth century favored a variant of this theory, in which Eve was tempted not by a snake but by a pre-Adamite black man (even, in one version, a "negro gardener").[13] Needless to say, more than an apple was on offer. Most southern Christians rejected as heretical the notion that Negroes were created before Adam (and were, therefore, soulless beasts incapable of salvation), but several influential post-Emancipation writers persisted in arguing precisely this point. Buckner H. Payne, a Nashville publisher and clergyman who wrote under the pseudonym Ariel, insisted that the tempter in the Garden was a talking beast—a black man—and his interactions with Eve the first cause of the Fall. Writing at the height of Radical Reconstruction in 1867, Ariel concluded his argument by reminding his readers that "a man can not commit so great an offense against his race, against his country, against his God, in any other way, as to give his daughter in marriage to a negro—a *beast*—or to take one of their females for his wife." Should America fail to heed his warning, Ariel predicted disaster: "The states or people that favor this equality and amalgamation of the white and black races, *God will exterminate.*"[14]

Although rebutted at the time and later, Ariel's argument remained current through the middle of the twentieth century, buttressed along the way by such widely read books as Charles Carroll's *The Negro a Beast* and *The Tempter of Eve*, both of which considered miscegenation the greatest of sins. Denounced for its acceptance of separate creations, *The Negro a Beast* was nonetheless enormously influential. Recalling the door-to-door sales campaign that brought the book to the notice of whites across the South, a historian of religion lamented: "During the opening years of the twentieth century it has become the Scripture of tens of thousands of poor whites, and its doctrine is maintained with an appalling stubbornness and persistence."[15] In this tradition, miscegenation—or, more commonly, *amalgamation* or *mongrelization*—was the original sin, the root of all corruption in humankind.[16]

The expulsion from Paradise did not solve the problem of miscegenation. By the time of Noah, race-mixing was so prevalent that, in the words of one civil rights–era pamphleteer, "God destroyed '*all flesh*' in that part of the world for that one sin. Only Noah was '*perfect in his generation*' . . . so God saved him and his family to rebuild the Adamic Race." That perfection did not last long, however; according to some traditions, the cursed son of Ham, already doomed to a life of servitude, mixed his blood with "pre-Adamite negroes" in the Land of Nod. Again and again God's wrath is aroused by the sin of miscegenation, and the people feel the awful weight of his punishment: Sodom and Gomorrah were destroyed for this sin, as was the Tower of Babel, where, in a failed effort to protect racial purity, God dispersed the peoples across the globe. King Solomon, "reputed to be the wisest of men, with a kingdom of matchless splendor and wealth was ruined as a direct result of his marrying women of many different races," and the "physical mixing of races" that occurred between the Israelites and the Egyptians who accompanied Moses into the wilderness "resulted in social and spiritual weakness," leading God to sentence the Exodus genera-tion to die before reaching the Promised Land.[17] For evidence that the God of Noah remained as adamantly opposed to racial mixing as ever, white southern believers could look back a mere fifteen years to the Holocaust. The liquidation of six million people was caused, D. B. Red explained in his pamphlet *Race Mixing a Religious Fraud*, by the sexual "mingling" of the Jews, who suffered what Red represented as God's final solution to the miscegenation problem: "Totally destroy the people involved." Here surely was proof that segregation was "divine law, enacted for the defense of society and civilization."[18]

Narratives like these had two key pedagogical aims: to make the case for seg-regation as divine law, and to warn that transgression of this law would inevita-bly be followed by divine punishment. In the 1950s and 1960s this punishment was imagined to be directed at the nation (in the form of the communist parti-sans of the Antichrist)[19] and at local communities and congregations. Referring to the fate of Sodom and Gomorrah, Carey Daniel, pastor of the First Baptist Church of West Dallas, Texas, who was active in his region's White Citizens' Council, explained: "Anyone familiar with the Biblical history of those cities during that period can readily understand why we here in the South are deter-mined to maintain segregation."[20] Rev. Burks of Norfolk was more explicit. As he lectured shortly after the Brown decision was announced,

spurning and rejecting the plain Truth of the Word of God has always resulted in the Judgment of God. Man, in overstepping the boundary lines God has drawn, has taken another step in the direction of inviting the Judgment of Almighty God. This step of racial integration is but another stepping stone toward the gross immorality and lawlessness that will be characteristic of the last days, just preceding the Return of the Lord Jesus Christ.[21]

If this happened, it would be the fault of no one but white southern Chris-tians themselves, for did not the Bible make clear, as the Mississippi senator Theodore G. Bilbo warned, that "miscegenation and amalgamation are sins of man in direct defiance with the will of God"?[22]

Racial extremists like Bilbo were not the only people who believed this. The 1955 opinion of Henry Louttit, the Episcopal bishop of South Florida, that only a few "sincere but deluded folk" would use scripture to back up their belief in segregation turned out to be optimistic. The argument that God was against sexual integration was articulated across a broad spectrum of education and respectability, by senators and Klansmen, by housewives, sorority sisters, and Rotarians, and, not least of all, by mainstream Protestant clergymen. Dr. W. M.

Caskey, a professor at Mississippi College, the state's leading Baptist institution, explained in 1960: "We . . . believe with Governor [Ross] Barnett, that our Southern segregation way is the Christian way. . . . [W]e believe that this Bible teaches that Thou wast the original segregationist. Segregationist ministers who believed that the Bible "gave clear guidance on the integration-segregation issue" were prominent in the crowds surrounding Little Rock's Central High.[23] Editorialists and congregations elsewhere spoke out as well. "In integrating the races in schools, we foster miscegenation, thereby changing God's plan and destroying His handiwork," resolved the Cameron Baptist Church in Cameron, South Carolina. David M. Gardner, writing in the *Baptist Standard*, agreed: "God created and established the color line in the races, and evidently meant for it to remain. Therefore, we have no right to try and eradicate it."[24]

As absurd as the argument for divine segregation may appear to today's readers, it had great power in its day. Evidence of the political and social power of these ideas is everywhere—in legal decisions, in personal correspondence, in sermons, pamphlets, speeches, and newspapers. Organizations acted on these assumptions: in 1958 the Daughters of the American Revolution denounced interracial marriage and resolved that "racial integrity" was a "fundamental Christian principle." Judges even incorporated these theological positions into legal decisions. Upholding segregation in a 1955 ruling, the Florida Supreme Court preferred its own reading of the Bible to that of the bishop of South Florida. "When God created man," the Florida justices explained, "He allotted each race to his own continent according to color, Europe to the white man, Asia to the yellow man, Africa to the Blackman, and America to the red man." A decade later, the circuit court judge Leon A. Bazile also appealed to divine sanction, in the case that would soon form the basis for the Supreme Court's ruling that antimiscegenation laws violated the Fourteenth Amendment. According to this federal judge,

> Almighty God created the races white, black, yellow, malay and red, and he placed them on separate continents. And but for the interference with his arrangement there would be no cause for such marriages. The fact that he separated the races shows that he did not intend for the races to mix.[25]

More than most sources, Leon Bazile's ruling in *Loving v. Commonwealth* provides a clear example of the importance of the sexual and theological nexus in the civil rights struggle. That nexus—visible to anyone who looked beneath the surface of southern race relations—burst out into the open in May 1954, with the Supreme Court's ruling in *Brown v. Board of Education*.

Like the chief executives of the other southern states, Governor Thomas B. Stanley of Virginia spent the spring of 1954 wrestling with the issue of state compliance with the *Brown* decision. Eager to communicate with their governor on this topic, hundreds of Virginians wrote to express their opinions about the ruling. Nearly everyone who wrote objected to integration. The most common argument of the dissenters was theological: integration facilitated miscegenation, which contradicted divine Word.[26]

On the face of things, this response seems surprising: the *Brown* decision, limited as it was to desegregation of public schools, looked to be about anything *but* sex and marriage. This impression was the result of a deliberate strategy on the part of *Brown's* architects, both within the NAACP and on the Supreme Court, which went to considerable trouble to limit the decision's language to public education. As was noted at the time, the Court failed to invoke John Marshall Harlan's famous dissent in *Plessy v. Ferguson* (1896): "Our Constitution is color-blind, and neither knows nor tolerates classes among its citizens." Nor did the Court claim that statutory considerations of race or color were impermissible in arenas other than public education. The justices who backed *Brown* also explicitly refused to rule on the constitutionality of antimiscegenation laws. The Court ducked a chance to evaluate restrictive marriage laws in 1955, a decision that was widely derided.[27] Felix Frankfurter's law clerk Alexander Bickel justified the Court's reluctance to rule on interracial marriage by insisting that the issue was "hardly of central importance in the civil rights struggle." But the justices knew better: they avoided ruling on miscegenation not because it was unimportant but because it was too hot to handle. As Justice John Marshall Harlan II (the grandson of the dissenting Harlan of 1896) put the matter in a 1955 note to his colleagues, "one bombshell at a time is enough."[28]

In avoiding the issue of miscegenation, the Warren Court was following the NAACP's strategy of attacking segregation first from its extremities. Certainly both the court and the NAACP recognized that restrictions on sex and marriage lay at the heart of Jim Crow. When the *Brown* decision was announced in May 1954, sex and marriage between those defined by the law as white and those defined as nonwhite were prohibited in twenty-seven states—and had been, with a few brief exceptions during Reconstruction, for the past three centuries.[29] These state antimiscegenation laws underpinned the edifice of racial segregation and discrimination in America, a fact advertised by students of southern social relations since the 1920s. James Weldon Johnson addressed the issue directly in 1933, writing: "in the core of the heart of the American race problem the sex factor is rooted; rooted so deeply that it is not always recognized when it shows at the surface." The Yale University professor John Dollard and the southern authors W. J. Cash and Lillian Smith all commented on the sexual foundation of segregation in bestselling books in the late 1930s and early 1940s. Gunnar Myrdal canonized the position in 1944, when he announced in *An American Dilemma* that sex was "the principle around which the whole structure of segregation of the Negroes ... [was] organized."[30]

Black southerners did not need Gunnar Myrdal to explain that sexual control was central to both the ideology and practice of white supremacy. Early black rights organizations, including the NAACP, set their sights on restrictive marriage laws. As a practical issue, however, the risks of addressing the sexual question outpaced the advantages. By 1940 the NAACP's new Legal Defense Fund had crafted a strategy of attacking Jim Crow from the outside in, through lawsuits focused on higher education and discriminatory voting practices such as the white primary. Sex was the last thing the NAACP wanted to talk about. But it was a topic that simply would not go away. Whether they fought for integrated public education at the graduate or primary level, civil rights groups opened themselves to the charge that they favored interracial sex and marriage. When he recalled the NAACP's successful campaign to get George W. McLaurin admitted to the graduate school of the University of Oklahoma in 1948, Thurgood Marshall noted that his strategy revolved in good measure around defusing whites' fears of racial mixing. "We had eight people who had applied and who were eligible to be plaintiffs, but we deliberately picked Professor McLaurin," Marshall explained, "because he was sixty-eight years old and we didn't think he was going to marry or intermarry. . . . They could not bring that one up on us, anyhow."[31]

Everyone connected with the school cases that became known collectively as *Brown v. Board of Education* understood how vital it was that they not be linked with sex. Despite the precautions of both the NAACP and the Warren Court, however, the *Brown* decision was interpreted by a large and vocal segment of white southerners in explicitly sexual terms. "The first reaction to the Supreme Court's decision was almost psychotic," Mark Ethridge, the editor of the *Louisville Courier-Journal*, recalled.[32] In a typical editorial comment, the Jackson, Mississippi, *Daily News* denounced the school decision as "the first step, or an opening wedge, toward mixed marriages, miscegenation, and the mongrelization of the human race." Walter C. Givhan, an Alabama state senator, interpreted the *Brown* decision the same way. "What is the real purpose of this? To open the bedroom doors of our white women to Negro men." Thousands of letters sent to southern governors struck the same theme. In a letter to the governor of Georgia, Herman E. Talmadge (who was on record as arguing that "God himself segregated the races"), William A. Robinson, Jr., worried about the future: "Of course, we may abolish the public schools," Robinson wrote, "but when the NAACP procures from an obliging Court, as seems quite likely in the near future, a ruling adverse to our marriage restrictions, we cannot meet that issue by abolishing marriage." Georgia's state attorney general, Eugene Cook, agreed with this line of reasoning and took it a step further, predicting "an amalgamation stampede" should the Supreme Court rule against state antimiscegenation laws. A popular pamphlet made the same point in a way any southern gardener could understand, warning of "Negroid blood like the jungle, steadily and completely swallowing up everything."[33]

It was within this highly charged sexual context that the battle for divine sanction between supporters and opponents of desegregation took place. While white southern opponents of *Brown* were making dire predictions of syphilis in the schools, southern moderates and reformers leapt to take the moral high ground. With southern newspapers and politicians almost unanimously opposed to the Supreme Court decision, *Brown's* supporters turned to the white churches.[34] The relative silence of white ministers on the race issue through 1954 may have encouraged moderates to try to coopt the church.[35] Mississippi's Hodding Carter—who won the Pulitzer Prize in 1946 for a series of antilynching editorials—made a claim for religious authority and linked Christianity to democracy when he wrote in the *Delta-Democrat Times* that "the Court could not have made a different decision in the light of democratic and Christian principles and against the background of today."[36] A group of thirty-seven college students and counselors attending the Southeastern Regional Methodist Student Conference in Virginia made the same rhetorical move in a letter to Governor Thomas Stanley. The *Brown* decision, the students explained, was "in keeping with the spirit of democracy and Christianity and should not be sidestepped in any way." Black southerners also tried to tie the *Brown* decision to Christian ideals. The National Baptist Convention, the leading forum of black Baptists, announced that on May 17, 1954: "the Social Gospel of Jesus received its endorsement by the Highest Court of the nation." Other African Americans reacted less reverently. The boxer Joe Louis, who had wandered into the office of *Ebony* magazine as editors there heard the news, smiled broadly and said, "Tell me, did Herman Talmadge drop dead?"[37]

Civil rights supporters understood immediately the importance of having God—and his spokesmen—on their side. "If the ministers speak out bravely, quietly, persuasively they can give direction to the feelings of millions of white southerners who don't know what to do or where to turn," wrote Lillian Smith from her home in Georgia. Although Smith was hardly representative of either southern Protestantism or white southern thought more generally, her hopes were not entirely unfounded: there is evidence that white Christian consciences were strained by many aspects of segregation. Certainly many southern religious leaders, especially those connected with seminaries or foreign mission work, had questioned segregation long before 1954.[38] Just two weeks after the announcement of the *Brown* decision, the ten thousand messengers of the

Southern Baptist Convention (SBC) endorsed the Supreme Court's decision, proclaiming it "in harmony with the constitutional guarantee of equal freedom to all citizens, and with the Christian principles of equal justice and love for all men." The Catholics, Methodists, and Presbyterians followed suit, although not without first addressing the trump argument: the Southern Presbyterian General Assembly accompanied its support for school integration with the assurance that interracial marriage would not follow.[39]

The proclamations of the national church organizations were useful to supporters of black civil rights. As one Virginia minister lectured his governor, in trying to circumvent the *Brown* decision Virginia was ignoring "the expressed wishes of the four, largest religious bodies in our State."[40] But these organizations—especially the SBC's progressive Christian Life Commission, which authored the denomination's official response to *Brown*—were not necessarily representative of the masses of white Christian Protestants or of the clergy. (As one white southerner remarked of the messengers to the writer Robert Penn Warren, "they were just a little bit exalted. When they got back with the home folks a lot of 'em wondered how they did it [voted in favor of the Christian Life Commission's report endorsing *Brown*].")[41] For every Protestant minister who declared that the *Brown* decision "showed the hand of God in it," there were others who saw the diabolical machinations of the Kremlin instead and who denounced "pinkos in the pulpit" for their support of integration.[42] Douglas Hudgins, the pastor of Jackson, Mississippi's enormously powerful First Baptist Church, was one of the few messengers to object to the report recommending support of the *Brown* decision. But he was surely not the only Baptist minister to preach the Sunday after the convention on the local autonomy of churches. Pastor of a congregation studded with state leaders, Hudgins almost never preached on contemporary events, but now he took the opportunity to remind his flock of the congregational autonomy at the heart of Baptist associational life. Decisions taken by the Southern Baptist Convention had no binding authority on local churches, he insisted. Furthermore, Hudgins explained, the Supreme Court decision was "a purely civic matter" and thus an inappropriate topic for the Christian Life Commission in the first place. In this Hudgins echoed J. W. Storer, the president of the SBC, who endorsed the *Brown* decision on civic rather than theological grounds. Repudiating the religious arguments of his organization's Christian Life Commission, Storer argued that Baptists should obey the Supreme Court decision because "we 'Render to Caesar the things that are Caesar's, and to God the things that are God's.'"[43]

Public schools belonged to Caesar. Racial purity belonged to God. In *Brown's* wake, many white southern Christian leaders tried to find a way to obey both the law of man and that of God and at the same time chart a middle course between massive resistance and capitulation to the theology of the emerging civil rights movement. Worried about the sexual and theological implications of the *Brown* decision and anxious about schism, in 1956 the Episcopal Church's National Council backtracked on its belief, expressed just a year earlier, that desegregation was "the will of God." Replacing this explicitly theological justification for desegregation with a civic concern for justice, the Episcopalians substituted "free access to institutions" for the goal of "integration"—a loaded term that suggested intermarriage, from which "the majority of church leaders still shrank."[44] In 1957 an interdenominational group of Atlanta clergymen published a statement that disavowed support for racial amalgamation but declared that "as Americans and Christians we have an obligation to obey the law."[45] The *Alabama Baptist*'s Leon Macon went further, arguing: "When we violate a law we hurt man and grieve God." Liberal clergymen in Little Rock during the integration crisis in September 1957 took the same tack, insisting that good Christians could disagree about segregation but not about upholding the law.[46]

But what were good Christians to do when the law of the land contradicted God's holy word? The *Brown* decision raised practical moral and theological issues for many southern white Christians. While liberal Presbyterians worried that "the courts have shown more sympathy toward the Negro than has the church" and admonished it to "strive to keep apace of its Master or become bereft of his spirit," segregationist Christians suspected that the state was following not the Master but his principal challenger.[47] Like Norfolk's Rev. Burks, who argued that "modern-day Christianity has substituted a social Gospel for the Blood-purchased Gospel of Christ," many white southerners considered the *Brown* decision at direct odds with God's moral codes.[48] Angry about the desegregation decision and the support liberal clergy had given it, a North Carolina man complained that "we the people . . . are being forced to disobey the laws of our GOD who created us." Insisting that "God is the author of segregation," the Miami resident Elmer M. Ramsey charged the Supreme Court with "exceed[ing] its authority" by interfering with divine law.[49]

This argument, it is important to note, was not about school integration per se but about its consequences, which segregationists considered to be interracial sex and marriage, leading to race corruption. The most common line of argument among the hundreds of letters that Governor Thomas B. Stanley of Virginia received in the two weeks following the *Brown* decision insisted that school integration led inevitably to intermarriage, which violated God's plans for the universe. Written largely by women, the letters to Governor Stanley represent a cross-section of popular opinion and echo the correspondence received by other southern governors in the weeks following the school decision. Mrs. Jessie L. West confessed that she had "never felt so strongly about anything before" and thus was compelled to write her governor even though she could not "phrase fancy statements." Mrs. West supported equal education for black Virginians ("they should have good, clean schools, buses to ride there, etc."), but she drew the line at integration, which she believed was a sin. "Having attended my beloved little county church from infancy I believe I know the fundamentals of the teachings of God's Holy Word. . . . [N]owhere can I find anything to convince me that God intended us living together as one big family in schools, churches and other public places." Mrs. G. P. Smith agreed. "My strong religious conviction tells me that God does not require this of us. He made us different and put us separate on His good earth." Should schools be integrated, she warned, "in less than ten years we will face the problem of intermarriage." Mr. and Mrs. J. W. Layne wrote straightforwardly that "integrated schools will lead to interracial marriage" and signed off with a benediction: "May the Lord direct you and others in doing what we believe to be right."[50]

Divine gubernatorial guidance was essential, these correspondents believed, because in integrating its public schools the nation was teetering on the brink of damnation. Fretting that "God's word is being made away with and people is believing in their selves and forgetting God," Mrs. R. E. Martin warned Governor Stanley that "the wicked shall be turned into hell, and all the Nations that forget God." Mrs. Henry Winter Davis was more explicit on the link between integration and hell.

> We consider this non segregation business comes directly from Satan, that old deceiver, the devil, to destroy *all peace in America forevermore!* . . . That is his business—to destroy *all good.* He whispered to that California man in [the] Supreme Court [Chief Justice Earl Warren] that it would be an advantage to abolish segregation—while one of our own statesmen would have known the danger, which is worse than any menace ever to threaten America . . . as it is in our *very midst, an every day menace.*[51]

As the civil rights movement left the courts and entered the streets, the struggle for cultural legitimacy became fiercer. Ministers often found themselves in the crosshairs on the segregation question, as congregants attempted to counteract the influence of clergymen in civic affairs and to capture the power of Christian righteousness for segregation. "It seems to me that there is a feeling among the clergy that you cannot be a Christian and oppose the integration of the negro and white races in our public schools," wrote R. D. Cook in June 1954. "I am sorry that I cannot see it their way." Pitting his own expertise against his pastor's, Cook continued, "although I may not be as good a Christian as I should be, I have belonged to the Board of Deacons in my church for a number of years and am now superintendent of the Sunday school." Then he got to the point:

> I believe that the integration of the races in our public schools will result in intermarriage of the negro and white races, and I am sure that the NAACP will next try to have the law repealed prohibiting intermarriage of the two races. I believe that the Lord would have made us all one color if he had intended that we be one race.

Cook's neighbor, J. D. Jones, wrote a similar letter.

> I know you have seen a lot about what the preachers have had to say about it [the *Brown* decision], but I do not believe that they are representing their congregations at all. . . . I have been a Baptist for forty years and have been a Deacon in my church for thirty odd years, and I know that our congregation is very much opposed to doing away with segregation in the public schools.

Local feeling on ministerial misrepresentation could run high. "The ministers of our country have been among the foremost advocates of this movement [to comply with *Brown*] and have falsely misrepresented their churches as being of the same opinion," wrote Mrs. James Beale. "They have passed resolutions at conventions where the delegates probably feel they would be most unchristlike to disagree and yet I do not know of a single instance where the minister has asked a vote in his individual church. He knows full well it would not support his opinion."[52]

Ministers who challenged their congregations on the segregation issue often found themselves without a pulpit. Thomas Thrasher, the rector of the Church of the Ascension in Montgomery, was forced out for talking too much about human brotherhood. As an Episcopalian and thus answerable to a bishop and not simply a local congregation, Thrasher perhaps thought he had greater freedom of speech. He found no ally in Rev. Charles Carpenter of Selma, however, who failed to use his Episcopal authority to come to Thrasher's aid.[53] Often presented in anticlerical terms as a clash between "pulpit and pew," the theological struggle over the rightness of desegregation spilled over into the sacristy, as Thomas Thrasher's case indicates. As one representative of the Southern Regional Council—which kept statistics on integrationist ministers run out of their churches—noted wryly, "in the South we have a new class of DPs—displaced parsons." Given these internal dynamics, is it any wonder that, as one civil rights worker complained, trying to fire up the white church was like "trying to strike a match on a wet windowpane?"[54]

Parishioners were not the only clerical critics. In April 1956 the *Citizens'*
Council complained that "many ministers of the Gospel and laymen are telling us that integration is the word of God. . . . Many others, equally devout
and, one is to assume, equally prayerful in their search for Divine guidance,
have received no word from the Throne of Grace that public school integration is God's wish." Admitting that there was ample biblical justification to
support notions of the brotherhood of man and the equality of all men in
God's sight, the official publication of the White Citizens' Council maintained,
nonetheless, that "it does not follow that God intended the different races of
men to inter-marry." It was this prospect of miscegenation that accounted for
"the strong opposition of thousands of devout Christians to public school
integration." Civil rights supporters, meanwhile, attacked the root argument,
and interpreted the more extreme manifestations of this "strong opposition" of
whites to integration as evidence of their irreligion. Referring to the bombing
of four churches associated with the Montgomery bus boycott, Martin Luther
King painted die-hard white supremacists as heathens, and tried to narrow
the ground Christian segregationists could occupy: "What manner of men are
these, men whose pagan impulses drive them to bomb ministers and desecrate
the House of the Lord?"[55]

It is not uncommon for accusations of heresy to strengthen resolve. After
Brown, Christian laypeople and many ministers clashed with their denominational bodies and with each other, and articulated "a newly self-conscious theology of segregationism."[56] Here again, worries about sexuality blended with
theological concerns. Informed that their position was "un-Christian" by their
denominational leaders and in many instances by the rising generation in the
form of youth conference declarations,[57] segregationists fought back. In North
Carolina, the Quarterly Conference of the Newton Grove Methodist Charge
wrote a resolution that upheld segregation as God's law and criticized the
"impractical idealists within our churches" who dared to speak for the whole
church. Integration, Newton Grove warned, could only lead to "the intermarry-
ing of the races, which we believe to be contrary to the very ordinance of God."[58]
Asked to implement his church's official policy on desegregation in denominational schools, the response of a Baltimore attorney—an alumnus of two
denominational schools and a trustee of three—reveals the theological, and not
just social and political, stakes involved in desegregation. "When the Church
steps forward as the champion of evil causes—as has happened in the long
course of history—there is nothing left to Christians but to cry out at whatever
peril to themselves, as their Lord cried out against the hierarchy of his day,
which crucified him," declared the lawyer. "Where in particular do Christian
churchmen get the idea that there is anything sinful in segregation?"[59] Other
churches criticized their national bodies implicitly through the publication of

church resolutions that stressed the biblical defense of segregation. Quoting the Apostle Paul's proclamation in Acts 17:26, South Carolina's Summerton Baptist Church resolved in October 1957 that integration was wrong because

> (1). God made men of different races and ordained the basic difference between races; (2). Race has a purpose in the Divine plan, each race having a unique purpose and a distinctive mission in God's plan; (3). God meant for people of different races to maintain their race purity and racial identity and seek the highest development of their racial group. God has determined "the bounds of their habitation."[60]

The desire to have God on their side motivated secular organizations dedicated to the maintenance of segregation as well. The minutes for the Jackson chapter of Americans for the Preservation of the White Race reveal an absorbing preoccupation with determining God's will on segregation. In between voting to inscribe "If God be for us who can be against us" on their organizational letterhead and erecting highway billboards denouncing Martin Luther King as a communist, this all-male association listened to an astonishing number of guest lectures dedicated to "the Bible and segregation" and "the scripture and how it applies to present problems."[61] Far from "sens[ing] the limitations of the Bible," religious segregationists grounded their defense of segregation firmly in their reading of that holy text, and pitted their own interpretations of it against their more liberal coreligionists.[62]

•   •   •

Surveying the *Brown* decision through the combined optic of sex and religion helps bring into focus both the political and the sacred worldview of many white southern Christians on the eve of the modern civil rights movement. Over the course of the next decade, while some southern whites tried to find a middle way, to obey the new desegregation laws without betraying their faith, others put theology to use both to push for black rights or to forcefully resist them. A particularly salient example of how sexualized theology shaped the nature of the struggle between segregationists and desegregationists is the Selma-to-Montgomery march of March 21–25, 1965. Viewing the Selma march through this intersection of sex and religion helps makes sense of the strategy of the SCLC, the specific shape the march took, and the ways in which opponents of the march articulated their claims.

Rising from the northern banks of the Alabama River in the heart of the black belt, the small town of Selma seemed an unlikely site for the climax of the civil rights movement. Although described by Martin Luther King in early 1965 as the "symbol of bitter-end resistance to the civil rights movement in the Deep South," Selma was at that point already deep in political transition. Aided by the Student Non-violent Coordinating Committee (SNCC), the city had seen voting rights demonstrations since 1962, organized by the local Dallas County Voters League. The 1964 mayoral race—Selma's first truly competitive municipal election since 1932—ended with the defeat of the local machine. The new mayor, an enterprising small businessman named Joe Smitherman, was elected with the support of the black community, which also posted the first black candidates for municipal office since Reconstruction.[63]

Drawn by this vital local movement, in late 1964 the SCLC focused its own voter registration efforts on Dallas County and its abusive sheriff, James G. Clark, Jr.—who could be relied on, the SCLC thought, to respond to the voter drive with an explosion that would catch the nation's attention the way Bull Connor's water hoses and police dogs had in Birmingham the previous year.[64] This reading of Clark was all too accurate: on February 18, 1965, four hundred activists in Marion, an outlying town, were attacked during a night march by a gang made up of Jim Clark's posse, state troopers, local police, and assorted hooligans. A twenty-six-year-old black man, Jimmie Lee Jackson—the youngest deacon in his small Baptist church—was shot while protecting his mother and eighty-two-year-old grandfather from state troopers. He died eight days later.[65]

Conceived in response to Jackson's death as a protest against the violence of the state, the first Selma-to-Montgomery march on March 7 became the most famous example of that violence when Sheriff Clark's mounted posse and Alabama state troopers met the marchers on the Edmund Pettus Bridge and gassed, clubbed, and trampled them. Caught on film, the grainy images of gas-masked, blue-helmeted state troopers and whip-wielding mounted police bludgeoning African Americans who, moments before, had been kneeling in prayer transfixed the nation. What was immediately dubbed "Bloody Sunday" ignited sympathy demonstrations across the country. The participation of religious leaders in these demonstrations visually struck observers. Two hundred nuns marched alongside 15,000 other people in Harlem; 150 clergymen joined SCLC's Walter Fauntroy and the Episcopal bishop Paul Moore in a denunciation of President Lyndon Johnson's passivity.[66]

The SCLC was determined to march again. But this time it would be more than a march: it would be a procession, and, like all proper processions, it would be led by holy men. Shrewdly building on the reaction of religious leaders outside the South, Martin Luther King issued a national call to clergymen to join him in Alabama. This call represented a significant rhetorical shift. Prior to Bloody Sunday, the SCLC presented the Selma voting rights campaign in terms of citizenship and equal justice. A nine-by-sixteen-inch advertisement published in the *New York Times* on February 5, titled "A Letter from MARTIN

LUTHER KING from a Selma, Alabama Jail," called for help from "all decent Americans" to support equal rights and "to advance dignity in the United States." What had been a secular campaign for civil rights was now transformed into a holy crusade to redeem the blood spilled in Selma. On the evening of Sunday, March 7, King sent telegrams to clergy around the country. Insisting that "no American is without responsibility" for what happened at Selma, King continued: "The people of Selma will struggle on for the soul of the nation, but it is fitting that all Americans help to bear the burden. I call therefore, on clergy of all faiths . . . to join me in Selma for a ministers march to Montgomery on Tuesday morning, March ninth."[67]

The response was overwhelming: more than 450 white clergymen, rabbis, and religious women (including a contingent of nuns) gathered in Selma, with more on the way. Contemporaries remarked on the sense of pilgrimage shared by those who traveled to Selma that March. Arriving from New York, the NAACP lawyer and longtime King adviser Stanley Levison was "struck by the unfamiliarity of the participants. They were not long-committed white liberals and Negroes. They were new forces from all faiths and classes."[68] As an article in *Newsweek* described it, "like the lame to Lourdes they came—bishops, rabbis, ministers, priests, and nuns—several thousand in all, sensing that somehow God was stirring the waters in Selma, Ala." Believers who did not themselves journey to Selma could still participate vicariously in the march: denominational leaders in New York and Washington urged that the coming weekend's sermons be on Selma. And that Sunday (March 14) upward of 15,000 people gathered across the street from the White House in Lafayette Park to take part in an ecumenical protest sponsored by the National Council of Churches.[69]

There are many ways to interpret this march, but one way to understand it is as a contest over Christian orthodoxy—as a collision of religious communities presenting themselves as defenders of two conflicting theological views. As its very name implies, the SCLC was always aware that men of the cloth lent the movement moral and social power. As I have shown already, King and other SCLC preacher-politicians encouraged the conflation of black protest and Christian righteousness throughout the civil rights era; King used it to particularly good effect, as when he chose to be arrested in Birmingham on Good Friday, 1963. But religious leaders were equally important for their theological imprimatur. Calling the Selma march a "pilgrimage," as the black press and leading rights workers did (including King, in his end-of-the-march speech at the Alabama capitol), invested it with religious, and not just political, significance. So did SCLC's decision to call those who would be allowed to walk the entire fifty-mile distance "the chosen few." The ranks of marching priests, ministers, and rabbis represented a concrete witness to the rightness of integration, a walking testimony to an ecumenical belief in racial equality rooted in a common Judeo-Christian heritage. This, at least, is how *Ebony* saw it. Rev. King, the magazine declared, had "accomplished the virtually impossible: he had converted leaders of the so-called white church" to civil rights.[70] Here we may see the participation of the "pure-faced nuns" and "the clerics with high collars" in the march and SCLC's longstanding campaign to portray desegregation and black equality as right Christian doctrine as part of a single strategy: to assault at its root the most powerful language supporting segregation, a language that was thoroughly Christian.

Understanding the march in religious terms helps explain both the SCLC's tactics and segregationists' response to those tactics, which was to emphasize the allegedly sexual sins of the clergy and the desecration of holy spaces. Surely good Christians—Christians whose behavior found favor in the sight of the Lord—could not behave the way these supposedly religious supporters of civil rights did in Alabama. In a speech before the U.S. Congress, the Alabama representative William Dickinson denounced the morals of the SCLC's supporters and declared that "Negro and white freedom marchers invaded a Negro church in Montgomery and engaged in an all-night session of debauchery within the church itself." "I saw numerous instances of boys and girls of both races hugging, kissing and fondling one another openly in the church," another source reported. "On one occasion I saw a Negro boy and a white girl engaged in sexual intercourse on the floor of the church." As the marchers reached Montgomery, Governor George Wallace of Alabama sent all female state employees home.[71]

Worse yet was what the clergy were meant to be up to. Publications ranging from the *Fiery Cross* to the *Memphis Press-Scimitar* described the march as a week-long interracial orgy, with men of the cloth leading the way. These stories were picked up by the mainstream press; during the first week in May, *Newsweek, Time,* and *U.S. News and World Report* all carried features with titles like "Kiss and Tell," and "Orgies on the Rights March." Riffing on Martin Luther King's appeal for clergy to come to Selma, white supremacists charged that marchers were offered "$15 a day, 3 meals a day, and all the sex [they] could handle." In a letter to the Episcopal bishop of Alabama that made its way into the *New York Times*, Frances H. Hamilton complained about the behavior of Jon Daniels and other priests during the march, and claimed that a white girl had died of exhaustion after providing "sexual comfort to the visiting clergy."[72] As Rep. Dickinson summed things up a month later, in another speech before Congress, "Mr. Speaker, our modern Canterbury Tales make Chaucer's pilgrims look like veritable paragons of virtue and piety."[73]

Dickinson's version of events was widely available. More than 15,000 copies of the speech were mailed to Alabamans. The speech was also sold at newsstands. As one colleague of the immensely gratified Dickinson reported to *Time,* there were three bestsellers in Alabama that spring—"*Nugget, Playboy,* and the

Congressional Record!"[74] However widely disseminated this testimony should nonetheless not be read as descriptive of actual clerical behavior on the march. Indeed, Congressman Dickinson's allegations regarding sexual activity during the march were refuted at the time. Hearing the rumors during the march, Bob Craig, a South Carolina editor, worked hard to substantiate the stories but came up empty. "I spent the entire night trying to find an orgy in a church and checked a lot of churches and found no such thing," he reported.[75] Nuns, seminarians, and clergymen who had participated in the march insisted in telegrams and affidavits that they had observed no sexual misconduct. (Or sexual conduct of any sort: as one SNCC official noted wryly, "Baby, everyone was too tired from all that marching."[76]) When McBee Martin of Bristol, Virginia, complained that the *Presbyterian Survey* had failed to cover the sexual angle of the story, the *Survey's* editor replied soberly: "We seldom report rumors of sex orgies in connection with religious events."[77]

The ease with which the *Presbyterian Survey* referred to the Selma to Montgomery march as a religious event reveals the victory of Martin Luther King's vision of Christianity as firmly allied with the civil rights movement. Yet this victory should not obscure the conflict behind it. However inaccurate, representations of clerical sex orgies should be taken seriously as efforts to demonize civil rights activists in religious terms that would resonate with southern Christians—just as the SCLC's use of "pilgrims" was an attempt to sanctify them in the same language.[78] In casting the clergy in Selma and Montgomery as miscegenators, as sexual sinners, white opponents of integration were able to represent them as apostles of the Antichrist. This was William Dickinson's position: "I feel very deeply that when the genuine devout men and women devoted to God's work participate in activities as I have described and lend their dignity and prestige they are doing themselves and those whom they represent"—including, presumably, Jesus—" a very grave disservice."[79]

Recognizing the religious dynamics of the conflict between segregationists and integrationists not as one of ungodly versus godly but as a yet undecided struggle for the crown of orthodoxy helps us understand the reaction to the *Brown* decision, the Selma march, and much of the shape that the civil rights movement took—both in terms of the strategic decisions of its leaders and in the strategies of resistance adopted by its opponents. It also helps contextualize certain contemporary issues. As anticipated in many reactions to *Brown*, sexualized Christian theology continues to be a way of championing segregation. At the congregational level, the debate has raged over the issue of integrated churches—a question that was raised only after the mid-1950s, when many white Protestant churches adopted closed-door policies in response to the civil rights movement. This problem gained national attention in 1976, when the deacons of Plains Baptist Church, the home church of the Democratic presidential candidate Jimmy Carter of Georgia, enforced its closed-door policy against Rev. Clennon King and three other African Americans. The specter haunting Baptists wrangling over integrated churches was a familiar one: miscegenation. In 1971, the Baptist Sunday School Board revised 140,000 copies of *Becoming*, a quarterly magazine for teenagers, because it accompanied an article supporting open churches with a photograph of an African American boy talking to two white girls.[80]

More important than the way Christian theology has buttressed segregationist views within the church has been the effort to use the constitutional protection of religion to expand the social sphere in which segregation could remain. The main battleground here has been private religious schools.[81] In 1979 (against the counsel of the Christian Life Commission, still sounding from the wilderness) the Southern Baptist Convention adopted by an overwhelming margin a resolution that opposed a federal proposal to deny tax-exempt status to private schools that discriminated on the basis of race. While the SBC resolved, the federal government sued. Their target was well chosen: Bob Jones University in South Carolina, which until the spring of 2000 prohibited interracial dating among its students. Founded in 1927, Bob Jones excluded black students until 1971. Revealing a deep concern about interracial marriage, from 1971 to 1975 the university accepted a small number of black students who were already married to other African Americans. In 1975 the university began to accept unmarried black students but prohibited interracial dating and marriage, insisting that "God has separated people for His own purpose."[82]

Because of this policy, in 1976 the Internal Revenue Service stripped the university of its tax-exempt status, arguing that federally supported institutions could not advocate views "contrary to established public policy," even if those views were grounded in religious belief. In 1983 the Supreme Court upheld this decision in *Bob Jones University v. United States*.[83] In this important ruling, the Court failed to grant constitutional protection to the expansion of religious privacy into other associational areas.

Although the federal government declined to subsidize the racially discriminatory behavior of Bob Jones, the Supreme Court recognized in its 1983 decision that some Americans might "engage in racial discrimination on the basis of sincerely-held religious beliefs." White supremacists and other defenders of segregation have not been shy about embracing such beliefs, especially if such a move gains them the protection of the Religion Clause and the Fourteenth Amendment's "zone of privacy." In 1984, Senator Trent Lott of Mississippi insisted that the main issue in the Bob Jones case was "not a racial question, but a religious question. And yet the Internal Revenue Service is going in, making a determination of that school's tax-deductible status, based on a religious belief."[84]

If religion has been and continues to be so important to those arguing in favor of segregation as well as those resisting it, why have modern historians preferred to study scientific racism or white supremacist politics and ignored this more widespread and deeply held set of beliefs? Perhaps the answer lies in a scholarly inclination to take the historical teleology of secularization so seriously as to distort our own idea of what is important. Religion ends up being seen as an archaic vestige, at most a rhetorical plaything of ideologues in the modern age (as indeed it sometimes is) and not a coherent cosmology capable of providing modern people with an all-encompassing model of social relations. Such an outlook overlooks the "suppleness" of American religion and underplays its importance in modern America.[85]

An equally important reason for continued scholarly indifference to the religious roots of white resistance to black civil rights has to do with what can only be seen as the victory of the theology of the beloved community. For many scholars otherwise uninterested in seeing religion as a meaningful part of public life in post–World War II America, "true" Christianity has become synonymous with the vision of Martin Luther King and other Christian integrationists. In a recent issue of the New Yorker, Louis Menand argued:

> It was King's genius to see that in the matter of racial equality the teachings of the Christian Bible are on all fours with the promise of the Constitution and its amendments. With one brilliant stroke, he transformed what had been a legal struggle into a spiritual one, and lost nothing in the bargain.[86]

King certainly lost nothing in this bargain. But those scholars and students who uncritically treat King's Christianity as "orthodox" or "true" not only lose a great deal of historical and theological complexity but also miss most of the real drama in the monumental conflict between the integrationist Christian theology of liberation and its venerable counterpart, the theology of segregation.

Notes

My thanks for the timely and expert research aid of Catherine Jones, the lucid questions and comments of the Johns Hopkins History Seminar, and the thoughts, expertise, and encouragement of Karen Anderson, Tony Badger, David Chappell, Charles Eagles, David Garrow, Glenda Gilmore, Paul Harvey, Elizabeth McCrae, Michael O'Brien, Bryant Simon, Stephen Tuck, Clive Webb, and my own in-house theologian, the medieval historian David Nirenberg.

1. Andrew Young, *A Way Out of No Way: The Spiritual Memoirs of Andrew Young* (Nashville: Thomas Nelson, 1994), 60.

2. First King quotation in *The Papers of Martin Luther King Jr.*, ed. Clayborne Carson, 4 vols. (Berkeley: University of California Press, 1992–), 3:306; King on the prodigal son quoted in Ralph E. Luker, "Kingdom of God and Beloved Community in the Thought of Martin Luther King, Jr.," in *The Role of Ideas in the Civil Rights Movement*, ed. Ted Ownby (Jackson: University Press of Mississippi, 2002), 44.

3. Will Campbell quoted in *New York Times*, Jul. 14, 1958. Kester quoted in special edition of *Prophetic Religion* (spring 1955): 8, Howard A. Kester Papers, folder 233, series 4–9, coll. 3834, Southern Historical Collection, University of North Carolina at Chapel Hill.

4. "Body of Christ" quotation from sermon reprinted in *Student Voice* (Tougaloo College Student Movement paper), Apr. 1964, folder 3, box 3, Ed King Collection, Special Collections, J. D. Williams Library, University of Mississippi, Oxford; King quoted in Charles Marsh, "The Civil Rights Movement as Theological Drama," in Ownby, *Role of Ideas in the Civil Rights Movement*, 30.

5. Aldon D. Morris, *The Origins of the Civil Rights Movement: Black Communities Organizing for Change* (New York: Free Press, 1984), 4. For a nuanced argument of the importance of religion to the movement see, for example, Charles M. Payne, *I've Got the Light of Freedom: The Organizing Tradition and the Mississippi Freedom Struggle* (Berkeley: University of California Press, 1995), 257; for a qualification of its influence see Adam Fairclough, *To Redeem the Soul of America: The Southern Christian Leadership Conference and Martin Luther King Jr.* (Athens: University of Georgia Press, 1987). For the importance of distinguishing between church people and churches as institutions see Randy J. Sparks, *Religion in Mississippi* (Jackson: University Press of Mississippi, 2001), 221. For connections between the civil rights movement and other progressive struggles (including organized labor, the New Deal, and explicitly black rights–oriented organizations before the 1950s) see Patricia Sullivan, *Days of Hope: Race and Democracy in the New Deal Era* (Chapel Hill: University of North Carolina Press, 1996); Timothy B. Tyson, *Radio Free Dixie: Robert F. Williams and the Roots of Black Power* (Chapel Hill: University of North Carolina Press, 1999); Barbara Ransby, *Ella Baker and the Black Freedom Movement: A Radical Democratic Vision* (Chapel Hill: University of North Carolina Press, 2003); and Robert Rodgers Korstad, *Civil Rights Unionism: Tobacco Workers and the Struggle for Democracy in the Mid-Twentieth-Century South* (Chapel Hill: University of North Carolina Press, 2003).

6. David L. Chappell refers to the "strained arguments segregationists used to justify segregation on religious grounds," in *A Stone of Hope: Prophetic Religion and the Death of Jim Crow* (Chapel Hill: University of North Carolina Press, 2004), 3; see also 8; and David L. Chappell, "Religious Ideas of the Segregationists," *Journal of American Studies* 32 (1998): 253. Paul Harvey refers to the "theology of segregationism" in "Religion, Race, and the Right in the Baptist South, 1945–1990," in *Religion and Politics in the South*, ed. Glenn Feldman (Tuscaloosa: University of Alabama Press, forthcoming), 5; on the "theology for racism" see Bill J. Leonard, "A Theology for Racism: Southern Fundamentalists and the Civil Rights Movement," in *Southern Landscapes*, ed. Tony Badger, Walter Edgar, and Jan Nordby Gretlund (Tübingen: Stauffenburg Verlag, 1996), 165–81. Wayne Flynt also refers to "segregationist theology," *Alabama Baptists: Southern Baptists in the*

Heart of Dixie (Tuscaloosa: University of Alabama Press, 1998), 458, and notes that "lay people charted the course on race relations. Laymen shaped the Baptist response to race from the *Brown* decision forward," 465. Andrew Michael Manis presents the civil rights movement in the South as an internal dispute among Baptists in which each side fought for sacred legitimacy; see Andrew Michael Manis, *Southern Civil Religions in Conflict: Black and White Baptists and Civil Rights, 1954–1957* (Athens: University of Georgia Press, 1987). Leonard argues a similar point, writing that "Southern fundamentalists . . . responded to the civil rights movement not merely as a national social crisis, but as a challenge to certain unchanging truths taught in Holy Scripture and required of all true Christians. Those who contradicted such teaching were not merely social deviants, they were also biblical apostates"; "Theology for Racism," 166–67.

7. Rev. James F. Burks, "Integration or Segregation," May 30, 1954, typescript, folder 1, box 100, General Correspondence, Executive Papers, Gov. Thomas B. Stanley (1954–1958), Library of Virginia, Richmond. Similar versions of this sermon were reprinted repeatedly, including in *Religious Herald* (May 3, 1956), cited in Mark Newman, *Getting Right with God: Southern Baptists and Desegregation, 1945–1995* (Tuscaloosa: University of Alabama Press, 2001), 56. Deuteronomy 32:8: "When the Most High gave the nations their inheritance, when he divided the sons of men, he fixed their bounds," Jerusalem Bible (1966); Acts 17:26: "From one single stock he not only created the whole human race so that they could occupy the entire earth, but he decreed how long each nation should flourish and what the boundaries of its territory should be."

8. Pastor of Highland Baptist Church of Montgomery quoted in Neil R. McMillen, *The Citizens' Council: Organized Resistance to the Second Reconstruction, 1954–64* (Urbana: University of Illinois Press, 1971), 174.

9. Harvey, "Religion, Race, and the Right," 5.

10. The integrationist T. B. Maston cites the anthropological work of Ruth Benedict and Gene Weltfish, *The Races of Mankind* (New York: Public Affairs Committee, 1943), on the unity of the peoples of the earth, in T. B. Maston, *Integration* (Nashville, 1956), 8.

11. For a specific reference to the Antichrist see Burks, "Integration or Segregation," in which the author asserts that "the amalgamation of races is part of the spirit of antichrist."

12. The biblical narrative is Genesis 3:1–7. Henry Ansgar Kelly, "The Metamorphosis of the Eden Serpent During the Middle Ages and Renaissance," *Viator* 2 (1971): 301–28.

13. The "Negro gardener" argument is from Samuel A. Cartwright, quoted in George M. Fredrickson, *The Black Image in the White Mind: The Debate on Afro-American Character and Destiny, 1817–1914* (New York: Harper and Row, 1971), 87–88.

14. "Ariel" [Buckner H. Payne], *The Negro: What Is His Ethnological Status?* (Cincinnati: published for the proprietor, 1867), in John David Smith, *The "Ariel" Controversy: Religion and "The Negro Problem"* (New York: Garland, 1993), 45, 48. See also Smith, *An Old Creed for the New South: Proslavery Ideology and Historiography, 1965–1918* (Westport, Conn.: Greenwood Press, 1985), 43, and Fredrickson, *Black Image in the White Mind*, 188–89.

15. Charles Carroll, *The Negro a Beast* (St. Louis: American Book and Bible House, 1900); Charles Carroll, *The Tempter of Eve* (St. Louis: Adamic, 1902). On those books, see Mason Stokes, *The Color of Sex: Whiteness, Heterosexuality, and the Fictions of White Supremacy* (Durham, N.C.: Duke University Press, 2001), 5, 95–98, and Fredrickson,

Black Image in the White Mind, 277. H. Paul Douglass, *Christian Reconstruction in the South* (Boston: Pilgrim Press, 1909), 114.

16. On the longevity of proslavery arguments, including religious arguments, and their applicability in the Jim Crow era see Smith, *Old Creed for the New South*, 286.

17. Early Van Deventer, *Perfection of the Races* [1954], pamphlet, folder 1, box 100, General Correspondence, Stanley Executive Papers; Burks, "Integration or Segregation?"

18. D. B. Red, "Race Mixing a Religious Fraud" [c. 1959], pamphlet, box 2, William D. McCain Papers, McCain Archives and Special Collections, Cook Library, University of Southern Mississippi, Hattiesburg; *Laurel Leader Call*, quoted in Charles Marsh, *God's Long Summer: Stories of Faith and Civil Rights* (Princeton, N.J.: Princeton University Press, 1997), 93.

19. Numerous pamphlets and private letters consider integration and miscegenation a communist plot—which, by virtue of communism's official atheism, was seen as synonymous with heresy. For example, in 1958 the Daughters of the Confederacy denounced miscegenation as a "Communist objective." Quoted in the monthly Citizens' Councils of Louisiana publication *Councilor Newsletter*, May 1958, p. 3, folder 1, Miscellaneous Papers—Race Relations, no. 517–38a, Southern Historical Collection, University of North Carolina at Chapel Hill.

20. Carey Daniel, "God the Original Segregationist," quoted in McMillen, *Citizens' Council*, 175.

21. Burks, "Integration or Segregation?"

22. Theodore G. Bilbo, *Take Your Choice: Separation or Mongrelization* (Poplarville, Miss.: Dream House, 1947), 109.

23. Henry Louttit quoted in Gardiner H. Shattuck, Jr., *Episcopalians and Race: Civil War to Civil Rights* (Lexington: University Press of Kentucky, 2000), 68; W. M. Caskey quoted in Sparks, *Religion in Mississippi*, 231. Ministers at Little Rock in Ernest Q. Campbell and Thomas F. Pettigrew, *Christians in Racial Crisis: A Study of Little Rock's Ministry* (Washington, D.C.: Public Affairs Press, 1959), 51.

24. Cameron Baptist Church quoted in Newman, *Getting Right with God*, 51; David M. Gardner quoted in Newman, *Getting Right with God*, 50.

25. Daughters of the American Revolution quoted in "Racial Integrity," flyer, p. 2 n. 15, no. 3551, E. A. Holt Papers, Southern Historical Collection, University of North Carolina at Chapel Hill. *Florida ex rel Hawkins v. Board of Control*, 1 RRLR 89 at 95 (1955), quoted in David L. Chappell, *Inside Agitators: White Southerners in the Civil Rights Movement* (Baltimore: Johns Hopkins University Press, 1994), 91; *Loving v. Commonwealth* (1965) (record no. 6163), 15.

26. See boxes 100 and 101, General Correspondence, Stanley Executive Papers.

27. On the reluctance of the Supreme Court to tackle the miscegenation issue while *Brown II* was pending, see interview of Philip Elman by Norman Silber, "The Solicitor General's Office, Justice Frankfurter, and Civil Rights Litigation, 1946–1960: An Oral History," *Harvard Law Review* 100 (Feb. 1987): 846. On reaction to the 1955 miscegenation case (*Naim v. Naim*, 350 U.S. 891) see Gerald Gunther, "The Subtle Vices of the 'Passive Virtues'—A Comment on the Principle and Expediency in Judicial Review," *Columbia Law Review* 1 (1964): 1–25.

28. Alexander M. Bickel, "Integrated Cohabitation," *New Republic*, May 30, 1964, 4. Bickel was referring to *McLaughlin v. Florida*, 379 U.S. 184 (1964). Memorandum from

Justice John Marshall Harlan II quoted in Rachel F. Moran, *Interracial Intimacy: The Regulation of Race and Romance* (Chicago: University of Chicago Press, 2001), 91.

29. On the history of antimiscegenation laws in America see Peter Wallenstein, *Tell the Court I Love My Wife: Race, Marriage, and Law: An American History* (New York: Palgrave Macmillan, 2002); Moran, *Interracial Intimacy*; and Walter Wadlington, "The *Loving* Case: Virginia's Anti-Miscegenation Statute in Historical Perspective," *Virginia Law Review* 52 (1966): 1189–23.

30. James Weldon Johnson, *Along This Way* (New York: Viking Press, 1933), 170; see also Johnson, *Negro Americans: What Now?* (New York: Da Capo Press, 1973); John Dollard, *Caste and Class in a Southern Town* (New Haven, Conn.: Yale University Press, 1937); Lillian Smith, *Killers of the Dream* (New York: Norton, 1949); Gunnar Myrdal, *An American Dilemma: The Negro Problem and Modern Democracy* (New York: Harper, 1944), 587.

31. For the NAACP position on intermarriage, see the correspondence between Walter White, Alfred Lewis (secretary of the Boston branch), and Florence H. Luscomb, Jun. 1–6, 1938, folder 247, box 11, Florence Hope Luscomb Papers, Schlesinger Library, Radcliffe Institute for Advanced Study, Cambridge, Mass. Thurgood Marshall quoted in Richard Kluger, *Simple Justice* (New York: Knopf, 1975), 266. On the NAACP's attempts to avoid cases involving sex offenses see Jack Greenberg, *Crusaders in the Courts: How a Dedicated Band of Lawyers Fought for the Civil Rights Revolution* (New York: Basic Books, 1994), 102.

32. Mark Ethridge, "A Call to the South," *Nieman Reports* 13 (Apr. 1959): 9.

33. *Jackson Daily News* quoted in Stephen J. Whitfield, *A Death in the Delta: The Story of Emmett Till* (Baltimore: Johns Hopkins University Press, 1991), 9. Walter C. Givhan quoted in Melissa Fay Greene, *The Temple Bombing* (Reading, Mass.: Addison-Wesley, 1996), 148. Herman E. Talmadge quoted in Stephen G. N. Tuck, *Beyond Atlanta: The Struggle for Racial Equality in Georgia* (Athens: University of Georgia Press, 2001), 77; Talmadge quoted in *Ebony* 12 (Apr. 1957): 78; William A. Robinson, Jr., to Talmadge, May 25, 1954 (copied to Thomas B. Stanley), in folder 2, box 100, General Correspondence, Stanley Executive Papers. Eugene Cook quoted in Greene, *Temple Bombing*, 149. *Racial Facts* (1964) quoted in Marsh, *God's Long Summer*, 84.

34. Of the thirty largest daily newspapers in the South, all were hostile to the *Brown* decision except for a dozen in the border states; see David R. Davies, *The Press and Race: Mississippi Journalists Confront the Movement* (Jackson: University Press of Mississippi, 2001), 9.

35. Keith Miller's survey of homiletic collections reveals few sermons concerned with race issues prior to the Montgomery bus boycott. Keith Miller, *Voice of Deliverance: The Language of Martin Luther King Jr. and Its Sources* (New York: Free Press, 1992), 53.

36. Hodding Carter quoted in Tony Badger, "The Crisis of Southern Liberalism, 1946–65," in *The Making of Martin Luther King and the Civil Rights Movement*, ed. Brian Ward and Tony Badger (New York: New York University Press, 1996), 69.

37. Southeastern Regional Methodist Student Conference (37 signatures) to Stanley, Jun. 11, 1954, folder 1, box 100, General Correspondence, Stanley Executive Papers. National Baptist Convention announcement quoted in Manis, *Southern Civil Religions in Conflict*, 61. Joe Louis quoted in "Backstage," *Ebony* 9 (Aug. 1954), 14.

38. Lillian Smith quoted in Pete Daniel, *Lost Revolutions: The South in the 1950s* (Chapel Hill: University of North Carolina Press, 2000), 182. A complaint representative of the concerns of those funding foreign missions was that "the practice of legal segregation on the basis of race weakens our Christian witness at home and abroad and lays a roadblock across the path of our missionaries": editor's page, *Alabama Baptist*, Nov. 4, 1954.

39. Joel L. Alvis, Jr., *Religion and Race: Southern Presbyterians, 1946–1983* (Tuscaloosa: University of Alabama Press, 1994), 57–58.

40. Rev. George E. Naff, Jr., Coeburn Methodist Church, to Stanley, Jul. 1, 1954, folder 1, box 101, General Correspondence, Stanley Executive Papers.

41. Robert Penn Warren, *Segregation: The Inner Conflict in the South* (New York: Random House, 1956).

42. "Hand of God" quoted in Daniel, *Lost Revolutions*, 184. "Pinkos in the Pulpit," *Citizens' Council*, Dec. 1956, quoted in David L. Chappell, "A Stone of Hope: Prophetic Faith, Liberalism, and the Death of Jim Crow," *Journal of the Historical Society* 3 (spring 2003): 152.

43. Douglas Hudgins quoted in Marsh, *God's Long Summer*, 100–101. J. W. Storer quoted in Newman, *Getting Right with God*, 23. This was the view as well of Leon Macon, the editor of the *Alabama Baptist*, who advised distinguishing between "being a Christian and performing a duty. Those who do right under the compulsion of law are performing a duty"; editor's page, *Alabama Baptist*, Nov. 4, 1954. King objected to this interpretation in his letter from the Birmingham Jail, insisting that Christians must embrace the civil rights movement on theological and moral grounds as well as civic ones. Martin Luther King, "Letter from Birmingham City Jail," in *A Testament of Hope: The Essential Writings of Martin Luther King, Jr.*, ed. James Melvin Washington (San Francisco: HarperCollins, 1986), 289–302.

44. Shattuck, *Episcopalians and Race*, 79–80.

45. Statement of Atlanta clergymen quoted in Newman, *Getting Right with God*, 45. Between 1957 and 1959, a number of groups of Protestant and Jewish clergy published statements supporting obedience to the law without specifically discussing the merits of desegregation. See Michael B. Friedland, *Lift Up Your Voice Like a Trumpet: White Clergy and the Civil Rights and Antiwar Movements, 1954–1973* (Chapel Hill: University of North Carolina Press, 1998), 36.

46. Editor's page, *Alabama Baptist*, Feb. 10, 1955; Campbell and Pettigrew, *Christians in Racial Crisis*, 100.

47. Special issue, "The Church and Segregation," *Presbyterian Outlook*, May 3, 1954, folder 1, box 100, General Correspondence, Stanley Executive Papers.

48. Burks, "Integration or Segregation?"

49. W. L. Trotten, Sr. to Stanley, Jun. 8, 1954; Elmer M. Ramsey to Stanley, Jun. 7, 1954, both in folder 1, box 100, General Correspondence, Stanley Executive Papers.

50. Mrs. Jesse L. West to Stanley, Jun. 3, 1954; Mrs. G. P. Smith to Stanley, Jun. 8, 1954; Mr. and Mrs. J. W. Layne to Stanley, Jun. 8, 1954, all in folder 1, box 100, General Correspondence, Stanley Executive Papers. For comparable arguments in North Carolina, see the examples in Elizabeth McRae, "Why White Women Want White Supremacy: Female Segregationists Respond to *Brown*," paper delivered at the annual meeting of the Southern Association for Women Historians, Athens, Georgia, Jun. 5–7, 2003, 4–5.

51. Mrs. R. E. Martin to Stanley, May 27, 1954,; Mrs. Henry Winter Davis to Stanley, Jun. 10, 1954, both in folder 1, box 100, General Correspondence, Stanley Executive Papers.

52. R. D. Cook to Stanley, Jun. 3, 1954, folder 2; J. D. Jones to Stanley, May 28, 1954, folder 1; Mrs. James Irving Beale to Stanley, Jun. 8, 1954, folder 1; all in box 100, General Correspondence, Stanley Executive Papers.

53. On Thrasher and more broadly on the Episcopal Church and desegregation see Shattuck, *Episcopalians and Race*, 77.

54. "Pulpit and pew" chapter title in Chappell, *Stone of Hope*. Regional council official quoted in Reed Sarratt, *The Ordeal of Desegregation: The First Decade* (New York: Harper and Row, 1966), 276. "Wet windowpane" quoted in Marshall Frady, "God and Man in the South," *Atlantic Monthly* 219 (Jan. 1967): 38.

55. *Citizens' Council*, 1 (Apr. 1956), folder 19, box 1, Ed King Collection. King in *Ebony* 12 (Apr. 1957), 120. Further evidence that miscegenation was at the root of much white southern resistance to school integration is the efforts by southern states to segregate their schools by gender. For examples from Georgia see Tuck, *Beyond Atlanta*, 203; for South Carolina see Mrs. Katherine H. Shane to Gov. Donald S. Russell, Sept. 6, 1963, quoted in Maxie Myron Cox, Jr., "1963—The Year of Decision: Desegregation in South Carolina" (Ph.D. diss., University of South Carolina at Columbia, 1996), 182–83. Denominational camps and conferences go the same sex-segregated route: for examples from the Episcopal church see David W. Coffee, "Episcopalians and the Civil Rights Movement in the Diocese of Southwestern Virginia, 1954–1964," unpublished paper in my possession, 30.

56. Harvey, "Religion, Race, and the Right," 5.

57. For example, Resolution of Methodist Youth from Eastern North Carolina, as reported in *Raleigh News and Observer*, Aug. 21, 1954.

58. "Resolution Adopted on December 12 by the Quarterly Conference of the Newton Grove charge and Wesley Circuit," Dec. 12, 1954, 1953–54 file, Nell Battle Lewis Collection, PS 255.40, North Carolina State Archives, Raleigh.

59. Lawyer quoted in Thomas F. Pettigrew, "Our Caste-Ridden Protestant Campuses," *Christianity and Crisis: Race in America* (1961): 88–91, folder 3, box 3, Ed King Collection. The denomination was probably the Episcopalians.

60. Summerton Baptist Church resolution quoted in Newman, *Getting Right with God*, 53. Generalizations across denominational boundaries are treacherous, but on the whole, ministers seem to have been more likely to support desegregation than their congregations were. On Episcopalians see Shattuck, *Episcopalians and Race*, 68; on southern Baptists see Newman, *Getting Right with God*, 41; overall see Chappell, "Stone of Hope," 151.

61. Minutes, 1964–1966, box 1, Americans for the Preservation of the White Race Collection, J. D. Williams Library, University of Mississippi, Oxford.

62. Chappell, "Religious Ideas of the Segregationists," 249.

63. King quoted in David J. Garrow, *Bearing the Cross: Martin Luther King and the Southern Christian Leadership Conference, 1955–1968* (New York: Morrow, 1986), 372. On Selma, see J. Mills Thornton III, *Dividing Lines: Municipal Politics and the Struggle for Civil Rights in Montgomery, Birmingham, and Selma* (Tuscaloosa: University of Alabama Press, 2002), 382, 433.

64. On the SCLC's desire to provoke a confrontation, see Garrow, *Bearing the Cross,* 360. On the ease with which such a provocation could arouse a firm reaction in Selma by Clark, see Thornton, *Dividing Lines,* 476. The extremist Clark was not necessarily representative of Selma whites, however: Selma's police chief, Wilson Baker, opposed Clark's violence, even to the point of protecting civil rights supporters. See David J. Garrow, *Protest at Selma: Martin Luther King, Jr., and the Voting Rights Act of 1965* (New Haven, Conn.: Yale University Press, 1978), 46, 72.

65. Fairclough, *To Redeem the Soul of America,* 239; Adam Fairclough, *Better Day Coming: Blacks and Equality, 1890–2000* (New York: Viking Press, 2001), 291.

66. *U.S. News and World Report,* Mar. 22, 1965, 32–33; Fairclough, *To Redeem the Soul of America,* 247. The *Washington Post* (following UPI) noted the "praying Negroes" in its story on the Selma march; see Garrow, *Protest at Selma,* 73–80.

67. King letter quoted in Garrow, *Protest at Selma,* 52; King telegram quoted in Garrow, *Protest at Selma,* 52; see also Garrow, *Bearing the Cross,* 399–400.

68. See Sister Thomas Marguerite Flanigan, "Nuns at Selma," *America,* Apr. 3, 1965, 454–56. Stanley Levison quoted in Fairclough, *To Redeem the Soul of America,* 250.

69. "Selma, Civil Rights, and the Church Militant," *Newsweek,* Mar. 29, 1965, 75–76. See also Garrow, *Protest at Selma,* 103.

70. See the many references to pilgrimage in Simeon Booker, "50,000 March on Montgomery," *Ebony* 20 (May 1965), 46–62, 75–86. Clergymen and nuns figure prominently in the many pictures that accompany this long article on the march. For King see *Pittsburgh Courier,* Apr. 3, 1965, 2; and Martin Luther King, Jr., "Our God Is Marching On," in Washington, *Testament of Hope,* 228. *Ebony* quotes from Booker, "50,000 March on Montgomery," 53, 55.

71. *Congressional Record,* 89th Cong., 1st sess., Mar. 30, 1965, 6333; sworn affidavit of anonymous black man, Apr. 12, 1965, read into *Congressional Record,* 89th Cong., 1st sess., Mar. 21, 1965, 8597. On Wallace and women workers in the capitol see Dan T. Carter, *The Politics of Rage: George Wallace, the Origins of the New Conservatism, and the Transformation of American Politics* (Baton Rouge: Louisiana State University Press, 1996), 256.

72. "Protest on Route 80," *Time,* Apr. 2, 1965, 21–22.

73. Cecil H. Atkinson affidavit, Nov. 17, 1965, quoted in *Fiery Cross* (winter 1965–66), 1; $15 a day from anonymous affidavit, Apr.12, *Congressional Record,* quoted in *Fiery Cross* (winter 1965–66), 1; clipping, *Memphis Press-Scimitar,* Mar. 21, 1965. See *Newsweek,* "Kiss and Tell?" May 10, 1965, 40; "Love on the Lawn?" *Time,* May 7, 1965, 27; and "What Really Happened on Alabama March?" *U.S. News and World Report,* May 10, 1965, 17. Frances H. Hamilton, letter to editor in *New York Times,* Mar. 30, 1965; see also Charles W. Eagles, *Outside Agitator: Jon Daniels and the Civil Rights Movement in Alabama* (Chapel Hill: University of North Carolina Press, 1993), 48; and Mary Stanton, *From Selma to Sorrow: The Life and Death of Viola Liuzzo* (Athens: University of Georgia Press, 1998), 137. Stories of clerical (and secular) sexual impropriety were gathered and published in Robert M. Mikell, *Selma* (Charlotte, N.C.: Citadel Press, 1965), esp. 8–19. Dickinson quoted in *Congressional Record,* 89th Cong., 1st sess., Apr. 27, 1965, 8593.

74. On the mass mailing see Carter, *Politics of Rage,* 260. Quote from "Mud in the House," *Time,* May 7, 1965, 27.

75. Bob Craig quoted in *Jackson Daily News,* Apr. 27, 1965.

76. *New York Times,* Apr. 29, 1965, May 5, 1965.

77. Alvis, *Religion and Race*, 113.

78. As was the Episcopal Church's addition of Jonathan Daniels—shot outside a grocery store in Lowndes County by a white Alabaman scandalized by Daniels's kissing a black female fellow civil rights worker—to the Calendar of Lesser Feasts and Fasts, which recognizes those who sacrifice their lives "for the faith of Christ." Eagles, *Outside Agitator*, 264, 220.

79. *Congressional Record*, 89th Cong., 1st sess., Apr. 27, 1965, p. 8596.

80. On *Becoming*, see Newman, *Getting Right with God*, 33. Considerable scholarly work on the integration of southern churches will have to be undertaken before it becomes possible to make more than speculative assertions about this debate. But it is clear at least that both sides recognized sacred space as a crucial frontier in the desegregation battle, and both sides made theological arguments in favor of their conflicting positions. Some denominational histories (e.g., Sparks, *Mississippi Baptists*; Newman, *Getting Right with God*) engage the issue, and there is an excellent account of the struggle at Jackson's largest Methodist church written by the minister at the time, W. J. Cunningham, *Agony at Galloway: One Church's Struggle with Social Change* (Jackson: University Press of Mississippi, 1980). Charles Eagles addresses the issue for Alabama in *Outside Agitator*. Otherwise, Charles Marsh's chapter on Rev. Ed King's "kneel-in" campaign is the most extensive treatment; see Marsh, *God's Long Summer*, 116–51.

81. A recent analysis of federal data on private school enrollments by the Civil Rights Project at Harvard University found that private religious schools are more racially segregated than public ones. "Study Finds Parochial Schools Segregated Along Racial Lines," *New York Times*, Aug. 30, 2002.

82. Admissions Office of Bob Jones University to James Landrith, Aug. 31, 1998, in *Multiracial Activist*, available online at: www.multiracial.com/letters/bobjonesuniversity.html (Dec. 11, 2003); see also Lynn Darlin, "Keeping to the Straight and Narrow When the Way Is Filled with Doubters," *New York Times*, May 10, 1982.

83. *Bob Jones University v. United States*, 461 U.S. 574 (1983).

84. Lott interview in *Southern Partisan* (fall 1984): 47.

85. Jon Butler, "Jack-in-the-Box Faith: The Religion Problem in Modern American History," *Journal of American History* 90 (Mar. 2004), 1357–78, esp. 1359.

86. Louis Menand, "Moses in Alabama," *New Yorker*, Sept. 8, 2003, 31.

NINE

White Womanhood, White Supremacy, and the Rise of Massive Resistance

Elizabeth Gillespie McRae

On September 30, 1962, white mothers and fathers across the state rushed to the University of Mississippi, to get their children out of Oxford and away from federal troops, James Meredith, and white rioters. The following month in the state capital, approximately two thousand white women gathered to protest the federal "invasion" of their state. Claiming that it was a white woman's responsibility to "preserve the good life for her children—life, liberty, and the pursuit of happiness," the protesters formed the Women for Constitutional Government (WCG), pledging to work for "constitutional government, free enterprise, the Christian faith, racial self-respect, and national sovereignty." Speaking at the inaugural meeting, Florence Sillers Ogden, a Mississippi journalist, planter, and longtime proponent of white supremacy, praised the ideals of the WCG and told her audience "you, the women . . . are the hope of the Nation."[1]

In emphasizing their political power, Ogden realized that white women were a powerful force for conservative principles, including white supremacy. Her address also implied that their dedication to white supremacy derived in part from their duties as white mothers. Taking a broader look at the politics of Florence Sillers Ogden suggests that the formation of the WCG was not an isolated or an anomalous event. Instead, her politics expose the presence of a malleable but powerful political language that linked white women to the maintenance of the Jim Crow order by suggesting that their sex-specific duties demanded that they teach and preserve the lessons of white supremacy. Invested in and even empowered by this ideology of white supremacy, southern white women fought to maintain racial segregation and in doing so played a central role in the rise of massive resistance and in the circumvention of racial equality.

Ogden's efforts on behalf of white supremacy were part of a long family history. She was no stranger to politics. Her great-uncle Charles Clark had served as Mississippi's wartime governor and had later organized a white man's party that "redeemed" Bolivar County from "Negro rule . . . [and] the corrupt and alien and traitorous renegades" otherwise known as Republicans. When Ogden was born in 1897, Bolivar County had approximately 3,222 white and 26,737 black residents. In order to eliminate the last vestiges of black political power, her father, Walter Sillers, Sr., worked hard to implement the disenfranchisement measures legalized in the Mississippi constitution of 1890. His efforts were successful, and in 1899 the last black elected official in Bolivar County left office. As she came of age, a whitewashed history of black political struggle, orchestrated in part by white women's control over public history, assured her that the Delta was a land legislated, owned, and operated by white men and labored on by black ones. The maintenance of such an economic and social system, however, required sustained political work. As part of that effort, her brother Walter Sillers served in Mississippi's state legislature from 1916 to 1966, securing the power of the white elite and becoming the most powerful voice in Mississippi politics.[2]

Ogden, who did not hold public office, nevertheless did her own political labor. Drawing on the Progressive-era language of maternalist politics, Ogden manipulated the duties of a public mother to build her own political reputation and to secure the Jim Crow order. Following in her mother's footsteps, Ogden became very active in the Daughters of the American Revolution (DAR). As the DAR became increasingly antiradical in the 1920s, Ogden lobbied her congressmen to pass more restrictive immigration policies. In Natchez, she fulfilled her role as historical guardian when she helped create a living reenactment of the Old South, replete with restored plantation homes, white women in hoop skirts, and black "pickaninnies." Looking out for the children in her community, Ogden successfully organized other Rosedale women to petition for a Works Projects Administration grant to build a swimming pool and park—for whites only.[3]

Her political efforts extended beyond the traditional purview of a public mother. In the 1930s, as her brother wrote legislation in Jackson, her husband left Rosedale for an administrative post overseeing the reconstruction of the levees, and Ogden took over the daily operation of the family's cotton plantation. In her own estimation, she successfully took care of forty-six black families that worked the cotton by "treat[ing] them like human beings." She called on Mississippi's political leaders to pay attention to cotton prices and trade policy, and she wrote to Mississippi governors encouraging lower tax rates on land. Then she became involved with the Farm Bureau, the Delta Council, and the Agricultural Adjustment Act administrators orchestrating planter-friendly policies. In the late 1930s, her desire to be a writer and her public reputation resulted in her Sunday column, "Dis an' Dat," with the region's largest daily newspaper, Greenville's *Delta Democrat-Times*. Ogden had long insisted that women had a place in politics, and now she used her column to lobby for the continued economic dominance of Delta planters by encouraging them to remain staunch supporters of President Franklin Roosevelt's New Deal.[4]

While Ogden could navigate the New Deal to reinforce the Jim Crow order, World War II brought changes to the Delta that forced her to alter her political strategies. Everywhere Ogden looked, she saw challenges to the South's social order and to planter power. During the war, the Democratic Party seemed to move left as it embraced labor and black civil rights. Under pressure from the civil rights activist A. Phillip Randolph, President Roosevelt formed the Fair Employment Practices Commission. Much to the alarm of some white southerners, Congress debated anti–poll tax legislation and the Soldier Voting Act. Anti–poll tax legislation threatened to alleviate the financial burden of voting as well as the logistical labyrinth set up in many southern communities to prevent black southerners, poor white southerners, and even white women from registering to vote. The congressional version of the Soldier Voting Act would eliminate the poll tax for military personnel voting by absentee ballot, enabling black soldiers to vote in southern states. Once the Supreme Court handed down the 1944 *Smith v. Allwright* decision declaring the all-white primary unconstitutional, the fear of enfranchised black southerners solidified the opposition of southern senators to the Soldier Voting Act, and they defeated the legislation. No longer legally barred from participating in the Democratic primaries, the only southern elections that mattered, more and more black southerners registered to vote. With the rising grassroots activism among black southerners and limited federal support for civil rights, agricultural subsidies and the restoration of plantation forms seemed woefully inadequate in the struggle to maintain white supremacy.[5]

With the wartime expansion of black and working-class political power, Ogden sought to bring more white women into the political sphere. Faced with the initial steps of the civil rights movement, Ogden moved toward massive resistance. In 1944, declaring that the "reason to vote the Democratic ticket no longer exists . . . if the New Deal and the Democratic party are as one," Ogden called on white women to get more involved in electoral politics. And they did. A group "of public-spirited women" met in a "serious enclave" to find out how they could become delegates to their state Democratic convention. Once educated, Ogden became first a delegate to the county convention and later to the state convention, where she supported the former suffragist Nellie Nugent Somerville's resolution to uphold the right of states to control elections and to collect a poll tax—measures that would effectively minimize black voting throughout the South. In Jackson, Ogden also voted to send an anti-Roosevelt slate of delegates to the Democratic National Convention.[6]

Ogden also worked outside of electoral politics to encourage white women to uphold the status quo by linking the duties of white womanhood to the political and cultural defense of white supremacy. As their sons fought the Axis powers overseas, those left at home, Ogden noted, had to "guard the homefront, keep it safe, and hold it free." As part of these vigilante duties, Ogden claimed that mothers must speak out against the class and racial strife that compromised the war effort. In contrast to strikers in the coal mines and black activists, Ogden noted that mothers "ask no special privileges for their sons." She called on them to "demand that every group, no matter how well organized make the same sacrifices that they and their sons are making." Ogden insisted: "When the Mothers of America speak, the world will listen—even the bureaucrats, the labor unions, the war profiteers, and the congress." "Mothers," she continued, "have no patience with organized selfish minorities." Although Ogden had no children, she joined the efforts of mothers when she began another weekly column entitled "My Dear Boys." In these open letters to local soldiers, Ogden told them of visiting their parents, seeing their sweethearts at local cafes, the water levels of the mighty Mississippi, and the prospects of the annual cotton crops. In her Christmas cards, along with pictures of white children sledding on the levees, she included bolls of cotton and pictures of black laborers picking cotton. "It's a great business being a mother of fighting men," she concluded, and she claimed responsibility for ensuring that "her boys" came home to a Delta that they recognized—one where Jim Crow was still alive.[7]

In the postwar period, however, Ogden's efforts to secure the Jim Crow order met opposition from the Democratic Party. In 1947, President Harry Truman's Committee on Civil Rights issued its report, "To Secure These Rights," condemning the precept of separate but equal and calling for an end to segregation in federal employment, the armed services, public housing, public accommodations, and public schools. Responding to this report, news of violence toward black veterans, and election pressures, Truman desegregated the military in 1948. Like some other white southerners, Ogden felt betrayed by Truman's civil rights platform and joined the Dixiecrats, a movement of white southern Democrats pledging to run a presidential candidate who would uphold states' rights and white supremacy.[8] While some Mississippi men charged that the president's policies made white women vulnerable to rape, mongrelization, and miscegenation, white women took a different approach. When garnering support for the states' rights movement, they emphasized their maternal duties as opposed to their sexual vulnerability and that of their daughters. At the first ever "WOMAN'S meeting" for the State Democratic turned Dixiecrat Party, Ogden delivered an address entitled "Civil Rights" to the eight hundred white women present. Highlighting the recommendations in "To Secure These Rights," Ogden warned white women that school integration would "affect you and your children and your children's children." "Race segregation is self-preservation," she claimed, and without it "mongrelization" would occur and erase the boundaries of white privilege. White women's activism, Ogden cried, "will mean much to our children and grandchildren." At this Jackson meeting, white Mississippi women translated their dedication to white supremacy into a commitment to the "uphill battle for States' Rights." "Women's power," the chairwoman claimed, had been used to "influence" and had "helped to elect men to office of whom we are justly proud." Intent on that power being used to support the Dixiecrat candidates Strom Thurmond and his vice-presidential running mate, the Mississippian Fielding Wright, Ogden spread the message of federal threats to white supremacy and states' rights to women's historical associations, civic organizations, and Parent Teacher Association (PTA) meetings.[9]

The Dixiecrat movement failed to build a permanent political party, and by 1952 Ogden began to look to the Republicans for a presidential candidate. That summer she returned from the Democratic National Convention determined to stop the Democratic Party's "disregard for constitutional government," their "benign attitude toward subversives," and, ironically, what she perceived as their promotion of "hatred between the races and classes." She pledged to work for Democrats for Eisenhower to "elect Ike all by myself—with the help of women." Building on women's political involvement in the Dixiecrat movement, Ogden organized Bolivar County women to send telegrams, knock on doors, and involve women from neighboring counties. And they did. Across the Delta, white women followed her lead and conducted voter drives, held rallies, and wrote editorials. Ogden conducted a one-woman speaking campaign for Eisenhower. Aware that some white Mississippians might resent white women's door-to-door campaigning, she advised women to evaluate the homes they were canvassing and, if necessary, send their husbands instead.[10] If other women did not have such a visceral reaction to the perceived constitutional piracy and racial liberalism of the Democratic Party, she sought to inspire them to political action in the name of motherhood. Attacking the hawkish policies of President Truman that had resulted in the Korean War, she called on mothers to join her because they did not want to "pour their sons into the insatiable maw of endless wars." Capitalizing on white men's patriarchal duty to protect, she also called on two male politicians—Charles Jacobs, a first-term state legislator, and Samuel Lumpkin, a Governor Hugh White appointee—to speak at the Rosedale rally for Eisenhower. Fearing admonition from the state's Democratic leadership, both men initially refused. Perhaps finding Ogden's political power over their districts more significant, however, the two men heeded her second demand and spoke at the rally. As Lumpkin had feared, he suffered political retribution by the state's Democratic leadership. Mississippi went for the Democrat Adlai Stevenson, but the Republican Eisenhower won nearly 40 percent of the vote. Bolivar County did go for Eisenhower—the first Republican presidential candidate ever elected in the county, a victory for which Ogden would take full credit. Mostly, Ogden was disappointed in Mississippi's loyalty to the Democratic Party. She felt it was a failure of male leadership and concluded that "as long as men are men, we are doomed to disappointments."[11]

Whereas her more liberal sisters sought to overturn white supremacy and in consequence white patriarchy, Ogden, in supporting white supremacy, was able to criticize male dominance and patriarchal power because it had failed to uphold its responsibilities to white women and children. Ogden believed that partisan politics and political ambition had corrupted most of Mississippi's male political leaders and rendered them impotent in the face of racial integration. Therefore, she capitalized on images of white women as mothers of future generations, as protectors of their homes, and as voting citizens to emphasize the role of women in defending the interests of the white South. Promoting women's political activism in terms of their gender-specific duties, however, left the patriarchal order intact.

In her efforts to inspire women, in the name of motherhood, to act politically, Ogden embraced a number of inconsistencies with apparent ease. On the eve of the 1952 national political conventions, she wrote: "A woman was put here for one great purpose. Into her hands was placed life's greatest responsibility—motherhood." Ignoring her own life as a very public figure, she claimed: "I am one of these old moss backs who believes that woman's place is in the home." But motherhood, according to Ogden, had explicitly political responsibilities as well. "It is hers," she continued, "to produce and train the men and women of the future.... her high school and college education better fit her for this enormous responsibility."[12] In addition, "now that woman has got the vote," Ogden said, "I think she should exercise her privilege for the good of her country."[13] Political mothers, however, did not mean working mothers, and Ogden reiterated the antifeminist messages of the 1950s by disparaging the idea of women as paid laborers. In addition to "losing the great privilege of making a home for their families," Ogden lamented that working mothers "lose the opportunity to teach their children—subconsciously teach as well as consciously."[14] "There is no substitute for mother's training," Ogden concluded, and "it is better to give your children fewer comforts and more maternal training."[15] According to Ogden, women's political involvement was an outgrowth of their status as mothers; wage labor was not.

Implicit in Ogden's vision of "maternal training" was the duty of white mothers to teach the practice of white supremacy. The family structure was central to the white supremacist order, and homes were to be sites of indoctrination where white mothers instructed their children in the racial customs of the segregated South. While public schools remained segregated, they could function as extensions of white homes, reinforcing white over black. As NAACP-sponsored court cases chipped away at segregated schooling in the 1950s, white southerners understood that public school integration would contradict maternal tutelage in the Jim Crow order. Ogden claimed that school integration interfered with the right of "free men and women to bring up their children in the manner they see fit, a manner that has prevailed for over one hundred and sixty-six years." With the Jim Crow order under siege, Ogden reinforced the power of white mothers when she wrote:

> It seems to me that what we need most in these United States today is more family life and less organization; more association of children with parents; more subconscious teaching of mother to child which comes from everyday association. Children cannot get it from schools, churches, or any other part of organized society. There is no substitute for parents in my book.[16]

Continuing to uphold patriarchal power, Ogden assured white women that their child-rearing work was vital to the politics of white supremacy.[17]

As the prospect of school integration loomed in the future, some Mississippians met this possibility with renewed efforts at school equalization. Ogden was not among them. Perhaps living in a region with an overwhelming black majority, Ogden had never been able to delude herself about the "equality" possible in a system of segregation. She stopped short of suggesting that those who had more children pay for schools, a proposal floated by her brother Walter Sillers, who was, like her, not a parent. Rather than assuming his position—one that would have alienated her from many white mothers—she simply predicted the impossibility of equalizing schools and instead, argued for the futility of a legislative fiat against racial practices. She dismissed all the discussion about equal opportunity and equal rights as simply unrealistic. Such conversation pushed for a society, she wrote, where "everything and everybody should be reduced to a no poor, no black, no white, no smart, no dull, and probably no men, no women, just something in between." Claiming that she had observed human nature as long "as most of the Mister Fix-Its," Ogden announced that equality "just can't be done." The natural order created by God, Ogden suggested, worked so that "some have to . . . be hewers of wood and drawers of water." "All cannot be at the top," she wrote. According to Ogden, school equalization could not mend the evolutionary and biological inequality of black men and women. Avoiding the issue of deplorable black schools and decades of unequal funding upheld by state legislatures, Ogden declared: "no body of men . . . can legislate that something within a person which makes him want to rise above the common level."[18]

In her subsequent columns, Ogden offered several reasons to oppose future integration. Before the Supreme Court ruled on the five integration cases that would later be known as *Brown*, she claimed that the mere consideration of the cases was unconstitutional. Since the Constitution did not mention schools or education, Ogden argued that those rights were reserved for the states. Ogden believed that the Constitution upheld white supremacy, unequal funding for public schools, and all other creations of the Jim Crow order. Federal interference in public schools challenged not only the Constitution but also evolution, God, and family autonomy—all justifications used in the maintenance of white supremacy.[19]

On May 17, 1954, the Supreme Court declared that segregation was unconstitutional. Ogden believed that the *Brown* decision was simply the latest step in the federal betrayal of the white South. Her lack of surprise about the decision, however, did not equal resignation. The potential widespread effect of the *Brown* decision on all white Mississippians allowed Ogden to expand her fight for white supremacy beyond the confines of the Delta. With her column now running in the Sunday issues of both the *Delta Democrat-Times* and the *Jackson Clarion-Ledger,* the state's largest paper, Ogden already had a statewide following. With the image of black boys attending school with white girls, Ogden exploited the duties of white femininity for the cause of white supremacy and stoked the fires of massive resistance. She presented white women's resistance to the *Brown* decision as a maternal responsibility to future generations, to public schools, and to politics. She called on women to uphold white supremacy with their votes, their public history work, and their Parent Teacher Associations. And she talked about white motherhood as if it was the key to national security.[20]

Reacting to the decision, Ogden wrote: "My friends, you will know now how it feels to live in a country that is not free." Calling the decision unconstitutional, Ogden addressed her column to both northerners and southerners—black and white—and contended that "social gains cannot compensate any group, class, or section for the loss of their constitutional rights under a Republic." In her correspondence, *Brown* even outweighed the Civil War in its devastating effect. She called it "the most outrageous seizure of power in all the history of our country" and contended that it was "absolutely a movement inspired by the Communists." To combat such a misuse of power, Ogden called on white southerners to speak up with open, strong, and civilized opposition. Ogden warned against reacting to the decision by "slipping up a dark alley or wearing a hood." Instead she encouraged southern whites not to "be afraid . . . to openly endorse a way of life that has existed from the day of the inception of the United States." And she called on white women to "protect their constitutional rights . . . as a mother protects her child" by joining the campaign of massive resistance.[21]

Some white southerners ignored her calls for dialogue, not violence. A little over a year after the *Brown* decision, a fourteen-year-old Chicago boy, Emmett Till, was murdered by white men in the Delta. While much of the United States and the international community condemned the murder, Ogden simply denied that the mutilated body was that of Till. She countered the Till murder with an alternative story of the Jim Crow South that erased racial violence and replaced it with white benevolence and interracial affection. In a series of stories about her grandmother adopting an orphaned "colored boy" and giving him the name Alex Sillers, Ogden celebrated the historical benevolence of the Sillers family's women toward their black neighbors. She even published letters from Alex's children declaring their fondness and affection for the Sillers family. She knew that how white women treated their black domestics, how they instilled the complicated etiquette of segregation in young black workers, and how they "took care" of their black neighbors was political work. By privileging an edited version of her relationships with black families, Ogden celebrated a society where white women met their duties in part by gently reminding black southerners of their subservient place.[22]

After the integration of Central High School in Little Rock, Arkansas, white supremacists expanded their efforts for massive resistance from electoral politics to an intensified public discourse over textbooks and history. Ogden worked with other white women to ensure that the lessons of white supremacy would be taught in Mississippi's schools. As early as 1956, she had suggested that Mississippians could subvert the *Brown* decision in a way that "even the Supreme Court will surely find . . . difficult to prevent" by adopting "such textbooks in Mississippi schools as we see fit." By 1959, Ogden's suggestion had been widely accepted. Capitalizing on the DAR's anticommunist censorship campaigns and the resentment among white southerners toward federal troops on southern soil, southern white women sought to purge schools of "unpatriotic" material. The Mississippi DAR chapter found that 44 of the 165 subversive texts named by the national organization were being used in their schools. They prepared an exhibit of the textbooks with evaluations that indicated that being an African American was in some cases as "subversive" as being a communist. Typical comments included: "Oblique propaganda in the text, such as give evidence that Negro people have done much to develop themselves." Another book was deemed inappropriate because it led grade school children to believe that "our world is really one great community." In order to "understand the past . . . to understand the present . . . [and] look to the future," Ogden called for "sound" textbooks and "old time patriotism." As one mother in Leland, Mississippi, wrote, these sound textbooks would emphasize that the cause of the Civil War was states' rights, not slavery. Ogden added that they "would show something of the development of the races" and celebrate white American heroes. To help establish such a curriculum, the DAR and the American Legion called on the state textbook selection committee to include "lay members competent to detect subversive authors and contents." The subversives that those lay members would hunt, however, clearly had more to do with racial equality than communist ideology. A segregated South simply could not have its children believe in either an interracial, intercultural community or the capabilities of their black neighbors.[23]

Again, however, Mississippi's white women needed the support of male politicians. Despite their admonitions, Governor J. P. Coleman seemed less alarmed than the DAR and the American Legion about these textbooks. One Mississippi woman took care to remind him of his promise to uphold segregation. "Shooting attempts backed by guns and bayonets would not have been nearly so detrimental to our children and to our State," she wrote, "as the books that have been placed in our schools."[24] She asked that he address this most important issue in his television broadcast that week. Coleman did not.

Soon Mississippians had a governor who would not only uphold racial segregation but who would also take a more substantial role in textbook matters. In 1960, Ogden encouraged the new governor, Ross Barnett, to pay more attention to public school textbooks. With increased funding from Barnett, the State Sovereignty Commission, a publicly funded organization that investigated civil rights activists, disseminated its own list of subversive textbooks and authors. Their list included authors who were "leftwingers, liberal, integrationists, and subversive writers." The list also included a number of "Negro" writers, members of the NAACP, and even Ogden's own editor at the *Delta-Democrat Times*, Hodding Carter, who had won a Pulitzer Prize for his editorials that promoted racial tolerance. Ogden praised Barnett's involvement in the textbook controversy and claimed that his efforts had resulted in "great strides ... for better textbooks in the Mississippi schools." She also complimented him on "his leadership in helping keep our schools American" when he appointed one of her recommendations, a Mr. Frank Hough, to the textbook rating committee.[25]

Ogden also used her various public service positions to promote a historical curriculum that reinforced a dying social system. As president of the Mississippi Historical Society for the 1959–60 term, Ogden called for a new history program in the public schools. She also encouraged Mississippians to join the organization in order "to become acquainted with the men and women who teach the youth of our state." She had urged Governor Coleman to establish American History Month. Although Coleman refused, he did offer to write a letter expressing "good wishes" for its success. In a speech to a state DAR chapter, Ogden praised the national Daughters for their support of consensus historians who did not try "to debunk our national heroes." She told members that they must "teach the children about the greatness of our country."[26]

Meanwhile, the Citizens' Council, an organization of white professional men who used political threats, economic pressure, and ultimately violence to minimize civil rights activism, tried to maintain a world of white power and privilege. Ogden used her columns, clubs, and, along with other women, her personal networks to push the all-male council to incorporate women-led education and youth activities into their campaign. As a result, the Citizens' Council established its Women's Activities and Youth Work, an organization directed by Mrs. Sam McCorkle. In this capacity, McCorkle created handbooks for elementary school children in order "to indoctrinate the nation's youth." As director, she spoke to students in nearly every Mississippi high school in 1958 and 1959. In 1959, the Citizens' Council Education Fund sponsored an essay contest for Mississippi's high school students, who wrote on the following topics: "Why I Believe in Social Separation of the Races of Mankind," "Subversion in Racial Unrest," "Why the Preservation of State Rights is Important to Every American," and "Why Separate Schools Should Be Maintained for the White and the Negro Races." Over eight thousand students from 163 Mississippi high schools participated in the Citizens' Council essay contest. The statewide winners, one boy and one girl, both received five hundred dollars—a sum that in 1959 would have paid a four-year tuition at the University of Mississippi.[27]

Not satisfied that the Citizens' Council could reach white Mississippians without additional help, in 1960, McCorkle called together thirty-one "ladies" to organize to "fight for our American way of life." The newly formed Paul Revere Ladies noted in their battle cry that "Washington has been taken, Little Rock has been occupied, and the Battle of New Orleans is raging wide." Therefore, "we in turn must save our children—we must stand and fight, or die." To save the "American way of life," women of the Educational Committee decided to sponsor prosegregation and states' rights speakers to appear at high schools, colleges, and mass meetings. To fund this project, Ogden suggested that the Paul Revere ladies petition the State Sovereignty Commission.[28]

Ogden soon believed that these efforts to promote a more "patriotic" education had experienced some success. After the state textbook committee threatened to pull some of its English textbooks, the publisher D. C. Heath released a revised edition of its English textbook for Mississippi schools with the "sensitive" material deleted.[29] In the late 1950s, Ogden had complained that the honor student papers read at a local high school were laden with socialistic propaganda and "not fit to be delivered in a truly American auditorium." After her investigation, she claimed, the school board and superintendent fired the principal who had allegedly written the papers. By 1963, the valedictorian at her local high school lamented the unpatriotic material in current textbooks, noting the disappearance of Patrick Henry's "Give me liberty or give me death" speech. The student's address served as evidence, Ogden believed, of the success of women's work in patriotic education.[30]

Ogden also capitalized on white women's roles as historical guardians to carry out the work of white supremacy. A member of the DAR, the United Daughters of the Confederacy, and the Colonial Dames, Ogden was perfectly situated to push a particular version of southern history that upheld the Jim Crow order. The work of this female legion of public historians was helped along by a coincidence of timing. Just as the civil rights movement gained momentum, historical societies and clubs across the South also worked on plans to celebrate the Civil War centennial. With an entire social system at stake, Mississippi women restored Vicksburg, rebuilt the plantation mansion of Rosalie in Natchez, and produced pageants in the nation's capital with cotton bales, black Delta sharecroppers posing as slaves, and southern belles. Ogden led a one-woman campaign to raise money for the restoration of Mississippi's oldest Presbyterian church at Rodney. Once a thriving antebellum port town on the Mississippi River, the Rodney church stood for an earlier era, and Ogden called on Mississippians to preserve it as history—slave balcony and all. As the South's female historical legion commemorated the values of the Old South, reconstructed the physical forms of the slave plantation, and linked the tragic consequences of the *Brown* decision to the martyred image of the Lost Cause, they attempted to instill in a new generation of white and black youth the values of a segregated society. In addition, their celebration of an old order—characterized in part by images of the white southern lady with her black domestics—reinforced the notion of sex-specific responsibilities and the preferential treatment that a racial hierarchy guaranteed white women.[31]

For Ogden, maintaining white supremacy and white femininity also meant extending the massive resistance campaign directly into the home, and she did her own educational work with her young female relatives. Just as the cultural politics of the 1960s led to the rewriting of certain folk songs and stories that celebrated the slave South, Ogden remained determined to teach her young relatives the original words to Stephen Foster songs such as *Old Black Joe, Camp Town Races, Massa's in the Cold, Cold Ground,* and *My Old Kentucky Home.* Although Ogden shared the astute observation that "it is a serious thing to wipe out folklore which has been 300 years in the making," she quickly illuminated a more politically unsavory reason for her resistance. The songs "reflect the best and most lovable impulses of a race." They were not meant to disparage black Americans, because they reflected such noble black characters that "Negroes, most of all, would resent it [the changed words]," she concluded. As black southerners struggled to gain the vote, to receive a better education, and to make public schools integrate, Ogden's constant reminders of the subservient place of African Americans reinforced the white supremacist values of a segregated society in a generation that would be the first participants in an integrated one.[32]

The legal dismantling of the Jim Crow system also dealt with more than just the end of racial segregation. Ogden knew it would erase social markers and the power of white women by erasing the barriers between the work of white women and the work of black women. In doing so, white and black women would have to compete openly for authority in public schools, in public history, and even in the home. Certainly black women had long pushed for civil rights using a political rhetoric that stressed maternal responsibility, patriotism, education, and equality, but segregation had politicized a racialized femininity and denied black women the opportunity to fulfill, on their terms, their understanding of their gender roles. Their work in white homes had allowed white women to construct an ideology of white femininity that celebrated white women in roles as public mothers. Integration threatened to integrate these constructions of femininity, and white women resisted such a move. In a telling example, Ogden, as president of the Mississippi Historical Society, noted in her introduction of a female professor that she hesitated to call her a lady because "it is the word lady which is in bad repute." Today, "when my cook comes in and says, Miss Flonce there's a lady in the kitchen to see you, I know this is someone seeking to get on the welfare roles of the ADC ... but when she says there's a woman in the parlor I know it is some Colonial Dame, UDC, DAR, or some historian or writer." At another time, Ogden asked her readers: "Now that the Commies and the do-gooders have got the lady out of the kitchen, who is going to do all the civic improvement, P.T.A., garden club, patriotic society, and sweet charity work that the lady in the parlor used to do?" "Will the former maids, released from domestic service," Ogden contemplated, "render the same community service once so freely given by the mistress of the House?" With these questions, Ogden exposed both the threat that black civil rights posed to white women's carefully constructed roles and to the contested nature of women's power in an integrated southern society.[33]

Having alerted white women to the need to fight for white supremacy in their homes, schools, and history, Ogden also alerted them to the threat that the United Nations posed to their authority. A nearly life-long worker in the DAR, Ogden echoed the DAR's national opposition to the United Nations (UN) when she wrote that it was against "white" civilization. Ogden's opposition to the UN involved, among other issues, her fear of newly independent African nations. By 1961, twenty-three African nations were members of the UN, and Ogden described them as "most of the tribal savage states." In conjunction with the civil rights movement at home, Ogden felt the rise of independent African

states was evidence of "an anti-white movement all over the world." By rais-
ing the specter of savage, heathen, even cannibalistic Africans, Ogden painted
the UN as a threat to white privilege and authority. Linked to the rise of black
authority, legitimized by the UN, was the demise of white authority.[34]

She also described the treaties sponsored by the UN and ratified by the
United States Senate as threats to the ability of individuals and women to teach
their children certain values. In particular, Ogden opposed the Universal Declaration of Human Rights Convention on the Prevention and Punishment of the
Crime of Genocide passed by the UN in 1948.[35] Contending that the UN was
a threat to private property, Christianity, and minority rights (in this case, she
noted that whites were a minority of the world's population), Ogden specifically attacked the genocide treaty because it defined genocide as a "crime which
does mental or bodily harm to a member of a racial minority." In addition to
making it illegal to make derogatory statements about the NAACP, Ogden contended that under it

> a Negro, a Chinese, or a member of any racial minority, could insult
> you, or your daughter. Your husband might shoot him, knock him
> down, or cuss him out. If so he could be tried in an international court.
> It would also make it a crime to prevent racial intermarriage and inter-
> marriage would destroy the white race which has brought Christianity
> to the world.[36]

To prevent this, Ogden encouraged them to write their congressmen and express
their support for a constitutional amendment that would prevent international
treaties from infringing on the rights guaranteed by the Constitution. Again
noting that it would be the children and grandchildren of DAR members who
would suffer the consequences of these treaties, she told her female audience:
"it is you who must rise up and lead the way."[37] "The women can do it," she said.
The question she posed was "Will they?"[38]

In addition to UN treaties, Ogden believed that the United Nations Education, Scientific and Cultural Organization (UNESCO) compromised public
school curricula. Under their influence, Ogden contended that the students
were being taught more about cooperation than competition, more about racial
unity than racial difference, and more about tolerance than Christianity. Even
UNICEF Christmas cards, Ogden contended, were a subtle effort to challenge
the traditions of white Christian nations. Youth, Ogden contended in many
speeches, had long been the focus of communist subversives, and now, working through the UN, these influences had filtered down to American schools.
Model UN meetings at Mississippi universities hid communist agendas under
the cloak of international understanding and tolerance. Ogden suggested that

the rise of African states in the UN created a world government run by non-whites, and she asked PTA members if this was "the kind of world government you want to hand down to your children?" [39] Those who did not fulfill their duties to American families, Ogden predicted, "will live to rue the day, or if they do not, certainly their unfortunate children and grandchildren will."[40]

In Ogden's construction of white femininity, oversight of public education was an extension of white women's maternal duties. When the UN took over this authority, they would not only be placing it in the hands of nonwhite leaders but also would be taking away the authority of white women in public education. In speeches to DAR clubs, Rotary Clubs, Parent-Teacher Associations, and historical societies, Ogden claimed that the UN's cultural programs produced educational materials that would "indoctrinate our children" with unpatriotic ideas. By interfering in public education, the UN would minimize white women's authority over their children and in effect control "other numerous matters that will affect your daily life." White women, however, could resist such a government takeover. As an example, Ogden highlighted the efforts of a fellow DAR member and Junior League docent at the Smithsonian Museum of American History, who, in 1959, used her position as a public historian to teach "the little chocolate drops . . . what the white people have done to build the country." Women, she implied, must through their work in education, prevent the demise of American freedom, an interracial democracy—all the while preserving the privileges of white femininity.[41]

In 1962, despite the diverse efforts of Ogden and other segregationists, James Meredith enrolled at the University of Mississippi. For many Mississippi segregationists, the armed integration of Ole Miss exemplified the widespread evil that had created racial integration—an intrusive federal government, a communist-inspired philosophy of racial equality, the betrayal of a region by its national government, and a condemnation of the white leadership of the state. For many white women, it was just one more example of the disregard for and erosion of their public authority. Far from defeating their resolve, this event clearly revealed how constructions of white femininity could be used for the forces of massive resistance. In response, Ogden organized "indignant Mississippi women" and representatives from seven other states into the WCG. In her keynote address, she charged that white children "have been denied their right to assemble and protest" and were treated like criminals by federal marshals. This was just the most egregious example of how the federal government sought to take over women's business—"the home, the schools, the prayers, the choice of association of our children." In the name of white womanhood, Ogden called on southern women to step up their public and political efforts. White womanhood meant, Ogden claimed, forgetting your "appointment at the Beauty Parlor, your Bridge Club meeting, your Garden Club convention."[42]

Instead, they should organize, vote, remove from office the men responsible for the federal invasion, and campaign for conservatives to take over political offices. While they should still ask men about candidates' ideological positions, and ask men for money, as a potential majority of voters, white women needed to take the lead in preserving racial segregation, constitutional government, and American freedoms.

White womanhood, for these women, meant working for conservative causes, and they defended their political actions in terms of their gendered responsibilities. In 1962, Ogden would sum up her position when she claimed that a woman's responsibility was the "protection of the family." "This is a woman's medium," she continued, and "we have every right to fight for it; every incentive." "If the men fail, we shall carry on," she said. "We are the mothers of men.... We are the builders of the future." "We have a duty to perform," she concluded, so "let's be up and about it!"[43] Believing that "women are capable of wielding unlimited power, especially when the welfare of their children is threatened," the WCG called upon white women to preserve constitutional government so that "our children's children will know freedom as we know it." By expanding the rhetoric of massive resistance from women's role in white supremacy to women's duty to a certain vision of America, Ogden and the WCG linked the forces of white femininity to a larger conservative ideology.[44]

In many ways, Ogden's hopes for both her state and her nation went unfulfilled. The integration of the public schools did finally come. Black Mississippians received the vote in 1965 and entered the electorate in unprecedented numbers. However, it was not until the 1985 amendment to the Voting Rights Act that black voters and black votes achieved tangible results that anywhere near approached their numbers.[45] Ogden lost even smaller battles in her state—the PTA supported federal aid to education despite her opposition. Even the Mississippi Educational Association did not adhere completely to the DAR's textbook watch list.

Ogden's failures, however, are only part of the story of massive resistance. Her story also reveals how the politics of white supremacy were intertwined with white women's sex-specific duties. In the postwar era, many southern white women understood that white supremacy helped define their roles in the private, public, and political domains, suggesting that as an ideology, white supremacy functioned as forcefully in the inner sanctum of homes as it did in legislative halls. Ogden and other southern white women manipulated or understood the duties of motherhood to justify female political authority *and* the Jim Crow order. Understanding that the ideology of white supremacy was central to the way they carried out their duties as private and public mothers, a fragmented and diverse mobilization of white women sabotaged, through their homes, schools, and civic and historical societies, the legal desegregation of the public schools for seventeen years. As they frustrated integration efforts, they seized the opportunity to educate another generation in lessons of white supremacy. Ogden's story also points to the long-functioning conservative political ideology that framed the activism of many white southern women. Sandwiched between the suffrage campaigns and the Equal Rights Amendment—the former foundered and the latter failed on southern soil, largely due to white women's opposition—women's efforts to maintain racial segregation hint at a malleable but powerful political ideology that linked women to a larger politics of conservatism: a politics in which even today race is still a salient force.

The historian Nell Painter wrote of the need "to see beyond racism as an individual, personal flaw, and view it instead as a way of life."[46] For Florence Sillers Ogden, the ideology of white supremacy was so central to her understanding of her world that it was a way of life. She was not alone. The powerful appeals of Ogden to the duties of white mothers suggest that many white southern women believed that segregation and the racism that supported it defined them, their place, and their power in society. While Ogden's political efforts on behalf of white supremacy made her a valuable figure to those opposed to segregation in state politics, many white women understood that their place in a Jim Crow world guaranteed them some public and political power, even if they remained unequal. By defining white women's politics in terms of their duties as mothers, Ogden validated their private and public work as essential to the state. The white supremacist politics of Ogden expose how constructions of femininity validated the vital work that white women performed in maintaining an entire system of race, gender, class, sexual, and political inequities. By not examining their work and its ideological foundations, our ability to understand the persistence of white supremacy, racism, and sexual inequality and to then fight those forces of injustice will remain severely compromised.

Notes

1. Undated columns, Florence Sillers Ogden file, State Sovereignty Commission (SSC) Files, Mississippi Department of Archives and History, Jackson, Mississippi. Ogden, speeches for WCG in Jackson, Oct. 30, 1962; Greenwood, Mar. 5, 1963; Greenville, Feb. 20, 1963, folder 113, Florence Sillers Ogden Papers, Charles W. Capps, Jr., Archives, Delta State University, Cleveland, Mississippi.

2. Ogden, "Memoirs" (typescript), and "Sillers Family Genealogy," Ogden Papers; Florence Warfield Sillers, comp., *History of Bolivar County, Mississippi*, ed. Wirt A. Williams (Jackson, Miss.: Hederman, 1948), 483–85. The population numbers come from the 1890 census and are quoted in Richard Aubrey McLemore, ed., *A History of Mississippi*, 2 vols. (Hattiesburg, Miss.: University and College Press of Mississippi, 1973),

2:3. William Gray, *Imperial Bolivar* (Cleveland, Miss.: Bolivar Commercial, 1923), 14–16; James C. Cobb, *The Most Southern Place on Earth: The Mississippi Delta and the Roots of Regional Identity* (New York: Oxford University Press, 1992), 85; Thomas R. Melton, "Mr. Speaker: A Biography of Walter Sillers" (M.A. thesis, University of Mississippi, 1972); William F. Winter, "New Directions in Politics, 1948–56," in McLemore, *History of Mississippi*, 141–42. On white women's roles as guardians of history see Karen Cox, *Dixie's Daughters: The United Daughters of the Confederacy and the Preservation of Confederate Culture* (Gainesville: University Press of Florida, 2003).

3. Ogden, "Immigration Speech to DAR," typescript, 1928, folder 123, Ogden Papers; Ogden to Mrs. Sam Knowlton and Members of the Mississippi Delta Chapter of the DAR, Nov. 4, 1937, folder 10, Ogden Papers. On the DAR's increasingly antiradical agenda, which stressed ethnic nationalism, see Francesca Morgan, "Home and Country: Women, Nation and the Daughters of the American Revolution, 1890–1939" (Ph.D. diss., Columbia University, 1998), 415–30. On Natchez see Jack Davis, *Race Against Time: Culture and Separation in Natchez Since 1930* (Baton Rouge: Louisiana State University Press, 2001), 51–82. On Ogden's WPA project see Sillers, *History of Bolivar County*, 359–61; "Golden Jubilee Edition," *Daily-Democrat Times* (Greenville, Miss.), Aug. 31, 1938.

4. Ogden, "Depression in Cotton" (n.d, typescript), folder 139, Ogden Papers. On the political agendas of Delta planters and political factions in the state see George B. Tindall, *The Emergence of the New South, 1913–1945* (Baton Rouge: Louisiana State University Press, 1967), 229–34; V. O. Key, *Southern Politics in State and Nation* (New York: Knopf, 1949), 229–53.

5. On the devastating effect that the poll tax had on white women see Sarah Wilkerson Freeman, "The Second Battle for Woman Suffrage: Alabama White Women, the Poll Tax, and V. O. Key's Master Narrative of Southern Politics," *Journal of Southern History* 68 (May 2002): 333–74. For more detail on the congressional debates surrounding the Soldier Voting Act see Stephen Lawson, *Black Ballots: Voting Rights in the South, 1944–1969* (New York: Columbia University Press, 1976), 61–76. Under the guidance of Walter Sillers, Mississippi did pass a Soldier Voting Act. The state version, however, allowed the state to determine which soldiers would receive absentee ballots, thereby leaving control of voting in the hands of white politicians. See Melton, "Mr. Speaker," 62–63.

6. "Dis an' Dat," *Delta Democrat-Times*, May 16, 1943; May 7, 28, 1944. The presidential election in Mississippi led to a crisis revolving around a discrepancy between the anticipated popular vote and the electors who would vote in the electoral college. The original slate of Democratic electors included the names of five "bolting electors" who said they would refuse to cast their votes for Roosevelt in the electoral college even if Roosevelt won a majority of Mississippi's votes. Governor Thomas Bailey called a special session of the state legislature to nominate an additional slate of Democratic electors who pledged to honor the popular vote. The names of the second slate of Democratic electors were printed on pink ballots. Mississippi voters could choose among thirty-six delegates from four slates—two Democratic slates (pro-Roosevelt and anti-Roosevelt) and the Lilly Whites and the Black and Tans. The pink ballot of pro-Roosevelt electors won in every Mississippi county, but Ogden's own Bolivar County led the Delta in votes for the anti-Roosevelt electors. See Roy H. Ruby, "The Presidential Election of 1944 in Mississippi: The Bolting Electors" (M.A. thesis, Mississippi State University, 1966), 39, 44–45.

7. "Dis an' Dat," *Delta Democrat-Times*, Oct. 18, Apr. 12, May 10, 1942; Florence Sillers Ogden, *Letters to the Boys* (Bolivar County, Miss.: Delta DAR Chapter, 1992), copy in my possession. Ogden's letters ran in the *Bolivar County Democrat* from February 1942 until February 1946. Ogden was not the only woman who wrote open letters to the soldiers. For another example see Keith Frazier Somerville, *Dear Boys: World War II Letters from a Woman Back Home*, ed. Judy Barrett Litoff and David C. Smith with an introduction by Martha Swain (Jackson: University Press of Mississippi, 1991).

8. In February 1948, Truman had made a civil rights speech that upheld many of the findings of his Committee on Civil Rights. He called for an end to poll taxes, the establishment of a Fair Employment Practice Commission, and statehood for Hawaii and Alaska. He also predicted the desegregation of the United States military. See John Egerton, *Speak Now Against the Day: The Generation Before the Civil Rights Movement in the South* (Chapel Hill: University of North Carolina Press, 1995), 475–79.

9. Ogden, "Women of Mississippi," address to States Rights Meeting, Jackson, Mississippi, 1948; Ogden, "State's Rights," speech to the Gunnison Parent-Teachers Association, undated, folder 119; Mrs. William Kendall and Mrs. O. H. Palmer to Ogden, Apr. 3, 1948, folder 20, all in Ogden Papers. See also Kari Frederickson, *The Dixiecrat Revolt and the End of the Solid South, 1932–1968* (Chapel Hill: University of North Carolina Press, 2001).

10. Gertrude to Ogden, Oct. 25, 1952, Ogden Papers.

11. "Dis an' Dat," *Delta Democrat-Times*, Jan. 11, 1953, Jan. 18, and Feb. 8, 1953; Marie Hemphill to Ogden, Sept. 1952; Katie Dee to Ogden, Sept. 24, 1952; Ogden, untitled speech, Sept. 22, 1952; Ogden to Mr. E. O. Spencer, Jun. 10, 1953; Ogden to Congressman Wint Smith, Mar. 7, 1959; Ogden to Samuel Lumpkin, Sept. 15, 1953, all in Ogden Papers; Frederickson, *Dixiecrat Revolt*, 118–49. Lumpkin is mentioned as a leader in the Democrats for Eisenhower in McLemore, *History of Mississippi*, 149. This brief account does not mention the role of Florence Ogden or other women in the organization. Nor does it note what happened to Lumpkin after the election. The letters between Ogden and Lumpkin, however, suggest some sort of political retribution. In Bolivar County Eisenhower received 2,096 votes to Stevenson's 1,843. Election results in Tip H. Allen, Jr., *Mississippi Votes: The Presidential and Gubernatorial Elections, 1947–1964* (State College, Miss.: Social Science Research Center at Mississippi State University, 1967).

12. "Dis an' Dat," *Jackson Clarion-Ledger*," Jun. 1, 1952. "Moss back" is a colloquial term for an extreme conservative who is very slow to change.

13. "Dis an' Dat," *Delta Democrat-Times*, Nov. 16, 1952.

14. "Dis an' Dat," *Jackson Clarion-Ledger*, May 11, 1958.

15. "Dis an' Dat," *Jackson Clarion-Ledger*," Jun. 1, 1952. This tone fit well with dominant media images during this period; see Susan Douglas, *Where the Girls Are: Growing Up Female with the Mass Media* (New York: Three Rivers Press, 1994), 21–42, 47–50.

16. "Dis an' Dat," *Jackson Clarion-Ledger*, Dec. 7, 1958. For the central role that families played in teaching values in Mississippi, including white supremacy, see Davis, *Race Against Time*, 71.

17. "Dis an' Dat," *Delta Democrat-Times*, Dec. 13, 1953.

18. "Dis an' Dat," *Delta Democrat-Times*, Dec. 6, 1953; Cobb, *Most Southern Place on Earth*, 227; Ogden, "Rosedale," in Sillers, *History of Bolivar County*, 352.

19. "Dis an' Dat," *Delta Democrat-Times*, Dec. 13, 1953.

20. Michael J. Klarman, "How *Brown* Changed Race Relations: The Backlash Thesis," *Journal of American History* 81 (Jun. 1994): 81–118; Ogden, "Women for Constitutional Government Speech," Drew, Mississippi, Jun. 10, 1963, Ogden Papers.

21. "Dis an' Dat," *Delta Democrat-Times*, Jun. 6, Sept. 12, 1954; Ogden to Francis Bartlett, Jun. 1, 1954, A. G. Paxton to Ogden, Jun. 9, 1954, R. Trabne Lawrence to Ogden, Jul. 4, 1954, Birney Imes to Ogden, Aug. 3, 1954, all in folder 26, Ogden Papers. In the letter of July 4, 1954, Lawrence notes his agreement with Ogden about the *Brown* decision and claims that "Washington has always been a bad *Nigger* town, but now it is most impossible." He even suggests that Ogden may soon have blacks in the DAR.

22. "Dis an' Dat," *Delta Democrat-Times*, Feb. 27, 1955.

23. "Dis an' Dat," *Delta Democrat-Times*, Apr. 8, 1956; the phrase referring to the Civil War comes from a letter to Ogden from Janice Neill of Leland, Mississippi, Oct. 18, 1959, folder 41; "Legion Will Take Textbook Action," *Jackson Clarion-Ledger*, Sept. 6, 1959; "DAR and Legion to Display All Questioned Books," *Jackson Clarion-Ledger*, Jul. 19, 1959.

24. M. N. Brown to Governor J. P. Coleman, Jun. 24, 1959, folder 39, Ogden Papers.

25. "Dis an' Dat," *Delta Democrat-Times*, Mar. 14, 1954, Mar. 11, 1956, Apr. 8, 1956; Janice Neill to Ogden, Oct. 18, 1959, Ogden Papers; list of textbook authors from the State Sovereignty Commission (postmarked Oct. 2, 1960), folder 42; Ogden to Ross Barnett, May 9, 1960, Ross Barnett to Ogden, Jun. 13, 1960, and Ogden to Barnett, Jun. 22, 1960, all in Ogden Papers; Yasuhiro Katagiri, *The Mississippi State Sovereignty Commission: Civil Rights and States' Rights* (Jackson: University Press of Mississippi, 2001), 86–94.

26. James Silver to Ogden, Oct. 8, 1959, folder 41; Ogden, "American History," typescript, speech to Ralph Humphreys DAR Chapter, 1959, both in Ogden Papers.

27. Neil R. McMillen, *The Citizen's Councils: Organized Resistance to the Second Reconstruction, 1954–1964* (Urbana: University of Illinois Press, 1971), 240–45. For the essay topics in 1959 see "Citizens' Council Essay Winners Told," *Jackson Clarion-Ledger*, Jul. 24, 1959. The 1959–60 University of Mississippi catalog lists the total fees, apparently including tuition, for a full-time undergraduate at $127.50. At that rate, four years would have cost $510.00. See 1959–60 University of Mississippi Catalog, 85, Special Collections, J. D. Williams Library, University of Mississippi, Oxford.

28. Dec. 14, 1960; May 28, 1960, SSC Files; McMillen, *Citizen's Councils*, 240–45; Katagiri, *State Sovereignty Commission*.

29. "Dis an' Dat," *Jackson Clarion-Ledger*, Oct. 20, 1963.

30. Ogden to Mrs. H. W. Gill of Mobile, Alabama, May 23, 1963, folder 52, Ogden Papers.

31. "Dis an' Dat," *Jackson Clarion-Ledger*, Oct. 5, 1958, Apr. 12, 1959, Mar. 20, 1960; "Dis an' Dat," *Delta Democrat-Times*, Apr. 7, 1955, Feb. 21, Jul. 25, 1954, Mar. 11, 1956. On the Civil War centennial see Robert Cook, "From Shiloh to Selma: The Impact of the Civil War Centennial on the Black Freedom Struggle in the United States, 1961–65," in *The Making of Martin Luther King and the Civil Rights Movement*, ed. Brian Ward and Tony Badger (New York: New York University Press, 1996), 131–45. At the time the Mississippi legislators were talking about their inability to fund certain projects, the state spent two million dollars on the centennial. Cook also mentions how politicians realized the value of political theater when federal intervention was eroding their own ability to maintain a caste system. He further notes that black civil rights activists, believing the centennial

celebrations were couched in such a way as to promote the ideology of white supremacy, encouraged federal agencies to stress emancipation. On the relationship between the Civil War, historical memory, and cultural politics see David Blight, *Race and Reunion: The Civil War in American Memory* (Cambridge, Mass.: Harvard University Press, 2001). For more on how tourist sites and historic renovation, replete with certain images of femininity, articulate racist values see Tara McPherson, "Reconstructing Dixie: Race, Place, and Femininity in the Deep South" (Ph.D. diss, University of Wisconsin at Milwaukee, 1996), 24–39.

32. "Dis an' Dat," *Jackson Clarion-Ledger*, Jun. 29, 1958.

33. Ogden, "Introduction," Mississipppi Historical Society [1960?], Introductory address to meeting of Mississippi Historical Society, typescript, folder 119, Ogden Papers; "Dis an' Dat," *Jackson Clarion-Ledger*, Oct. 11, 1959. For more on black women's involvement in teaching equality and in trying to subvert Jim Crow through their gender roles see Adam Fairclough, *Teaching Equality: Black Schools in the Age of Jim Crow* (Athens: University of Georgia Press, 2001), 51–55.

34. "Dis an' Dat," *Jackson Clarion-Ledger*, Oct. 16, 1965; Ogden, "Building Responsible Citizens Through Knowledge and Appreciation of Our Country and Its History," speech to Benoit Parent-Teachers Association, Feb. 20, 1961, folder 111, Ogden Papers.

35. "Dis an' Dat," *Delta Democrat-Times*, Apr. 27, 1952.

36. Various versions of this quotation appeared in her speeches at Yazoo and Lake Village, 1954, folder 105; Ogden, speech at State DAR Meeting and Madam Hodnett Chapter DAR Meeting, 1955, folder 106, both in Ogden Papers.

37. Ogden, Lake Village DAR speech, 1954, folder 105, Ogden Papers. See also "Dis an' Dat," *Delta Democrat-Times*, Mar. 14, 1954; "Dis an' Dat," *Delta Democrat-Times*, Apr. 27, 1952.

38. Ogden, "World Government and the United Nations," speech for Yazoo Chapter of the DAR (January 1954?), folder 105, Ogden Papers.

39. Ogden, "Building Responsible Citizens Through Knowledge and Appreciation of Our Country and Its History"; "The United Nations and Its Specialized Agencies," typescript of speech, Grenda, Oct. 19, 1962, folder 114, Ogden Papers.

40. "Dis an' Dat," *Delta Democrat-Times*, Mar. 14, 1954. Senator John W. Bricker to Ogden, Mar. 14, 1954, folder 26, Ogden Papers. This letter notes that one organization dedicated to securing favorable action on the amendment was "Vigilant Women for the Bricker Amendment" in Hinsdale, Illinois. James Eastland to Ogden, Jan. 21, 1954, folder 26, Ogden Papers.

41. Ogden, "United Nations," typescript of speech to Lake Village DAR meeting, 1954, Ogden Papers; "Dis and Dat," *Delta Democrat-Times*, Mar. 14, 1954. On the United Nations, UNESCO and taking over of public schools, Ogden, "Spiritual Values of the United Nations," typescript of speech to DAR, 1955; Ogden, "Building Responsible Citizens Through Knowledge and Appreciation of Our Country"; Ogden, "American History Month," typescript of speech to Ralph Humphreys Chapter of the DAR, 1959, all in Ogden Papers. For a broad discussion of white women's roles in an education for imperialism and white supremacy see Vron Ware, *Beyond the Pale: White Women, Racism and History* (London: Verso, 1992), 11–20.

42. Ogden, Untitled Speech for Women for Constitutional Government, typescript, Drew, Mississippi, folder 113, Jun. 10, 1963.

43. Ogden, "Address in Chicago to the Women for Constitutional Government," typescript, Oct. 4, 1963, Ogden Papers.

44. Undated columns, Florence Sillers Ogden file, SSC Files; Ogden's WCG speeches in Jackson, Oct. 30, 1962; Greenwood, Mar. 5, 1963; Greenville, Feb. 20, 1963, folder 113; Ogden, WCG speech, Montgomery, Alabama, Jan. 17, 1963; WCG speech, Mobile, Alabama, Feb. 11, 1965, all in Ogden Papers. For more on the WCG see Lisa Speer, "'Contrary Mary': The Life of Mary Dawson Cain" (Ph.D. diss., University of Mississippi, 1988).

45. Frank R. Parker, David C. Colby, and Minion K. C. Morrison, "Mississippi," in *Quiet Revolution in the South: The Impact of the Voting Rights Act, 1965–1990*, ed. Chandler Davidson and Bernard Goffman (Princeton, N.J.: Princeton University Press, 1994), 136–54. The authors argue that Mississippians diluted the Voting Rights Act of 1965 by erecting barriers to black electoral power and participation. After the passage of the act, these efforts increasingly included deceit, intimidation, violence, and legislation such as the mandating of at-large municipal elections. In a series of decisions, the Supreme Court ruled that Section 5 of the Voting Rights Act required that after 1965 any change to election procedures had to be approved or "predeclared" by either the United States Attorney General's office or through lawsuits decided in the United States District Court for the District of Columbia. Most Mississippi cities had adopted at-large voting prior to 1965 and thus were exempt from preclearance, however. A decision involving Mobile in 1980 nonetheless determined that prosecutors had to prove that at-large systems had been adopted for discriminatory purposes and with discriminatory intent—a difficult burden of proof. Parker, Colby, and Morrison concluded, on the basis of a study of 145 cities of over one thousand or more in Mississippi, that in the years following the Voting Rights Act, black electoral power was significantly reduced through these measures. In addition, between 1965 and 1980, fourteen of Mississippi's eighty-two counties switched to at-large elections for county supervisors, and twenty-two for school board members. Other disfranchising methods, such as dual registration with county and municipal clerk, were not abolished until 1984.

46. Nell Painter, "The Shoah and Southern History," in *Jumping Jim Crow: Southern Politics from Civil War to Civil Rights*, ed. Jane Dailey, Glenda Gilmore, and Bryant Simon (Princeton, N.J.: Princeton University Press, 2000), 310.

TEN

Massive Resistance, Violence, and Southern Social Relations: The Little Rock, Arkansas, School Integration Crisis, 1954–1960

Karen S. Anderson

In August 1957, the city of Little Rock, Arkansas, prepared to desegregate its schools by admitting African American students to the previously all-white Central High School. Fearful that this would involve violence and unwilling to have her daughter attend schools with African American students, Mrs. Clyde Thomason called the Little Rock school superintendent, Virgil Blossom, to request that her daughter, Louise, be allowed to transfer. He refused her request. Thomason, described by another segregationist activist as "a sweet little thing but a very stern person in the things she believes," called him back repeatedly. He did not return her calls.[1]

A working-class mother employed at Little Rock's Westinghouse plant, Thomason reacted angrily to Blossom's indifference to her concerns. On August 27, she filed suit in the Pulaski Chancery Court asking for a temporary injunction against the integration of the Little Rock schools. Although she clearly did so in collusion with the governor of Arkansas, Orval Faubus, she also acted for her own reasons. In an interview with the FBI, she related the story of her interactions with Blossom, alleging that the school official ignored her calls but "met at least twice a week with various Negro groups." Interpreting her political marginality in racial terms, she revealed the complex class relations that shaped the desegregation crisis in her Upper South community.[2]

Joining with other women, Thomason helped to form the Mothers' League of Central High, a segregationist women's organization composed primarily of working-class women. The Mothers' League, which claimed to be "group of Christian mothers opposed to violence," was instrumental in spreading rumors of impending violence, encouraging protestors to converge at the high school as desegregation began, and condemning integration as a threat to public order and white well-being. Moreover, the women's organization enabled segregationists to claim legitimacy, in part by denying the centrality of violence to their political position. Their mobilization of a Christian identity, whether it was an appeal to an encoded anti-Semitism or to an unspecified religious solidarity with other whites, was designed to render their values and actions unassailable.[3]

As elsewhere in the South, the Capital Citizens' Council in Little Rock claimed the mantle of "respectable resistance" by posing as exponents of non-violent opposition to a coercive federal government ostensibly controlled by subversives. At the same time, they and the Mothers' League also positioned themselves as the alternative to more violent groups, without providing names of the organizations or information to authorities so that they could investigate. In February 1957, the Citizens' Council president, Amis Guthridge, told Blossom that a group of men would not join his organization because it was nonviolent, "but at the proper time, they would take over with guns and pistols." In a letter to Faubus written on August 28, Guthridge assured the governor that he had told his members that any who participated in violence would be removed from the organization. He also predicted that desegregation would cause "blood shed" [sic] and worried that it would be blamed on the Citizens' Council. On September 9, 1957, L. D. Poynter, president of the Association of Citizens' Councils of Arkansas, told the FBI that his group was trying to achieve its goals legally but that if those efforts failed, he believed that "other more drastic organizations would be formed to work in an underground manner." He denied any intention of leading such an effort. Divided within and among themselves, the arch segregationists disclaimed and desired violence in equal measure. They and other segregationist leaders, including Governor Orval Faubus, crafted an ideology centered on the idea that most whites did not want desegregation and, because they were the majority in Arkansas, their views should prevail even in the face of adverse rulings from the federal courts. Segregationists implicitly linked their ideology of white majoritarianism to the idea that violent resistance to racial change was inevitable.[4]

In Arkansas, rhetoric centered on race, resistance, and violence had first surfaced in the small northeastern town of Hoxie, where school officials announced in 1955 that they were going to integrate their schools. Segregation had been costly for Hoxie, which had paid tuition and transportation costs for its African American high school students to attend segregated schools in Jonesboro and had shouldered the expenses of operating a one-room grade school for blacks rather than incorporate them into its existing white schools. In 1955, school officials there faced a looming budget deficit. Moreover, equalizing facilities for the twenty-five black students in the district, which also had one thousand white students, would have been prohibitively expensive. So the Hoxie School Board decided to integrate its schools because, as one official put it, "it's the law of the land, it's inevitable, it's God's will, and it's cheaper." In July 1955, at the beginning of the split school session that was common in cotton-producing areas, black students attended the public schools of Hoxie for the first time. Despite some local complaints, the experiment seemed peaceful at first.[5]

Then *Life* magazine featured the integrated schools in a story that touted the small town as an example of a white community that had made "a 'morally right' decision" to accept racial change, eliciting a powerful segregationist backlash. In response, segregationists from Hoxie and elsewhere, including Jim Johnson of Crossett and Amis Guthridge of Little Rock, deployed a repertoire of tactics designed to stop integration, including inflammatory racial rhetoric and a politics of intimidation directed at those in the community deemed to be supportive of desegregation. The Hoxie School Board refused to meet with them regarding its policy, intensifying local resistance. Speaking at a protest rally in Hoxie, Johnson told the crowd that he feared sending a child to an integrated school because "I'm afraid I might see the day when I'll be bouncing a half-Negro on my knee and have him call me Grandpa."[6]

His fear—that desegregation portended a loss of patriarchal control so serious that it could lead to consensual interracial sex on the part of one's own children—was broadly shared with other segregationists, giving emotional power to the states' rights arguments used by some to justify extreme measures. Another militant segregationist threatened to use the South's historic weapons of racial resistance, imagining that "blood would run knee-deep all over Arkansas" unless whites used guns and "grass ropes" to keep the "nigger out of the white bedroom." Guthridge said he would not take the responsibility should someone throw a rock through a school board member's windshield, blinding him. A Hoxie minister told his congregation that God would overlook violence committed in defense of white racial "purity," providing religious sanction for a politics of threat and intimidation. Segregationist rhetoric in the Hoxie crisis, therefore, revealed the centrality of a sexualized and patriarchal racism to calls for states' rights, local control, and violence in response to the twin perils of federal authority and racial change.[7]

For his part, Governor Faubus declared that Hoxie was a local matter, leaving him vulnerable to charges that he was "weak" on the question of integration. Jim Johnson, who would use the issue in his 1956 campaign for governor, charged that Faubus had been supine in the face of federal "tyranny" in Hoxie. A charismatic race-baiter and arch conservative, Johnson became the state segregationists' most important leader and spokesman. Johnson liked to claim that his politics of resistance would create such a dilemma for federal authorities that "there wouldn't have been enough jails to hold all the resist-ers!" In fact, like Faubus after him, Johnson was unwilling to violate a federal court injunction or risk being imprisoned for his principles. In the civil rights struggles of the 1950s and 1960s, it was African Americans, not white segrega-tionists, who were willing to sacrifice individual freedom in large numbers for their cause. As Adam Fairclough concluded, "their huffing and puffing was so much hot air."[8]

Johnson stayed out of Hoxie, but he did not choose to construe the Hoxie conflict as a defeat. Instead, he and other segregationists used it as a rallying cry and a precedent for future mobilization. This was true even as they advanced a conspiratorial view regarding the forces they confronted. Guthridge, for example, claimed later that events in Hoxie were "all a setup" in which those supporting segregation were "predestined to lose." Ironically, the masculin-ist rhetoric of honor and power they invoked in this and other conflicts with federal authority reinforced active resistance rather than passive acquiescence, despite the setbacks they experienced.[9]

While a sexually freighted fear of racial change aroused moral outrage, segregationists' ideology of victimization by federal authorities provided addi-tional emotional impetus for resistance by associating defiance with manhood. Indeed, only resistance could redeem that manhood. Marvin Hamilton, for example, wrote to the Little Rock School Board in 1956 to commend its victory in a lawsuit brought by the local branch of the NAACP: "I am truly glad that we have at least a few school boards that have the manhood and courage to stand for the right, and try to protect the rights of the white people." In fact, segre-gationists' defiance would be more successful in Little Rock, where the school board members would demonstrate much less courage and conviction than Hoxie's officials when it came to desegregating the schools.[10]

In most areas of the South, the "conservative lawbreaking" that characterized massive resistance was predicated on a perceived class division among whites in which the middle class claimed and used institutional political and economic power while extralegal threats and methods were attributed to, and sometimes enacted by, working-class and rural whites. Middle-class whites organized Citi-zens' Councils and similar organizations to threaten the livelihoods of African Americans and whites who dared to support desegregation and to exert pres-sure on politicians. Within the southern context, this division became the means whereby mainstream politicians like Faubus attempted to threaten and deploy "grassroots" violence while disclaiming accountability for it.[11]

In Little Rock and Arkansas, massive resistance was closely tied to class politics, but those politics operated somewhat differently there from many other parts of the South. Little Rock was unusual in that the Capital Citizens' Council and the Mothers' League consisted primarily of working-class whites, along with some marginal professionals, including ministers from small Baptist churches. Excluded from any meaningful power in Little Rock School Board decisions, they bitterly resented the board's decision to open Hall High School, a new all-white institution in the affluent western section of the city, at the same time that they made Central the locus of integration. Many white working-class people interpreted this as a form of social leveling that would cost them prestige and opportunity, while threatening a sense of morality and worth constructed on the basis of whiteness. To be meaningful, this whiteness had to be shared across class boundaries. Expressing the class grievance felt by his constituents, the Citizens' Council leader Amis Guthridge complained a few days before the 1957 academic year began that "the rich and well-to-do were going to see to it that the 'only' race mixing that is going to be done is in the districts where the so-called rednecks live." Indeed, one segregationist woman wrote to the businessman Herbert Thomas: "I personally am sick of so-called 'successful businessmen' integrating white people against their will and against our United States Constitution; white people from whom your so-called success has been drawn." Although her class-conscious racism differed from the economic conservatism of most segregationist leaders in the South, she readily closed ranks with that leadership in Arkansas, in part because she saw it as the best means to undermine the power of business elites in local politics.[12]

Racial competition for scarce jobs also concerned those who opposed racial change. In an anonymous letter, one segregationist wrote to Virgil Blossom that African Americans were not "working for equality but supremacy— with *your* help, they will get it." The message was written on a comic strip depicting an inversion of existing class relations between blacks and whites. In them, "The White Man of Tomorrow" worked either as a chauffeur, shoeshine boy, or policeman for blacks whose economic supremacy was signified by their affluent attire as well as their ability to secure service and deference from whites. One frame depicted an African American man marrying a white woman (labeled "Blossom's daughter" by the letter's author) while her hapless father watched. White men's gendered losses, therefore, were complete; they included economic privilege, sexual control over white women, and a social esteem that derived from an economic supremacy closely linked to racial dominance. For this author, the stakes of the desegregation struggle included white manhood itself.[13]

The cartoon, moreover, revealed that segregationists occupied a "rule or be ruled" racial order that echoed the Darwinian political world they evoked in their confrontations with moderates and with the federal government. Like the Cold War system, theirs was a morally and politically divided world beset with peril. The comic strip pictured "The White Man of Today" standing hat in hand under a tree, defying a bird to drop a load on him, with the words "Go ahead, I've let everyone else." The message was obvious enough—white men facing racial and political challenges from African Americans could choose either supremacy or a humiliating capitulation. Within this worldview, which was forged equally from class oppression and racial privilege, white men's freedom required African Americans' oppression.[14]

According to the journalist Roy Reed, the top-down philosophy of the Blossom-dominated school board constituted the "fatal flaw" in its effort to implement school desegregation in Little Rock: "That approach by Blossom with the school board going along with him because he was a very dominant personality . . . simply ignored Margaret Jackson [of the Mothers' League] and all those folks out there who had always felt, I think, that they had no say in how their town was run." Indeed, segregationist activists were correct to assume that the school board reflected the interests and goals of those elites. From the beginning, Blossom cultivated close ties to business leaders in Little Rock, who played a critical role in recruiting him for his new job. Once in his job, Blossom reciprocated, speaking before men's civic groups, whom he urged to provide "citizen leadership" for the public schools, and offering his support for local businesses and the development strategies advanced by local elites. In return for his efforts on their behalf, he was named the Little Rock Man of the Year for 1955.[15]

Segregationists' sense of disempowerment, especially at the local level, exacerbated their tendency to threaten violence. At the same time, the identification of the Citizens' Council and massive resistance with working-class whites made it easy for the established leadership of Little Rock to disdain them and to condemn the violent crowds that gathered at Central in September 1957. Hugh Patterson, Jr., publisher of the *Arkansas Gazette,* described Little Rock's segregationists as "people who crawl out of the holes and appear to gain a respectability during a time of strife and stress." At the same time, he noted that they were "tolerated by people who have found them to be disreputable and sort of unclean before," because those people "don't themselves want to expose a profile for attack."[16]

Some in Little Rock who opposed Faubus's actions and the behavior of the crowds concluded that the governor had enabled the rule of poor whites. Adolphine Fletcher Terry, the seventy-five-year-old leader of Little Rock's civic activists, wrote of her reaction as follows: "For days I walked about, unable to concentrate on anything, except the fact that we had been disgraced by a group of poor whites and a portion of the lunatic fringe that every town possesses. I wondered where the better class had been while this was being concocted." J. O. Powell, the vice principal of Central High School, described the demonstrators at the high school as a "cluster of unidentifiable and apparently unemployed white civilians [who] had accumulated with other debris in the gutters and dirty by-ways near and on the campus" while Faubus did nothing about them. In 1959, the *Washington Post* editorialized that the demonstrations against the resumption of desegregation in Little Rock revealed that "Governor Faubus was in the ambivalent position of having said that he deplored violence while egging on the mob."[17]

The stress on the racial violence of the working class ignored the support, tacit and overt, given them by "the better class" in Little Rock. Although the crowds that gathered at Central were predominantly working class, their leaders included ministers and lawyers, as well as the merchant Jimmy Karam, who was regarded by many as Faubus's surrogate leader in the mob actions. As one Little Rock businessman told the reporter Gertrude Samuels later, "I have no use for Faubus or Guthridge. Yet I feel a bit of comfort whenever a roadblock is thrown up to stop the plans of the N.A.A.C.P., and they're the biggest roadblocks to have come along." The strength of segregationist sentiments among business leaders and other moderates made them ambivalent regarding the resistance to racial change provided by the arch segregationists. As Rev. Robert Brown noted, many business leaders "admitted publicly that they did not mind saying they were for law and order, but that they were still going to stop integration in Little Rock if they could."[18]

Gender also shaped observers' perceptions of the meanings of violence in the crisis, although it did so in contradictory ways. Representations of women's actions in the mobs at Central High School reveal the intense ambivalence experienced by some whites who observed their participation in violence. The mainstream media, as well as the critics of violent resistance, often described women's behavior in the crowds as both hyperfeminine in its extreme emotionality and as unfeminine in all its appearances: dress, demeanor, hatefulness, and unruliness. In the process, mob violence itself was feminized, described as "belligerent, shrieking and hysterical." A *New York Times* account also noted that some of the women in the crowd used a vocabulary of gender to provoke more violent resistance by the men, taunting them with the question: "Are you men?" Their words also suggest that the women felt constrained as women from using the force that they believed the situation required.[19]

However strongly this may suggest that the women's intentions were not entirely pacific, for some observers the participation of women endowed the mobs with benign intent. Writing for the *Arkansas Democrat*, Bascom N. Timmons discounted the dangerous possibilities of the crowds at Central High School by peopling them with innocent mothers and children:

> But some of the Little Rock "mob" were school children, armed with nothing more lethal than school books. And there was a preponderance of women. One does not ordinarily think of the raw material for

mobs as coming from mothers who bear children, nurture them to school age, sacrifice for them, wish them trained and educated in the best environment.[20]

The Mothers' League reinforced this perspective by speaking out against segregationists who threatened violence. In an August 1957 meeting of the Mothers' League, a man wanted to know how many would show up at Central High School when desegregation began—to "push back" any blacks who dared to enter. When he added that he "[imagined] there are a few shotguns in Little Rock, too," Mrs. O. R. Aaron, president of the Mothers' League, told him that her organization was "trying to keep down violence."[21]

The Mothers' League's fear of violence extended beyond that which might come from adult segregationists. In their interviews with the FBI and in other statements, Mothers' League leaders repeatedly expressed the view that the threat of violence came from high school students of both races and from the provocative presence of blacks in "white" spaces. One woman who expressed sympathy with the Mothers' League said that she thought violence would occur when African American students participated in school social activities, naturalizing the connection between sexual fears and violent responses. Even as they sought to repress white violence in their ranks, they rationalized and tacitly encouraged it.[22]

The strategy of mobilizing large numbers of segregationist women to converge at Central High School as desegregation began had some resonance in high places. By early October 1957, J. Edgar Hoover, the director of the FBI, was advising the Eisenhower administration to take no further legal action to enjoin the segregationists, on the grounds that Central High School was then peaceful and that the crowds had included large numbers of ministers and women; he believed that the federal government could not legitimately target them. The maternalist respectability with which the Mothers' League hoped to cloak the cause of massive resistance was clearly achieved in this case.[23]

Segregationists interpreted women as the victims of integration and of the violence that accompanied it in Little Rock. In a speech before the Capital Citizens' Council in January 1958, Roy V. Harris of Georgia, leader of the Citizens' Councils, said that whites throughout the South were grateful to the resisters in Little Rock as they confronted ostensibly abusive federal troopers: "Pictures flashed all over the world of innocent young high school girls being pushed along the sidewalks of your city by the bayonets of paratroopers. Pictures flashed all over the world showing a man in your town with blood streaming down his face while under arrest by the federal troops." A segregationist wrote anonymously to the Arkansas NAACP leader Daisy Bates asking whether her organization intended "to use bayonets, now, to force those white girls to go to bed with the black boy," alleging that "if you've gone this far you will probably go to the finish."[24]

The picture of the troops following young girls going to school was widely used as a photographic image and a political icon, captioned with the words "Remember Little Rock." This representation of the situation had great resonance in the South, where "Remember Little Rock" became a rallying cry for massive resistance, appearing on envelopes, fliers, and other documents. The *Arkansas Democrat*, the pro-Faubus newspaper in Little Rock, used pictures, including one suggesting that federal troops had bayoneted school girls, and headlines, such as "Spectator Bayoneted, Another Clubbed by Tough Paratroopers" and "CHS Emptied by Bomb Scare Shortly after U.S. Troops Force Integration," in its coverage of the arrival of the troops in 1957. Faubus's statements that the picture of the girls confirmed that the "naked force of the Federal Government is here apparent in these unsheathed bayonets in the backs of schoolgirls" created, in the words of Phoebe Godfrey, "a clear sexual image reverberating no doubt back to Civil War fears of the Yankee rapist." The various images reinforced the message that the actions and purposes of the federal government were violent and coercive, while representing those in the mobs around the high school as peaceable spectators. The use of little girls in the "Brotherhood by Bayonet" image illustrates the tenacity of an imagery of victimization that was gendered female even when the political vocabulary of equality—brotherhood—was gendered male.[25]

The segregationist representation of women as innocent victims of a brutal federal authority expressed segregationist fears rather than documenting actual violence against white women, whether occasioned by desegregation or the presence of federal authorities. As Phoebe Godfrey has perceptively noted, "Faubus's genius was to seal the two fears together—federal authority and miscegenation—in one sizzling and politically efficacious package." He did so by linking federal agents and troops with desegregation, sexual threats, and a loss of parental authority. When he claimed that FBI agents in Little Rock had taken into custody adolescent school girls who had been "held incommunicado for hours of questioning while their frantic parents knew nothing of their whereabouts," he expressed parents' fears regarding the vulnerability of their daughters in a context of racial change while "disseminating falsehood," in the words of the aggrieved J. Edgar Hoover. As Godfrey has noted, the girls' vulnerability derived not only from desegregation but also from the budding cultural and sexual autonomy of adolescent girls. The parents' inability to exercise power over school politics in Little Rock combined with the "moral panic" engendered by sexual and family changes to fuel a powerful politics of rage evidenced by the women and men of the segregationist movement.[26]

While white women enacted the role of passive and nonviolent "victims of integration," white men assumed the roles of "protectors" and defenders of segregation. Paradoxically, this allowed white women to assume critical roles in organizing segregationist politics in Little Rock without apparently violating southern white gender norms. At the same time, it displaced men's sense of victimization and, thus, of masculine failure, onto female figures. Otherwise the figures of federal troops—associated in history with southern men's defeat in the Civil War—might have carried a different message. As David Goldfield and others have concluded, that southern defeat was redeemed only through representations of planter culture as the height of genteel civilization and Reconstruction as the epitome of a jackbooted military and social oppression of whites. In Little Rock, where bumper stickers with the words "Occupied Arkansas" proliferated, white men transformed their fear of victimization into a righteous defiance of tyrants and denied that fear through the feminized iconography they circulated throughout the South. "Remember Little Rock" had become a sexually loaded slogan.[27]

Employing maternalist rhetoric centered on the safety and welfare of their children in the schools, the Mothers' League sought to confer legitimacy on segregationist efforts. Their rhetoric focused on themes of sexual and other dangers posed to whites by integration. Acting with the Citizens' Council, they deployed vintage stereotypes of African American men as sexual predators prone to violence, focusing constantly on what they believed to be the imminent threat of interracial dating and marriage.[28]

The Mothers' League and other segregationists fanned popular fears about student violence, hoping that the threat of disorder would justify a refusal to comply with the *Brown* decision. Their conviction that integration was unthinkable and their fear that the legitimately constituted authorities would compromise their cause meant that the arch segregationists needed and wanted the threat of violence. Most of them also recoiled from the implications of this position, routinely projecting violent feelings and impulses onto others, usually unnamed "students." Their claim to the mantle of "respectable resistance" required that they maintain the appearance of lawfulness. That appearance also served their efforts to elude legal accountability for attempting to obstruct a federal court order. At the same time, the power of their dissent rested with an apocalyptic vision of the consequences of racial change—consequences so ominous that they had to be prevented at all cost. In their view, that change threatened untold harm to whites, to "civilization," to the meaning of America—in short, to the moral order they embraced.[29]

Shortly after Eisenhower ordered troops to Little Rock to enforce the federal court order, Margaret Jackson, another of the leaders in the Mothers' League, filed a lawsuit to have the troops removed. She alleged that the troops "did intimidate, mutilate, bayonet and bludgeon private citizens and endanger the lives and safety of the petitioners." The journalist Bob Considine concluded that a minor injury to one man from a soldier's bayonet had given the "mob something to pin their rage on." A federal district court and a federal appeals court, apparently agreed, concluding that Jackson's charges lacked credibility. In late September, Jackson complained that the white mothers' "children [were] attending classes under the watchful eye of hardened soldiers who are acting under stern orders." In fact, the troops were not allowed in classrooms, gym classes, cafeterias, and restrooms and had become less evident in the hallways as President Eisenhower moved to decrease their numbers and visibility by the end of fall term of 1957. In February 1958, Everett Barnes, a science teacher at Central who opposed desegregation, told the Arkansas State Police that he found it difficult to teach "with the 'ring of steel around the school' and further that he did not like being constantly guarded and the feeling of being constantly watched became 'sickening.'" Clearly, he and other segregationists experienced the federal presence itself as violence.[30]

Faubus and other segregationist men used a powerful rhetoric of invasion and emasculation to express their convictions regarding the harmful effects of federal authority in matters of race. The governor, for example, saw his inability to find a face-saving way to avert federal intervention as a humiliating personal defeat. The vocabulary of states' rights and gubernatorial autonomy that he employed not only expressed the white South's historic support for states' rights but also supported his personal claim to immunity from subjection to the authority of others. That claim was important because Faubus's actions in assigning state National Guard troops to Central High School in order to prevent the entry of African American students had prompted a federal court order enjoining him from any further interference in Little Rock's school desegregation plan. In addition, he well knew that other segregationist leaders viewed his failure not only as a humiliating capitulation to the South's enemies but also as the occasion for his own abasement.[31]

Fearful that he could be jailed for contempt of court should he use the state for further segregationist resistance, and anxious to maintain his political legitimacy in Arkansas, Faubus lodged wild charges against federal officials, accusing them of engaging in "unwarranted interference" in his actions and adding that he had dependable information that federal authorities in Little Rock had been considering plans to "take into custody by force the head of a sovereign state." Representing the federal government, the attorney Osro Cobb denied the governor's charges. Personalizing the federal-state confrontation in which he was embroiled, Faubus further said that he could no more "surrender his rights" in the dispute than Eisenhower could his. As the school board member Wayne Upton put it, Faubus was "hellbent on letting the whole wide world know that he was in charge of this state and the federal government just wasn't going to interfere with him and with his operation of the state of Arkansas." Although Faubus's fears regarding the consequences of his choice to violate a federal court order were not entirely groundless, they were quite exaggerated. His claim that the federal government had no legitimate authority over him, which was quite dubious legally, made more sense as a politics of masculine protest against the power of other men in a hierarchical system.[32]

After the court enjoined Faubus and the Arkansas State National Guard from interfering with integration, Jim Johnson, speaking for the states' arch segregationists, begged Faubus "not to humiliate" the state *and himself* by submitting to the jurisdiction of the federal court. According to Johnson, "such action of submission will be an unwarranted surrender of rights reserved to the states." Rev. Wesley Pruden, a segregationist leader, later said that Faubus was set up in the late September meeting with President Eisenhower for the "surrender of his position." In a later discussion of his uneven power struggle with the president, Faubus said that he did not "believe in degrading anyone or putting anyone in a subservient role to another." Harry Ashmore, the editor of the *Arkansas Gazette*, wrote that after the meeting between the governor and the president "there remained some doubt as to who emerged with whose sword." Once federal troops arrived, however, no doubt remained. The language of submission and surrender, indeed the common recourse to military metaphors to describe the encounter, suggest that federal-state confrontation also involved a contest for manhood, one that Faubus (and the South) had apparently lost, at least for the moment.[33]

In the spring and summer of 1959, exponents of massive resistance in Arkansas experienced a series of setbacks. In May, moderates swept the Little Rock School Board recall elections, assuring them control of school policies in the short term. In June, a federal court declared that the state's school closing laws were unconstitutional. In early August, the managing board for Raney High School, the state's first white flight academy, announced it would be closing for lack of money. The school board announced the same month that the public high schools would open one month early so that Faubus could not call a special session of the legislature to pass obstructionist legislation. On August 12, three African American students entered Hall High School, and one went to Central, as the Little Rock police forcefully restrained segregationist resisters. It seemed that the protesters had run out of options.[34]

On September 7, 1959, bombs exploded at the school board offices and two other locations associated with city officials. Within a few days, the police had arrested and charged five white men with ties to the Citizens' Council and the

Ku Klux Klan. The defendant E. A. Lauderdale, the owner of a lumber and roofing company, was a member of the board of the Capital Citizens' Council who had run twice for the City Manager Board, losing both times. He had recruited others to the bombing plot at Klan meetings, including the truck driver J. D. Sims, who told the police that he did not want his daughter "to go to school with niggers."[35]

Citizens' Council leaders were quick to defend Lauderdale, one of their own, and to allege that the charges against him were a plot to discredit the segregation movement. Dr. Malcolm G. Taylor, president of the Capital Citizens' Council, praised Lauderdale as "a hard-working Christian patriot" whose arrest revealed the machinations of despotic local leaders. According to Taylor, "if Mr. Lauderdale can be selected as the scape goat and railroaded to prison, then no American can dare voice his honest resentment to police state tactics nor hope to find refuge in the time-honored laws and constitutional rights of this once-great land." Amis Guthridge, who provided legal assistance to some of the defendants, accused the prosecutors of charging Lauderdale "because of his prominence as a segregation leader."[36]

As the bombings demonstrated, the line between respectable resistance and violent defiance was a thin one in Little Rock and Arkansas. The trials revealed segregationists' use of the Klan and its "confidential squad" as the site for their "disreputable" resistance. If their goal was to insulate the Citizens' Council from any association with violence, they failed, as Lauderdale's active role in both groups created public suspicions that the two organizations were closely connected. Indeed, the *Washington Post* reporter Robert E. Baker concluded that with the arrests, the Citizens' Council's "last vestige of respectability was gone." The politics of masculinist protest had gone too far.[37]

Gender affected massive resistance and the social relations in which it was embedded in complex ways. It is hard to prove conclusively that the working-class nature of massive resistance in Little Rock made the presence and activism of women more necessary to its attempts to construct a credible and ostensibly peaceable politics of resistance, but it seems likely that this was so. Segregationists used women to claim respectability and nonviolence for a movement that relied on the idea of a spontaneous and potentially violent popular racism to justify state resistance to federal court orders. Symbolically, women also stood in as archetypal victims, enabling men to enact the protector role while obscuring their own inability as men to defend either the personal or state sovereignty they had claimed. Ultimately, however, the thin veneer of "Christian" respectability they gave the movement could not protect it from its own excesses, as the politics of masculine protest enacted by a few in the fall of 1959 led not to redemption but to political failure and public disgrace.

Notes

1. Mrs. Clyde Thomason, interview report, Sept. 4, 1957, FBI, file 44–12284; "Integration in Public Schools in Little Rock," MS 1027, both in Federal Bureau of Investigation Records, Investigative Reports, 1957, Special Collections Division, University of Arkansas Libraries, Fayetteville (hereafter FBI-UAF); Mrs. Abby Edwards, Dermott, to Jim Johnson, Apr. 28, 1958, box 6, Papers of Jim Johnson, Arkansas History Commission, Little Rock.

2. Mrs. Clyde Thomason, interview report, Sept. 4, 1957; Tony Freyer, *The Little Rock Crisis: A Constitutional Interpretation* (Westport, Conn.: Greenwood Press, 1984), 101–102; *Arkansas Gazette*, Aug. 28, 1957; Graeme Cope, "'A Thorn in the Side'? The Mothers' League of Central High School and the Little Rock Desegregation Crisis of 1957," *Arkansas Historical Quarterly* 57 (summer 1998): 160–90. Thomason was hardly the only one to find that Blossom failed to hear her concerns. Forrest Rozzell, head of the Arkansas Education Association, later observed: "Mr. Blossom wasn't the kind of person you conferred with. Mr. Blossom was the kind of person you listened to." John Pagan, interview by Forrest Rozzell, Dec. 29, 1972, box 3, Papers of Sarah Murphy, Special Collections Division, University of Arkansas Libraries, Fayetteville. See also oral history interview with Nat R. Griswold, Aug. 21, 1971, Little Rock Desegregation Crisis, 1957–1959, oral history interview transcripts, 1972–1973, MS L720 310 Little Rock, Special Collections Division, University of Arkansas Libraries, Fayetteville.

3. Cope, "'A Thorn in the Side'?" 160–90; *Arkansas Gazette*, Aug. 28, 30, Sept. 3, 4, 8, 1957; Elizabeth Huckaby oral history, Columbia University Oral History Project (CUOHP), Papers of Elizabeth Paisley Huckaby, Special Collections Division, University of Arkansas at Little Rock; Sewell, notes, Sept. 30, 1957, White House Office, Office of the Staff Secretary, Subject Series: Alphabetical Subseries, box 13, Dwight D. Eisenhower Library, Abilene, Kansas (hereafter DDEL).

4. Graeme Cope, "'Honest White People of the Middle and Lower Classes'? A Profile of the Capital Citizens' Council During the Little Rock Crisis of 1957," *Arkansas Historical Quarterly* 61 (spring 2002): 36–58; Numan V. Bartley, *The Rise of Massive Resistance: Race and Politics in the South During the 1950s* (Baton Rouge: Louisiana State University Press, 1969), 104; *Arkansas Gazette*, Aug. 30, 1957; *Arkansas Gazette*, Sept. 3–4, 1957; clipping, no citation, Jun. 18, 1958, Huckaby Papers; L. D. Poynter, interview report, Sept. 9, 1957, FBI-UAF; "FBI Investigation Instituted at Request of Judge Ronald L. Davies," clipping, box 1, FBI Records, Special Collections Division, University of Arkansas at Little Rock (hereafter FBI-UALR); Amis Guthridge to Orval E. Faubus, Aug. 28, 1957, box 589, Orval E. Faubus Papers, Special Collections Division, University of Arkansas Libraries, Fayetteville. Anita Sedberry of the Mothers' League, by contrast, told the FBI that she would be willing to use violence; "FBI Investigation Instituted at Request of Judge Ronald L. Davies." The Capital Citizens' Council rhetoric regarding violence resembled that in other parts of the South. David R. Goldfield, *Black, White, and Southern: Race Relations and Southern Culture 1940 to the Present* (Baton Rouge: Louisiana State University Press, 1990), 83–84. Both the Mothers' League and the Citizens' Council professed their commitment to nonviolence frequently in the days before classes started at Central. *Arkansas Gazette*, Aug 28, 1957, Aug. 30, 1957; Amis Guthridge to Orval E. Faubus, Aug. 28, 1957, box 589, Faubus Papers.

5. Roy Reed, *Faubus: The Life and Times of an American Prodigal* (Fayetteville: University of Arkansas Press, 1997), 172–74; Harry S. Ashmore, *Civil Rights and Wrongs: A Memoir of Race and Politics, 1944–1994* (New York: Pantheon Books, 1994), 113. In split sessions, students would start school in the summer, take a few weeks off to help in the fall harvest, and then resume their interrupted studies.

6. Reed, *Faubus*, 172–74; *Life*, Jul. 25, 1955, 29–31; John T. Elliff, "The United States Department of Justice and Individual Rights, 1937–1962" (New York: Garland, 1987; reprint of Ph.D. diss., Harvard University, 1967), 407–20; *New York Times Magazine*, Sept. 25, 1955; Freyer, *Little Rock Crisis*, 65; *Arkansas Gazette*, Sept. 18, 1955.

7. Reed, *Faubus*, 172–74; Elliff, "United States Department of Justice and Individual Rights," 407–20; *New York Times Magazine*, Sept. 25, 1955; Freyer, *Little Rock Crisis*, 65. The *Arkansas Gazette* reporter in Hoxie refused to publish the sexualized and violent rhetoric of the segregationists there because he believed their remarks were "unfit for publication." Nathan Griswold, manuscript, chapter 1, p. 29, Murphy Papers, box 11. Elizabeth Jacoway's characterization of segregationists primarily as advocates of local control obscures the connections between segregationists' understandings of race, sex, and gender and their enthusiasm for state power, then a monopoly of white men. She herself concludes that the "trouble with the Jim Johnsons of the world was that they believed the things they said about integration leading inevitably to miscegenation." Elizabeth Jacoway, "Jim Johnson of Arkansas: Segregationist Prototype," in *The Role of Ideas in the Civil Rights South*, ed. Ted Ownby (Jackson: University Press of Mississippi, 2002), 137–55.

8. Reed, *Faubus*, pp. 172–74; Jacoway, "Jim Johnson of Arkansas," 148; Adam Fairclough, "The Little Rock Crisis: Success or Failure for the NAACP?" *Arkansas Historical Quarterly* 56 (autumn 1997): 371–75.

9. Reed, *Faubus*, 172–74; Virgil T. Blossom, *It Has Happened Here* (New York: Harper, 1959), 38; interview with Amis Guthridge, CUOHP, OH-186, Aug. 19, 1971, DDEL.

10. Marvin M. Hamilton to the School Board Members of Little Rock, Aug. 16, 1956, box 3, Virgil T. Blossom Papers, MS 1364, Special Collections Division, University of Arkansas Libraries, Fayetteville. As David Goldfield notes, one "would think that the exaltation of death and defeat would generate depression, but it proved exhilarating to southern society"; *Still Fighting the Civil War* (Baton Rouge: Louisiana State University Press, 2002), 29.

11. Joel Williamson, *A Rage for Order: Black/White Relations in the American South Since Emancipation* (New York: Oxford University Press, 1986), 150. The South Carolina author James McBride Dabbs, for example, concluded that "the part about violence is always said publicly . . . so that the lower-class whites know what is expected of them." Goldfield, *Black, White, and Southern*, 84. The phrase "conservative lawbreaking" is from Goldfield, *Black, White, and Southern*, 81.

12. Dale Alford and L'Moore Alford, *The Case of the Sleeping People (Finally Awakened by Little Rock School Frustrations)* (Little Rock: n. p., 1959), 125; Orval E. Faubus to Herbert Thomas, Apr. 14, 1959, MC 437, box 4, Papers of Herbert L. Thomas, Special Collections Division, University of Arkansas Libraries, Fayetteville; Bartley, *Rise of Massive Resistance*, 253–54; *Arkansas Gazette*, Sept. 1, 1957; Mrs. Bob O. Cook to Herbert Thomas, Apr. 11, 1958, MC 437, box 4, Herbert Thomas Papers, Special Collections Division, University of Arkansas Libraries, Fayetteville; Pete Daniel, *Lost Revolutions: The South in the*

1950s (Chapel Hill: University of North Carolina Press, 2000), 197; Scott D. H . [Hamilton], manager, Little Rock Chamber of Commerce, to Virgil Blossom, Feb. 10, 1953; Dave Grundfest to Virgil Blossom, Dec. 28, 1953; Glenn A. Green to Virgil Blossom, Mar. 31, 1954; Herbert L. Thomas, Jr., to John A. Riggs, Jr., Jul. 28, 1955; Everett Tucker, Jr., to Virgil T. Blossom, Feb. 1, 1956, all in box 1, Blossom Papers.

13. Anonymous letter and cartoons, n.d., box 7, Blossom Papers. An unmarked copy of this cartoon can also be found in box 48, Johnson Papers.

14. Anonymous letter and cartoon, n.d., box 7, Blossom Papers.

15. My interview with Roy Reed, Jun. 19, 1995.

16. *Arkansas Gazette*, Sept. 5, 1957; David Thoreau Wieck, "Report from Little Rock," *Liberation* (Oct. 1958): 4–9; *New York Times*, Sept. 6, 1957; *Arkansas Democrat*, Sept. 29, 1987; Cope, "'Honest White People of the Middle and Lower Classes'?" 44–45. Journalists from outside the South also viewed segregationist activists as disreputable poor whites. The political reporter Bob Considine, for example, called the women of the Mothers' League "slatternly housewives." The crowd was "so ticked at him" that they went after a row of glass telephone booths occupied by him and other reporters at 16th and Park . . . and tried to push them over. "They took great offense at that and gave him a tough time particularly. . . . The crowd was so incensed at that point about reproters that some of them came over and started rocking these booths." Ernest Dumas, interview by Jerry Dhonau, Mar. 3, 2000, available online at: http://libinfo.urk.edu/SpecialCollections/ACOVH/dhonau.pdf, accessed on Sept. 14, 2003, Gazette Project, University of Arkansas-Fayetteville; Dan Wakefield, "Siege at Little Rock: The Brave Ones," *Nation*, Oct. 11, 1958, 204–6.

17. Terry, *Life Is My Song, Also*, 231, typescript, Fletcher-Terry Papers, RG A-13, Special Collections Division, University of Arkansas at Little Rock; J. O. Powell, "Central High Inside Out (A Study in Disintegration)," unpublished manuscript, Velma and J. O. Powell Collection, MS 1367, box 1, Special Collections Division, University of Arkansas Libraries, Fayetteville; *Washington Post*, Aug. 13, 1959.

18. Gertrude Samuels, "The Silent Fear in Little Rock," *New York Times Magazine*, Mar. 30, 1958, 11, 78–79; oral history interview with Henry Woods, Dec. 8, 1972, CUOHP; Liz to Bill, October, 1957, file entitled "Letters to Bill, 1957–1958," Huckaby Papers; Robert R. Brown, *Bigger Than Little Rock* (Greenwich, Conn.: Seabury Press, SPCK, 1958), 62.

19. The classic example of the feminized mob is in Benjamin Fine's front-page story on the disorders of September 23, 1957. In it, women screamed and men yelled. "Hysteria swept from the shrieking girls to members of the crowd. Women cried hysterically, tears running down their faces." *New York Times*, Sept. 24, 1957. In a *New York Post* article reprinted in the *Arkansas Gazette*, Murray Kempton described women demonstrating against integration in Nashville as "on parade, in sweat socks one, in formless cotton sacking others," sending "up their tribal cries." *Arkansas Gazette*, Sept. 16, 1957.

20. *Arkansas Democrat*, Oct. 25, 1957.

21. *Arkansas Gazette*, Aug. 23, 28, 1957.

22. Interview with Mrs. Margaret Jackson, Sept. 6, 1957; interview with Mrs. A. T. Forbess, Sept. 7, 1957; interview with Mrs. T. H. Dame, Sept. 8, 1957, all in box 1, FBI-UALR.

23. John Edgar Hoover, memorandum for Mr. Tolson, et al., Oct. 7, 1957, FBI Record on Orval Faubus, unprocessed collection, Special Collections Division, University of Arkansas Libraries, Fayetteville. The peace he claimed for CHS obtained only with

respect to the absence of white crowds in the vicinity of the school. A systematic effort to intimidate and harass African American students continued in and around the school.

24. Anonymous to the President of the N.A.C.P.A. [*sic*], Sept. 30, 1957, Papers of Daisy Bates, box 1, State Historical Society of Wisconsin, Madison; Harris concluded that "Little Rock has proved to the crazy bunch in Washington that they haven't got enough soldiers to station troops in every white school in the south." Speech of Roy V. Harris Before Capital Citizens' Council, Little Rock, Arkansas, Jan. 14, 1958, box 589, Faubus Papers.

25. *Arkansas Democrat*, Sept. 25, 1957; clipping, 1982, Huckaby Papers; Phoebe Godfrey, "Bayonets, Brainwashing, and Bathrooms: The Discourse of Race, Gender, and Sexuality in the Desegregation of Little Rock's Central High," *Arkansas Historical Quarterly* 62 (spring 2003): 42–67; quotation, 50–51. Elizabeth Huckaby's interpretation of the picture diverged considerably from that advanced by segregationists. She saw "two laughing girls, absent from school without their mothers' knowledge I found later, being moved along by soldiers with bayonets pointed toward them." Elizabeth Huckaby, *Crisis at Central High, 1957–58* (Baton Rouge: Louisiana State University Press, 1980), 45.

26. Speech, Sept. 26, 1957, box 496, Faubus Papers; Godfrey, "Bayonets, Brainwashing, and Bathrooms," 42–67.

27. Goldfield, *Still Fighting the Civil War*, 2, 28.

28. Interview with Mrs. Margaret Jackson, Sept. 6, 1957; interview with Mrs. A. T. Forbess, Sept. 7, 1957, both in box 1, FBI-UALR; *Arkansas Gazette*, August 28, 30, 1957; Godfrey, "Bayonets, Brainwashing, and Bathrooms," 42–67.

29. Goldfield, *Black, White, and Southern*, 83; Daniel, *Lost Revolutions*, 251–83.

30. *Arkansas Gazette*, Nov. 17, 1957; *New York Times*, Sept. 28, 1957; Dumas, interview by Jerry Dhonau; "Investigation to Determine Leaders and Instigators of Violence at Central High School," box 1, FBI-UALR; Everett Barnes, interview, Feb. 7, 1958, box 497, Faubus Papers.

31. The touchy negotiations prior to the meeting between the president and the governor, centering on who was to request the meeting and how, also bespeak the freighted emotional subtext of the encounter. Brooks Hays, *A Southern Moderate Speaks* (Chapel Hill: University of North Carolina Press, 1959), 138–65. The women of the Mothers' League also experienced federal intervention as humiliating, but did not invest it with the concern for masculine dignity and autonomy expressed by the men. Cope, "'A Thorn in the Side'?" 168.

32. *Arkansas Gazette*, Sept. 5, 1957; Wayne Upton, oral history, 1971, MS 720310, CUOHP.

33. *Arkansas Gazette*, Sept. 20, 1957; Wesley Pruden, oral history, CUOHP, OH-264, 1970, DDEL; John Ward interview with Orval Faubus and Brooks Hays, Jun. 4, 1976, series 3, subseries 1, box 45, MS H334P, Papers of L. Brooks Hays, Special Collections Division, University of Arkansas Libraries, Fayetteville; Harry Ashmore, "The Untold Story Behind Little Rock," *Harper's*, Jun. 1958, 16. A scholarship on masculinity, southern culture and identity, and white racial privilege is now beginning to emerge. See Kari Frederickson, "'As a Man, I Am Interested in States' Rights': Gender, Race, and the Family in the Dixiecrat Party," in *Jumpin' Jim Crow: Southern Politics from Civil War to Civil Rights*, ed. Jane Dailey, Glenda Elizabeth Gilmore, and Bryant Simon (Princeton, N.J.: Princeton University Press, 2000), 260–74; Nancy Bercaw, ed., *Gender and the Southern*

Body Politic: Essays and Comments (Jackson: University Press of Mississippi, 2000); William F. Pinar, *The Gender of Racial Politics and Violence in America: Lynching, Prison Rape, and the Crisis of Masculinity* (New York: Peter Lang, 2001); Ted Ownby, *Subduing Satan: Religion, Recreation, and Manhood in the Rural South, 1865–1920* (Chapel Hill: University of North Carolina Press, 1990); Bryant Simon, "The Appeal of Cole Blease of South Carolina: Race, Class, and Sex in the New South," in *Sex, Love, Race: Crossing Boundaries in North American History*, ed. Martha Hodes (New York: New York University Press, 1999), 373–98. The former Arkansas governor Sid McMath saw Eisenhower's decision to meet with Faubus as an inappropriate elevation of the governor's status, commenting that the president "met with him and negotiated with him as if he were ambassador of some foreign country, you know, and gave him prestige and recognition—he should never have called him up there and conferred with him and given him recognition." Oral history interview with Sidney McMath, Dec. 30, 1970, OH-202, MS L720 310, CUOHP.

34. *John Aaron, et al., v. Ed. Il McKinley, Jr., et al.,* Jun. 18, 1959, U.S. District Court, box 17, group 3, National Association for the Advancement of Colored People Papers, Library of Congress, Washington, D.C.; *Arkansas Gazette*, Jun. 19, 1959; Freyer, *Little Rock Crisis*, 162; *Arkansas Gazette*, Aug. 5, 1959; *Arkansas Gazette*, Aug. 13, 1959; Reed, *Faubus*, 256.

35. *Arkansas Gazette*, Sept. 10, 1959; *Arkansas Gazette*, Sept. 12, 1959; *Arkansas Gazette*, Oct. 10, 1959; *Arkansas Democrat*, Nov. 3, 1959; *Arkansas Gazette*, Oct. 28, 1959.

36. *Arkansas Gazette*, Sept. 11, 1959; *Arkansas Democrat*, Oct. 28, 1959; *Arkansas Gazette*, Nov. 28, 1959; *Arkansas Democrat*, Jul. 10, 1961; *Arkansas Gazette*, Sept. 10, 1959; *Arkansas Gazette*, Oct. 30, 1959.

37. *Arkansas Gazette*, Sept. 9, 1959; *Arkansas Gazette*, Oct. 29, 1959; Robert E. Baker, "Passions Calmer in Little Rock," *Washington Post*, undated clipping in Women's Emergency Committee Papers, box 14, Arkansas History Commission, Little Rock; clipping, no citation, Huckaby Papers; *New York Times*, Nov. 29, 1959.

BIBLIOGRAPHICAL ESSAY

This essay is intended to facilitate further research on massive resistance. Although much of the literature on the civil rights struggle has focused on the activists who pushed for racial reform, there are a number of important published works on southern segregationists. Some of the most important literature on massive resistance has appeared in the last few years, a clear indication of increased scholarly interest in the subject.

Race Relations before *Brown*

One of the most important debates about massive resistance is whether or not the Supreme Court decision retarded a gradual reform process in southern race relations that was underway before 1954. For readers interested in assessing the conflicting interpretations of Michael Klarman and Tony Badger in this collection, the following works will help to place the massive resistance era in historical context: John Egerton, *Speak Now Against the Day: The Generation Before the Civil Rights Movement in the South* (New York: Knopf, 1994); Neil R. McMillen, ed., *Remaking Dixie: The Impact of World War II on the American South* (Jackson: University Press of Mississippi, 1996); Charles D. Chamberlain, *Victory at Home: Manpower and Race in the American South During World War II* (Athens: University of Georgia Press, 2003); Gail Williams O'Brien, *The Color of the Law: Race, Violence, and Justice in the Post–World War II South* (Chapel Hill: University of North Carolina Press, 1999); Kari A. Frederickson, *The Dixiecrat Revolt and the End of the Solid South, 1932–1968* (Chapel Hill: University of North Carolina Press, 2001); and Robert Rogers Korstad, *Civil Rights Unionism: Tobacco Workers and the Struggle for Democracy in the Mid-Twentieth-Century South* (Chapel Hill: University of North

Carolina Press, 2003). Although unpublished at the time of compilation of this bibliographical essay, another book that promises to be of considerable importance is Glenn Feldman, ed., *Before Brown: Civil Rights and White Backlash in the Modern South* (Tuscaloosa: University of Alabama Press, 2004). This collection assesses the increased civil rights activism of southern blacks in the 1930s and 1940s and the white conservative backlash against it. It includes an essay by Feldman, "Ugly Roots: Race, Emotion, and the Rise of the Modern Republican Party in Alabama and the South," that demonstrates how massive resistance contributed to the political conversion of the South from a Democratic region to a Republican stronghold.

The Civil Rights Movement

The literature on the civil rights movement is enormous, and the outpouring of publications on the subject shows no sign of abating. One of the best places to start is Harvard Sitkoff, *The Struggle for Black Equality, 1954–1992* (New York: Hill and Wang, 1980), a stylishly written narrative. Another outstanding introduction to the subject is Robert Cook, *Sweet Land of Liberty? The African-American Struggle for Civil Rights in the Twentieth Century* (New York: Longman, 1998), which places the movement within a broader history of black activism. My students also find extremely useful the interpretive debate between Steven F. Lawson and Charles Payne in *Debating the Civil Rights Movement, 1954–1968* (Lanham, Md.: Rowman and Littlefield, 1998).

Other broad interpretive treatments of civil rights activism include Clayborne Carson, *In Struggle: SNCC and the Black Awakening of the 1960s* (Cambridge, Mass.: Harvard University Press, 1981); Taylor Branch, *Parting the Waters: America in the King Years, 1954–63* (New York: Simon and Schuster, 1988); Adam Fairclough, *To Redeem the Soul of America: The Southern Christian Leadership Conference and Martin Luther King, Jr.* (Athens: University of Georgia Press, 1987); and David J. Garrow, *Bearing the Cross: Martin Luther King, Jr. and the Southern Christian Leadership Conference* (New York: Morrow, 1986).

Some of the best research on the civil rights movement in recent years has been case studies of black protest in specific communities and states. These studies include John Dittmer, *Local People: The Struggle for Civil Rights in Mississippi* (Urbana: University of Illinois Press, 1994); Adam Fairclough, *Race and Democracy: The Civil Rights Struggle in Louisiana, 1915–1972* (Athens: University of Georgia Press, 1995); John A. Kirk, *Redefining the Color Line: Black Activism in Little Rock, Arkansas, 1940–1970* (Gainesville: University Press of Florida, 2002); Peter B. Levy, *Civil War on Race Street: The Civil Rights Movement in Cambridge, Maryland* (Gainesville: University Press of Florida, 2003); Charles

Payne, *I've Got the Light of Freedom: The Organizing Tradition and the Mississippi Freedom Struggle* (Berkeley: University of California Press, 1995); and Stephen G. N. Tuck, *Beyond Atlanta: The Struggle for Racial Equality in Georgia, 1940–1980* (Athens: University of Georgia Press, 2001).

Brown v. Board of Education

The best study of the origins and impact of the Supreme Court decision outlawing segregation in public schools is Richard Kluger's monumental *Simple Justice: The History of Brown v. Board of Education and Black America's Struggle for Equality* (New York: Knopf, 1976). An expanded edition of the book, published to coincide with the fiftieth anniversary of the court decision, contains a sobering assessment of the resegregation of public schools. A more concise, but still extremely informative, study is James T. Patterson, *Brown v. Board of Education: A Civil Rights Milestone and Its Troubled Legacy* (New York: Oxford University Press, 2001).

The southern federal judges entrusted with the responsibility of overseeing implementation of the *Brown* decision suffered death threats and public censure. Their tales of individual and collective bravery are told in J. W. Peltason, *Fifty-Eight Lonely Men: Southern Federal Judges and School Desegregation* (New York: Harcourt, Brace and World, 1961), and Jack Bass, *Unlikely Heroes: The Dramatic Story of the Southern Judges of the Fifth Circuit Who Translated the Supreme Court's Brown Decision into a Revolution for Equality* (New York: Simon and Schuster, 1981).

Other key texts on the Supreme Court decision and the unresolved dilemma of racial segregation in American schools include J. Harvie Wilkinson III, *From Brown to Bakke: The Supreme Court and School Integration, 1954–1978* (New York: Oxford University Press, 1979); Raymond Wolters, *The Burden of Brown: Thirty Years of School Desegregation* (Knoxville: University of Tennessee Press, 1984); Mark V. Tushnet, *Making Civil Rights Law: Thurgood Marshall and the Supreme Court, 1936–1961* (New York: Oxford University Press, 1994); Austin Sarat, ed., *Race, Law, and Culture: Reflections on Brown v. Board of Education* (New York: Oxford University Press, 1997); Gary Orfield, Susan E. Eaton, and Elaine R. Jones, *Dismantling Desegregation: The Quiet Reversal of Brown v. Board of Education* (New York: New Press, 1996); and Peter H. Irons, *Jim Crow's Children: The Broken Promise of the Brown Decision* (New York: Viking Press, 2002).

One of the most controversial assessments of the *Brown* decision is Michael J. Klarman, "How *Brown* Changed Race Relations: The Backlash Thesis," *Journal of American History* 81 (Jun. 1994): 81–118. Klarman contends that the Supreme

Court impeded the gradual process of racial change that had been taking place in the South since the late 1940s. By focusing on school desegregation, rather than the less emotive issue of voting rights or public transportation, the Warren Court precipitated a militant counterattack from southern conservatives. A response to this interpretation can be found in the essay by Tony Badger included in this collection. Another study that emphasizes the limited impact of the *Brown* decision is Gerald N. Rosenberg, *The Hollow Hope: Can Courts Bring About Social Change?* (Chicago: University of Chicago Press, 1991).

Primary Sources on Massive Resistance

There are only a limited number of accessible works written in defense of southern segregation. The most thorough and lucid arguments in defense of the racial status quo are William D. Workman, Jr., *The Case for the South* (New York: Devin-Adair, 1960); and Edward P. Lawton, *The South and the Nation* (Fort Myers Beach, Fl.: Island Press, 1963). One of the most venomous attacks on the Supreme Court, characterized by its unconcealed racism, is Tom P. Brady, *Black Monday* (Jackson, Miss.: Citizens' Council of America, 1955). Excerpts from this booklet can be found in Clayborne Carson, et al., eds. *The Eyes on the Prize Civil Rights Reader: Documents, Speeches, and Firsthand Accounts from the Black Freedom Struggle, 1954–1990* (New York: Penguin Books, 1991). A more temperate defense of segregation, drawing not on base appeals to white racial prejudice but the doctrine of states' rights, is James J. Kilpatrick, *The Southern Case for School Segregation* (New York: Crowell-Collier Press, 1962). A small but important selection of segregationist sources is also included in Jack E. Davis, ed., *The Civil Rights Movement* (Malden, Mass.: Blackwell, 2001).

Some of the students and teachers involved in the desegregation of southern schools wrote autobiographical accounts of their experiences. Melba Patillo Beals, *Warriors Don't Cry: A Searing Memoir of the Battle to Integrate Little Rock's Central High* (New York: Pocket Books, 1994) is a moving narrative written by one of the "Little Rock Nine." Margaret Anderson, *Children of the South* (New York: Farrar, Straus, and Giroux, 1966) is an account of the Clinton, Tennessee, school desegregation crisis from the perspective of one of the high school's teachers.

Journalism on Massive Resistance

Some of the most insightful contemporary analyses of southern segregationists came from reporters whose work benefited from firsthand observation and extensive interviews with both the political elite and ordinary people.

The best of these journalistic accounts include Robert Penn Warren, *Segregation: The Inner Conflict in the South* (New York: Random House, 1956); John Bartlow Martin, *The Deep South Says "Never"* (New York: Ballantine, 1957); Wilma Dykeman and James Stokely, *Neither Black nor White* (New York: Rinehart, 1957); Dan Wakefield, *Revolt in the South* (New York: Grove, 1960); and James Graham Cook, *The Segregationists* (New York: Appleton-Century-Crofts, 1962). A selection of the finest media coverage of the civil rights crisis is also included in Clayborne Carson, David Garrow, Bill Kovach, and Carol Polsgrove, eds., *Reporting Civil Rights*, 2 vols. (New York: Library of America, 2003).

Academic Studies of Massive Resistance

Although more than thirty years have elapsed since its publication, the most important study of segregationist politics is still Numan V. Bartley, *The Rise of Massive Resistance: Race and Politics in the South During the 1950s* (Baton Rouge: Louisiana State University Press, 1969). The book demonstrates that white southerners did not stand in united opposition to the Supreme Court. On the contrary, the defense of segregation differed from state to state, and the forces of massive resistance were fractured by ideological and strategic divisions.

A number of more recent works have added substantially to our understanding of massive resistance. The role of class politics is particularly well explored in Pete Daniel, *Lost Revolutions: The American South in the 1950s* (Chapel Hill: University of North Carolina Press, 2000) and Allison Graham, *Framing the South: Hollywood, Television, and Race During the Civil Rights Struggle* (Baltimore: Johns Hopkins University Press, 2001). Southern efforts to discredit the civil rights movement as a communist conspiracy are thoroughly detailed in Jeff Woods, *Black Struggle, Red Scare: Segregation and Anti-Communism in the South, 1948–1968* (Baton Rouge: Louisiana State University Press, 2004). One of the most arresting interpretations of massive resistance is David L. Chappell, *A Stone of Hope: Prophetic Religion and the Death of Jim Crow* (Chapel Hill: University of North Carolina Press, 2004). In an elaboration of the chapter written for this collection, Chappell argues that the failure of white southern clergymen to bestow segregation with cultural legitimacy caused a crippling lack of confidence among massive resisters. The impact of global politics on southern segregationists has not been explored in proper detail, but an excellent starting point is Thomas Noer, "Segregationists and the World: The Foreign Policy of the White Resistance," in *Window on Freedom: Race, Civil Rights, and Foreign Affairs, 1945–1988*, ed. Brenda Gayle Plummer (Chapel Hill: University of North

Carolina Press, 2003). Noer assesses the influence of African decolonization on the ideological defense of Jim Crow and notes how the massive resistance leadership saw itself as standing shoulder to shoulder with the white supremacist regimes in South Africa and Rhodesia.

White southerners sought to safeguard against the incursions of the federal government and civil rights movement through the formation of numerous segregationist organizations. The largest and most influential of these political bodies is the subject of Neil R. McMillen, *The Citizens' Council: Organized Resistance to the Second Reconstruction, 1954–1964* (Urbana: University of Illinois Press, 1971). The sorts of men and women who joined the Citizens' Councils is assessed in Graeme Cope, "'Honest White People of the Middle and Lower Classes?' A Profile of the Capital Citizens' Council During the Little Rock Crisis of 1957," *Arkansas Historical Quarterly* 61 (2002): 36–58. One of the more unusual public relations campaigns launched by the Citizens' Councils is discussed in Clive Webb, "'A Cheap Trafficking in Human Misery': The Reverse Freedom Rides of 1962," *Journal of American Studies* 38 (2004): 249–71. Another important study of institutional opposition to racial reform is Yasuhiro Katagiri, *The Mississippi State Sovereignty Commission: Civil Rights and States' Rights* (Jackson: University Press of Mississippi, 2001). Katagiri was the first scholar to throw light on this shadowy surveillance force as a result of his access to thousands of recently declassified documents.

Both the White Citizens' Council and the Mississippi State Sovereignty Commission ostensibly operated within the parameters of the law. While scholars have written in some detail about these instruments of supposedly "respectable resistance," more extremist groups such as the National States Rights' Party and the National Association for the Advancement of White People have suffered relative neglect. The most infamous of these radical white segregationist organizations was the Ku Klux Klan. David Chalmers, *Backfire: How the Ku Klux Klan Helped the Civil Rights Movement* (Lanham, Md.: Rowman and Littlefield, 2003), demonstrates how Klan violence against civil rights activists proved counterproductive to the segregationist cause, since it forced the federal government to assume a more interventionist role in the southern race issue. Federal authorities were still frequently guilty of doing too little, too late, to abate acts of racial terrorism, as demonstrated by Michal R. Belknap, *Federal Law and Southern Order: Racial Violence and Constitutional Conflict in the Post-Brown South* (Athens: University of Georgia Press, 1987). One of the most notorious racial extremists who advocated violence as a legitimate political tool was Asa Carter. His story is told in Dan T. Carter, "Southern History, American Fiction: The Secret Life of Southwestern Novelist Forrest Carter," in *Rewriting the South: History and Fiction,* ed. Lothar Hönnighausen and Valeria Gennaro Lerda (Tübingen: Francke Verlag, 1993), 286–304; and Jeff Roche, "Asa/Forrest Carter and Regional/Political Identity," in *The Southern Albatross: Race and Ethnicity in the American South,* ed. Philip D. Dillard and Randal L. Hall (Macon, Ga.: Mercer University Press, 1999), 235–74.

Carter was one of many segregationists seized by the moral panic over the new rock-and-roll music that emerged during the 1950s. The colorblind-ness of this new youth culture led to pronounced fears of miscegenation. For insight into this phenomenon see Brian Ward, *Just My Soul Responding: Rhythm and Blues, Black Consciousness, and Race Relations* (Berkeley: University of California Press, 1998); and Michael T. Bertrand, *Race, Rock, and Elvis* (Urbana: University of Illinois Press, 2000).

Other important studies of massive resistance politics include Hugh Davis Graham, *Crisis in Print: Desegregation and the Press in Tennessee* (Nashville: Vanderbilt University Press, 1967); I. A. Newby, *Challenge to the Court: Social Scientists and the Defense of Segregation, 1954–1966* (Baton Rouge: Louisiana State University Press, 1967); Francis M. Wilhoit, *The Politics of Massive Resistance* (New York: Brazilier, 1973); and Earl Black, *Southern Governors and Civil Rights: Racial Segregation as a Campaign Issue in the Second Reconstruction* (Cambridge, Mass.: Harvard University Press, 1976).

Biographies

There are numerous biographical studies of segregationist politicians. The best of these is Dan T. Carter, *The Politics of Rage: George Wallace, the Origins of the New Conservatism, and the Transformation of American Politics* (New York: Simon and Schuster, 1995), which demonstrates the influence of the Alabama governor in the rise of the New Right since the late 1960s. Other studies of individual segregationist leaders include Nadine Cohodas, *Strom Thurmond and the Politics of Southern Change* (Macon, Ga.: Mercer University Press, 1994); James W. Ely, *The Crisis of Conservative Virginia: The Byrd Organization and the Politics of Massive Resistance* (Knoxville: University of Tennessee Press, 1976); Gilbert C. Fite, *Richard B. Russell, Jr., Senator from Georgia* (Chapel Hill: University of North Carolina Press, 1991); Ronald L. Heinemann, *Harry Byrd of Virginia* (Charlottesville: University Press of Virginia, 1996); Elizabeth Jacoway, "Jim Johnson of Arkansas: Segregationist Prototype," in *The Role of Ideas in the Civil Rights South,* ed. Ted Ownby (Jackson: University Press of Mississippi, 2002), 137–55; Glen Jeansonne, *Leander Perez: Boss of the Delta* (Baton Rouge: Louisiana State University Press, 1977); William A. Nunnelly, *Bull Connor* (Tuscaloosa: University of Alabama Press, 1991); Harold Paulk Henderson, *Ernest Vandiver, Governor of Georgia* (Athens: University of Georgia Press, 2000); Roy Reed, *Faubus: Life and Times of an American Prodigal* (Fayetteville: University of Arkansas Press, 1997); Bob Short, *Everything Is Pickrick: The Life of Lester Maddox* (Macon, Ga.: Mercer University Press, 1999); and Clive Webb, "Charles Bloch: Jewish White Supremacist," *Georgia Historical Quarterly* 83 (1999): 267–92.

Case Studies

The most substantial research on southern opposition to black civil rights is in the form of case studies of specific communities. Much of this literature focuses on Virginia, the state most responsible for shaping an ideology of massive resistance. The most impressive of these works is Matthew D. Lassiter and Andrew B. Lewis, eds., *The Moderates' Dilemma: Massive Resistance to School Desegregation in Virginia* (Charlottesville: University Press of Virginia, 1998). Other useful studies of desegregation in Virginia include Benjamin Muse, *Virginia's Massive Resistance* (Bloomington: Indiana University Press, 1961); Robert C. Smith, *They Closed Their Schools: Prince Edward County, Virginia 1951–1964* (Chapel Hill: University of North Carolina Press, 1965); Forrest R. White, *Pride and Prejudice: School Desegregation and Urban Renewal in Norfolk, 1950–1959* (Westport, Conn.: Praeger, 1992); and Alexander Leidholt, *Standing Before the Shouting Mob: Lenoir Chambers and Virginia's Massive Resistance to Public-School Integration* (Tuscaloosa: University of Alabama Press, 1997). The Little Rock school crisis, as the most notorious incident of its kind, has attracted considerable attention from scholars. See, in particular, Elizabeth Jacoway and C. Fred Williams, eds., *Understanding the Little Rock School Crisis: An Exercise in Remembrance and Reconciliation* (Fayetteville: University of Arkansas Press, 1999). Also recommended are Graeme Cope, "'A Thorn in the Side?' The Mothers' League of Central High School and the Little Rock Desegregation Crisis of 1957," *Arkansas Historical Quarterly* 57 (1998): 160–90; and Phoebe Godfrey, "Bayonets, Brainwashing, and Bathrooms: The Discourse of Gender, Race, and Sexuality in the Desegregation of Little Rock's Central High," *Arkansas Historical Quarterly* 62 (2003): 42–67, which shows how segregationist appeals to protect white women from predatory black males and federal troops united local whites across socioeconomic lines in opposition to desegregation. I. Wilmer Counts, *A Life Is More Than a Moment: The Desegregation of Little Rock's Central High* (Bloomington: Indiana University Press, 1999), a collection of photographs, provides an excellent visual record of the school crisis.

Other informative case studies of school and university desegregation include June N. Adamson, "Few Black Voices Heard: The Black Community and the Desegregation Crisis in Clinton, Tennessee, 1956," *Tennessee Historical Quarterly* 53 (1994): 30–41; Robyn Duff Ladino, *Desegregating Texas Schools: Eisenhower, Shivers, and the Crisis at Mansfield High* (Austin: University of Texas Press, 1996); Jeff Roche, *Restructured Resistance: The Sibley Commission and the Politics of Desegregation in Georgia* (Athens: University of Georgia Press, 1998); and William Doyle, *An American Insurrection: The Battle of Oxford, Mississippi, 1962* (New York: Doubleday, 2001).

Race and the Church

The role of southern white churches in obstructing or advancing the civil rights cause is discussed in Donald E. Collins, *When the Church Bell Rang Racist: The Methodist Church and the Civil Rights Movement in Alabama* (Macon, Ga.: Mercer University Press, 1998); J. Wayne Flynt, *Alabama Baptists: Southern Baptists in the Heart of Dixie* (Tuscaloosa: University of Alabama Press, 1998); Mark Newman, *Getting Right with God: Southern Baptists and Desegregation, 1945–1995* (Tuscaloosa: University of Alabama Press, 2001); Andrew M. Manis, *Southern Civil Religions in Conflict: Civil Rights and the Culture Wars* (Macon, Ga.: Mercer University Press, 2002). The position of the Catholic Church is discussed in Fairclough, *Race and Democracy.* Further references to the role of the church can be found in the notes to the chapters 7 and 8 in this collection.

Southern Liberals

The mobilization of massive resistance against integration created a climate of political intolerance that forced southern white liberals into retreat. Their travails are documented in Morton Sosna, *In Search of the Silent South: Southern Liberals and the Race Issue* (New York: Columbia University Press, 1977); Charles W. Eagles, *Jonathan Daniels and Race Relations: The Evolution of a Southern Liberal* (Knoxville: University of Tennessee Press, 1982); Irwin Klibaner, *Conscience of a Troubled South: The Southern Conference Educational Fund, 1946–1966* (Brooklyn: Carlson, 1989); Frank T. Adams, *James A. Dombrowski: An American Heretic, 1897–1983* (Knoxville: University of Tennessee Press, 1992); David L. Chappell, *Inside Agitators: White Southerners in the Civil Rights Movement* (Baltimore: Johns Hopkins University Press, 1994); Sarah Hart Brown, *Standing Against Dragons: Three Southern Lawyers in an Era of Fear* (Baton Rouge:

Louisiana State University Press, 1998); Catherine Fosl, *Subversive Southerner: Anne Braden and the Struggle for Racial Justice in the Cold War South* (New York: Palgrave, 2002); and Gail S. Murray, *Throwing Off the Cloak of Privilege: White Southern Women Activists in the Civil Rights Era* (Gainesville: University Press of Florida, 2004).

INDEX

Aaron, Mrs. O. R., 210
Aaron v. Cooper, 84–85
ACCA. *See* Associated Citizens' Councils of Arkansas
accommodationists. *See* politics and politicians
Agricultural Adjustment Act, 182
Alabama Baptist, 162, 177n43
Alaska statehood, 199n8
Alexander, T. M., 50
Alexander v. Holmes County Board of Education, xiv
Alford, Dale, 128
Allen, Clifton, 139
Almond, Lindsay, 30, 31
amalgamation. *See* miscegenation
American Association of University Women, 86
American Baptist Convention, 150n32
American Christian, 141
American Dilemma, An (Gunnar Myrdal), 159
American History Month, 190
American Institute of Public Opinion, 5
American Legion, 190
Americans for the Preservation of the White Race, 15, 166
amicus curiae for *Briggs v. Elliott*, 44
Anderson, Karen S., 203–220
anti-Catholicism, 144–145
anticlericalism, 141–142, 148n16-17, 164–165
anticommunism, 118, 127–130
antimiscegenation laws, 157, 158, 160. *See also* miscegenation

anti-poll tax. *See* poll tax
anti-Roosevelt slate, 184, 198n6
anti-Semitism, 70–71, 204
Ariel. *See* Payne, Buckner H.
Arkansas Democrat, 92, 209, 211
Arkansas Education Association, 216n2
Arkansas Gazette, 43, 208, 214
Arkansas General Assembly, 80
Arkansas Plan, 43
Arkansas State Conference of NAACP, 84
Arkansas State National Guard. *See* National Guard
Arkansas State Police, 213
Arkansas State Press, 79
Arlington County, Virginia, 24
Arnall, Ellis, 45
Articles of Confederation, 65
ASC. *See* Arkansas State Conference of NAACP
Ashmore, Harry, 39, 43, 214
Associated Citizens' Councils of Arkansas, 83–84, 204
Association of Citizens' Councils, 141
Atlanta, Georgia, 10, 99–114
Atlanta Board of Education, 103, 104
"Atlanta Compromise," 110
Atlanta Constitution, 21, 106, 107, 109
Atlanta University, 50
"Awful Faubus." *See* Faubus, Orval

Badger, Tony, 9–10, 39–55
Bailey, Thomas, 198n6
Baker, Robert E., 215

Women for Constitutional Government,
41, 181, 196
Women's Activities and Youth Work, 191
Women's Emergency Committee to Open
Our Schools, 90
Woods, Jeff, 118, 129, 132n7
Woodward, C. Vann, 56
Worker (Communist), 124
Workman, William D., 46, 142

Works Project Administration, 182
Wright, Fielding, 185
Wright, J. Skelly, 69–70

Young, Andrew, 107, 151
Young, Whitney, 43

Zaire, independence of, 132n9
Zambia, independence of, 132n9